The Newfoundland Railway, 1898–1969

The Newfoundland Railway, 1898–1969

A History

LES HARDING

McFarland & Company, Inc., Publishers
Jefferson, North Carolina, and London

LIBRARY OF CONGRESS CATALOGUING-IN-PUBLICATION DATA

Harding, Les.
The Newfoundland Railway, 1898–1969 : a history / Les Harding.
p.   cm.
Includes bibliographical references and index.

ISBN 978-0-7864-3261-5
Softcover : 50# alkaline paper ∞

1. Railroads — Newfoundland and Labrador — History.
2. Newfoundland Railway Company — History.   I. Title.
TF27.N42H36   2008   385.5'209718 — dc22   2007046479

British Library cataloguing data are available

©2008 Les Harding. All rights reserved

No part of this book may be reproduced or transmitted in any form or by any means, electronic or mechanical, including photocopying or recording, or by any information storage and retrieval system, without permission in writing from the publisher.

Cover photograph: Locomotive on a trestle bridge at North Arm, early 1900s (Provincial Archives of Newfoundland and Labrador); Tilted railway symbol on a boxcar (CNR)

Manufactured in the United States of America

*McFarland & Company, Inc., Publishers
Box 611, Jefferson, North Carolina 28640
www.mcfarlandpub.com*

Acknowledgments

I would like to thank the staff at the Centre for Newfoundland Studies, Queen Elizabeth II Library, Memorial University of Newfoundland for their assistance. The same for the folks at the Provincial Archives of Newfoundland and Labrador, the C.N.R. Archives and Library and Archives Canada. Hollis Harding and Dianne Taylor-Harding get thank-yous for their photography and for helping an admitted computer illiterate. Jennifer Fowler of the map library, Memorial University earns a thank-you for preparing the map of the Newfoundland Railway system.

Table of Contents

Introduction 1

ONE. A Somewhat Startling Notion 7

TWO. The Battle of Foxtrap 15

THREE. The Great American and Shortline Railway 24

FOUR. The Surveys 27

FIVE. The Harbour Grace Railway 35

SIX. The Placentia Railway 51

SEVEN. Enter R. G. Reid 58

EIGHT. Life on the Line 62

NINE. King Reid 66

TEN. The Contract of 1898 76

ELEVEN. The Cross-Country Express 86

TWELVE. The New Century 96

THIRTEEN. July 2, 1969, The Last Run 119

FOURTEEN. Railway Mail Service, Dispatching Office, Locomotive Shop, Coastal Boats and More 132

FIFTEEN. Wrecks, Collisions and Close Calls 150

Appendix One: Travelers, Eyewitnesses and Shameless Boosters 157

Appendix Two: To the Old Capitals by the New Way: Crossing the Ancient Colony by Rail, 1899–1900 187

Appendix Three: Poetry and Song 200

Appendix Four: Connections Far and Wide in 1900 204

Appendix Five: Miscellaneous 207

Chronology 213

Glossary 215

Notes 219

Bibliography 223

Index 227

Introduction

What do Sir Sandford Fleming, the inventor of Standard Time, the American movie actress Joan Blondell and an old-timer and professional windsniffer by the name of Lauchie McDougall have in common?

Answer: "The Bullet."

What was the only train in the world which could have served such a diverse collection of places as Foxtrap, Kelligrews, Bareneed, Harbour Grace, Goobies, Come by Chance, Rattling Brook, Heart's Content, Heart's Delight, Heart's Desire and Tickle Harbour; not to mention Dildo, Dildo South and Dildo Arm?

Again: "The Bullet."

Lovingly called "the slowest crack train in civilization" and "the streak of rust," the Express, as it was known officially, came into existence on the evening of June 29, 1898. For the next seventy-one years, the "Bullet"—as it later came to be known—meandered, rattled, rocked, swayed, thumped, shook and banged its way across the island of Newfoundland and into the realms of railroad folklore.

The building of a narrow-gauge trans-island railway in nineteenth-century Newfoundland was a reckless and even desperate experiment. The island was poor and the population small, scattered and rent by bitter sectarian conflict. Until 1949, when it finally agreed by the narrowest of margins to become the tenth province of Canada, Newfoundland was determined to go it alone as a semi-independent British dominion. Poor as it was, the island had issued its own currency and its own postage stamps and conducted relations with foreign governments. Although the coastlines had been settled for centuries, the interior of Newfoundland was virtually unknown, and as far as anyone knew, unsuited for settlement or development of any kind. It was hoped that the rails would accomplish what the centuries had been unable to do — bring prosperity and unite the people of Newfoundland. In order to batter down the walls of isolation between settlements, the track was planned to reach as many of the island's great bays as possible. Unfortunately, the circuitous route, uneconomical branch lines and the resulting cost of construction, maintenance and "snow-fighting" canceled forever any hope of a profitable operation.

From the beginning, both the railway and the government of Newfoundland, which was ultimately responsible for it, were driven to the brink of bankruptcy. Yet, confounding most predictions, the railway in Newfoundland was built and operated successfully. During World War II the Newfoundland Railway was a vital cog in the Allied war effort, hauling supplies, fuel and troops to American and Canadian bases established in St. John's, Gander, Stephenville, Botwood, Argentia and elsewhere. After confederation with Canada in 1949, the Newfoundland Railway, renamed Terra Transport, was operated as a division of the Canadian National Railways system. The passenger train sarcastically nicknamed the "Bullet" because of its supposedly relaxed schedule continued daily operation until July 3, 1969. It is a sad comment on our time that on that date, the proud old train, which had survived riots, forty-foot snowdrifts, butting contests with moose, endemic derailments caused by sleeping cows and a track that could be bent out of shape by the weight of the locomotives, succumbed to progress in a no less prosaic form than a fleet of gleaming new Roadcruiser buses.

Although I live in Newfoundland, rode the train across the island as a child, have relatives who worked for the railway and pass by its physical remains almost daily, for the longest time I did not give the train much thought. The idea for this book came from a visit to the Canada Science and Technology Museum in Ottawa, Ontario. The museum has an excellent display on the Newfoundland Railway and while examining it I developed a sudden craving to know more about the subject. It did not take me long to discover that there was very little that was conveniently available. So I went to work combing archives and university libraries, enduring eyestrain from reading microfilmed newspapers. The original manuscript was prepared on a typewriter! Yes, that long ago. I won't bore you with the depressing and sordid details but if the manuscript had been published when it was supposed to be it would have been the first book on the history of the Newfoundland Railway. Alas, that was not to be.

Since I completed my original research there has arisen a minor cottage industry in Newfoundland of retired trainmen issuing their memoirs and earnest academics contributing scholarly articles. The books usually went out of print almost immediately and the academic journals never reached a wide audience.

Who would have guessed that it would take McFarland, a publisher in North Carolina, of all places, to revive my history of the Newfoundland Railway. With their encouragement I went back to the libraries and rare book rooms and completely rewrote my manuscript, incorporating the new material that had become available. The chapters have been expanded, new chapters have been added, as have appendices, a map and a number of historic photographs. An extensive and up-to-date bibliography is at the end. The result of my efforts is in your hands and I believe it to be a better book as a result of the long delay.

Newfoundland is the sixteenth largest island in the world. Within the memory of persons still living large tracts of her land were mere blanks on the map. It was the railway which changed this forever and it is a story which cries out to be told, particularly

Lauchie McDougall, the world's only professional windsniffer (Canada Science and Technology Museum).

to those who do not live in Newfoundland. It is my wish that this book will bring the epic story of the island's railway to the widest possible audience.

I have attempted to combine the usefulness of a history with the stimulus of a book which is fun and interesting to read. Whether or not I have succeeded is for the reader to decide. I have endeavored to be as thorough and accurate as possible. Any deficiencies or omissions are entirely mine.

There is a plaque in honor of the "human wind sniffer," Lauchie McDougall, mounted on the wall of the Marine Atlantic ferry terminal, Port aux Basques, Newfoundland. It reads:

> This plaque is dedicated to the memory of
> LAUCHIE McDOUGALL
> (1896–1965)

Mr. McDougall, a trapper and farmer, lived at Wreckhouse which was probably named for the 140 kilometers per hour winds which funnel down the 1700-foot Table Mountains often lifting rail cars off their tracks as they passed through the natural wind tunnel which exists there. McDougall had extraordinary skills in determining wind velocities without the use of instruments and he was contracted by the railway to determine if it was safe for the trains to pass through this area. Often called the "human wind gauge," McDougall provided this service to the railway for over 30 years. When he died in 1965 his wife Emily continued the practice until 1972.

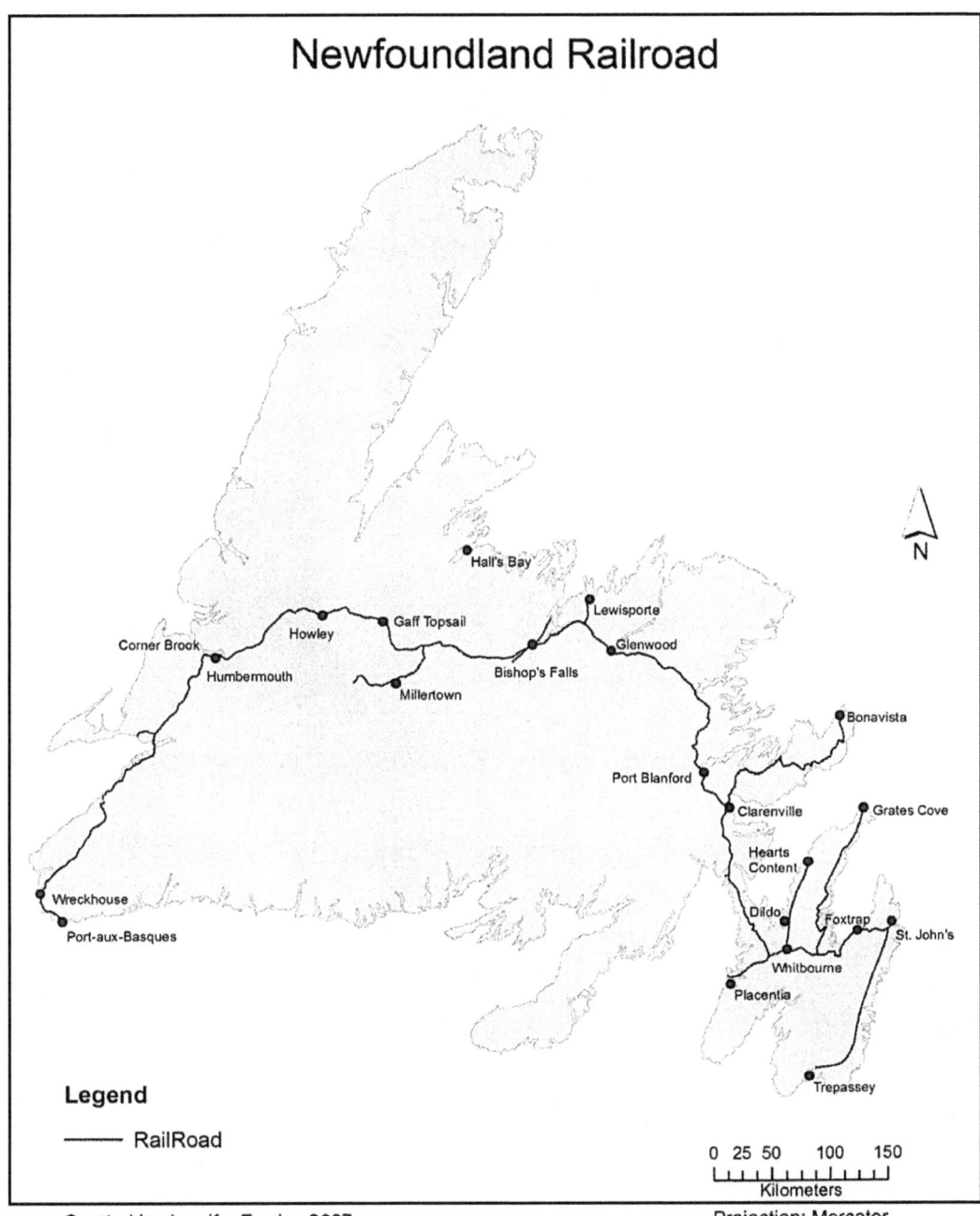

One

A Somewhat Startling Notion

The beginnings of Newfoundland's history, which are the European beginnings of North America's history, have long been lost in the dense fogs of the North Atlantic Ocean. No one knows who was the first pale-skinned intruder from the east. It might have been a nameless fisherman caught in a gale or an Irish Celt bobbing across the sea in a skin-covered curragh. Whoever the pathfinder was, we do know that beginning in the eleventh century A.D. the rugged Newfoundland coasts were begrudgingly yielding anchorages to the longships of the Northmen. Hardy Vikings from the Iceland and Greenland colonies, driven to the west as much by their chronic need for timber as by fierce mid–Atlantic storms, wintered and fitfully attempted settlement in the remote bays and coves of the Great Northern Peninsula. The only authenticated Norse site in North America can be seen today at L'Anse aux Meadows, at the northernmost tip of Newfoundland. The island's aboriginal inhabitants, the Beothuks, the original "Savage Red Men" after whom all the others were named so called because they smeared red ocher pigment on their bodies, had trekked across the wild interior since time immemorial. But even these people occupied the shorelines for nine or ten months each year. Eventually the Beothuks yielded the shores and then their lives to the tread of the white intruders, their guns and their microbes. The ultimate fate of these earliest trespassers is unknown, but throughout the dark centuries of Europe the western isle and its rich fishing grounds were whispered about and certainly visited by others. At least a full century before an obscure Italian navigator in English employ, a mercenary adventurer by the name of John Cabot (or Giovanni Caboto), forty days outward bound from the port of Bristol, "discovered" the New Founde Land in 1497 and claimed it for King Henry VII, fishermen from the English West Country, Brittany, Portugal and the Basque lands were drying their catches on shore and sometimes wintering there.

Eventually, fed up with the servitude of Europe, a few of the fishermen stayed on permanently and brought their families out. Though forbidden by jealous fish merchants from settling within six miles of the coast and even barred from building a sod hut, the people still came. Imperceptibly, settlers began to trickle into the most remote inlets they could find on Newfoundland's six thousand miles of rock-bound coastline. Remoteness was seen as an advantage. By 1550, despite all edicts to the contrary, the

Newfoundland coast was occupied by "liveyers"— permanent inhabitants of European stock. A hundred years before New York was a village, St. John's, the island's capital, was a thriving small community.

Nevertheless the island slumbered throughout most of its history. By the height of the railway age, Newfoundland lagged far behind most of the western world. Though Newfoundland is one of the largest islands in the world, 42,000 square miles, its population in 1890 was but 200,000. Isolation, sectarian division and privation were a daily part of the people's lives. Scattered along an unrelenting and craggy coastline, the Newfoundlanders, bold and fearless when afloat, lived in tiny hamlets called outports, often as unknown to each other as their island was unknown to the world at large.

The interior of Newfoundland was almost totally unknown, even to the "liveyers." Someone said that Newfoundland was "a husk without a kernel."[1] It was not until 1822 that the first white man — W. E. Cormack, in a futile attempt to find the last surviving Beothuk Indians — crossed the center of Newfoundland on foot. Aside from short trips for caribou hunting and wood cutting the settlers never penetrated far from the coast and the sea they understood so completely. The interior, with its gloomy forests, bottomless bogs and trackless barrens, was a place of terror and mystery. The interior was the home of headless specters, phantoms, nameless creeping things, unearthly noises and the bloodcurdling banshee. For such a people as the Newfoundlanders, to even think of building a railway smack in the teeth of four hundred years of seafaring history was nothing short of astonishing — some would say mad!

Not surprisingly, the policy of railway building faced stiff opposition. It was not until 1825 that the first rude cart-track was built. And that too faced opposition. One English West Country merchant remarked sourly, "They are making roads in Newfoundland. Next thing they will be having carriages and driving about."[2]

On May 22, 1847, the St. John's *Morning Post* commented on the benefits that a railway would bring to Newfoundland. Privately, the somewhat startling notion of bringing an iron horse to this, the oldest of British colonies, had been bandied about for some time, but this was the first public endorsement. The *Morning Post* was humble enough in its request. The railway they envisioned would certainly be nothing grand, a mere ten or twelve miles in length; just long enough to link St. John's, the capital, with the little town of Portugal Cove to the west and the lucrative traffic of Conception Bay. Nothing came of the suggestion. St. John's had only barely survived a disastrous fire the year before and the worst gale in living memory. Only a madman would suggest building a railway at a time like that. However, the idea of a railway was never entirely forgotten. A railway to Newfoundland's west coast, with connections to Canada and from there to the United States, was proposed in a public lecture by Dr. Henry Stabb, medical superintendent of the Mental Asylum, in 1865. Some wags must have seen an immediate linkage between the doctor's position at the asylum and his opinions on public transport. Dr. Stabb suggested that a standard-gauge railroad be constructed from St. John's to Newfoundland's west coast, where it could serve as a connecting link to Canada. In 1866 a Roman Catholic prelate, the Right Reverend Dr. John Mullock, Bishop of Newfoundland and well-known political agitator, "firebrand and disturber of the peace," spoke out in the name of good government, civilization and the Christian religion in favor of modern steamships, improved roads, telegraphs, and a railway that would connect Conception Bay with St. John's. Both of these pleas were ignored, but the word *railway* soon came to haunt every Newfoundland government.

Newfoundland had a great deal of catching up to do. By 1846 and the "Great Fire" of St. John's, the Stockton and Darlington Line had been operating in England for more than twenty years. Railway construction had been part of official French government policy for at least fifteen years. In the United States, the Delaware and Hudson Line had been running since 1832. Canada was not far behind. For at least nine years a small railway had been running at St. John's, Québec. Only twenty years after the fire, the United States had its "ribbon of steel" stretching from coast to coast. By 1887 it was possible to ride the rails from Montréal, Québec to Vancouver, British Columbia on the Canadian Pacific. It took forty long years for railway fever in Newfoundland to percolate under the surface. When it finally boiled over, Newfoundland, like St. John's during the fire, almost died of the consequences.

Part of the problem was that railways were seen by many in Newfoundland as a cunning Canadian plot to link the island to the mainland. Once emotions began to run rampant there was little time for serious talk of railways. Thirty years were spent in a bitter struggle for responsible government and in keeping the dreaded "Canadian Wolf" at bay. It was not until 1881 that work began on a very modest line of track. The government seemed actually embarrassed that Newfoundland was the only "Colony of equal importance under the Crown without a Railroad, and the advantages thereby conferred elsewhere in the enhancement of the value of property and labour."[3] As the Newfoundland government completely lacked experience in engineering, financing and big business, an American syndicate was contracted to build a line of narrow-gauge track from St. John's to a point on the northeast coast of the island. This was to be the first in a series of disastrous business deals entered into by the Newfoundland government. With the laying of the track, the railroad's supporters gave voice to the high objectives of joining up the outports, opening up new timber areas, farms, mines, inland settlements and vast new industries which would give gainful employment to all.

> Conjecture what this country would be in twenty-five years if railways were snorting across vast areas of cultivated land, well water-margined and timber-bordered. Who can say what station this country will occupy in the future? Who can say what station in the new colonial empire she may not assume? Who can deny that the advancement offers a field for the most rational conjecture?[4]

These great hopes soon came tumbling down. For after the first sixty miles of track were laid, in a somewhat slapdash fashion, the American railway syndicate promptly went broke. Mismanagement, bungling, and the unexpected rigors of the

Newfoundland climate were more than the Americans had bargained for. The half-completed railway reverted to its creditors. The Newfoundland government, poorer but, as we shall see, not much wiser, found itself embroiled in decades of lawsuits and counter-lawsuits that ranged all the way to the supreme arbiter, the Privy Council in London. By the time it was all over, it would have been cheaper for Newfoundland to have built the railway by itself!

But railway fever had bitten, and once bitten there was no cure. As one of the St. John's newspapers correctly observed, "Railways — when once introduced into a country have a pertinacious way of getting extended — they invariably push on."[5] The government of Newfoundland was determined to build a railway come hell or high water. It obviously subscribed to the theory of Lord Thomas Babington Macaulay, the English writer and historian who wrote, "Every improvement in the means of locomotion benefits mankind morally and intellectually as well as materially."[6] After the debacle with the Americans, it would take another seventeen years of nineteenth-century Newfoundland-style politics — scandal, patronage, arm-twisting, character assassination and shameless demagoguery — before the rusty thirty-five pound rails of the Newfoundland Railway spanned the island. But span the island they did.

The effort was herculean and it almost ruined the country. By the time the first

First excursion trip on the Newfoundland Railway. "Train About to Start." (Harvey, 1883)

Cross-Country Express from St. John's to Port aux Basques steamed proudly into the western terminal, the government had been bankrupted. Seventy percent of all government revenue went toward meeting interest payments on unpaid debts. In a desperate attempt to pay the bills and avoid any new ones, the resources and future of the entire island and its people were virtually given away to a single man, Robert Gillespie Reid, a Canadian capitalist and empire builder in the grand style of Cecil Rhodes. This agreement, signed in 1898, known by its many detractors as the Reid deal, was even worse than the contract signed with the Americans. By signing his name to the agreement R. G. Reid made himself nothing short of the "uncrowned czar" of Newfoundland. He owned the entire railway system, the telegraphs, the mail steamers, one in every six acres of land with full mineral rights, the hydroelectric system and sundry other investments ranging from a skating rink, quarries, the St. John's tramways, and hotels, to cold storage plants and, so many alleged, the government itself. Such a virtual abdication of authority by a democratically elected government was without precedent.

The Newfoundland Railway was built, mostly by hand, through some of the most rugged country imaginable. Labor, at one dollar a day, being cheaper and more readily available than heavy equipment, the railway was built by pick and shovel, and of necessity to the cheapest specifications. The Newfoundlanders were obliged to construct their railroad with track that was only three and one-half feet apart. This was done with full knowledge that the standard rail gauge in most of North America was and is four feet, eight and one-half inches. The track of the railway in Newfoundland was thus a full fourteen and one-half inches narrower than that of railways in Canada and the United States and remained so for the life of the line. The Bullet thereby earned for itself the undisputed claim of being the longest narrow-gauge railway in the Western Hemisphere.

Destined to be more thrown into place than properly constructed, the Newfoundland line had the curviest roadbed of any railroad in North America. Of its seven hundred miles of track, almost six hundred were expended in curves. Other railroaders were incredulous when they were told that in some parts of Newfoundland it was possible for a train to be in a process of negotiating three curves at the same time. Railway engineers in Canada and the United States balked at the idea of building curves of ten degrees — six degrees is considered the optimal maximum. But in Newfoundland, curves of fourteen degrees were commonplace. Moreover, the builders could not afford expensive frills like tunnels and signals. There was a bridge every four miles on average and for a time there was but one signal on the whole line. On the entire length of the Bullet's track there was not a single tunnel, though steep hills were common. It was found to be much cheaper to build curves around things than tunnels through things. In situations where it was impossible to go around an obstacle, the accepted alternative was to go up and over it. Though the highest elevation in Newfoundland is less than 3,000 feet, the rate of climb, as much as two and a half percent, was steeper than most gradients found in the Rocky Mountains. As one might expect from such a railway, the sharpest curves had the malicious tendency to appear on the steepest inclines. The legislation passed by the Colony of Newfoundland in 1878 was not exaggerating when it stated, "The railway intended to be constructed shall not be what is deemed in England or the United States a first-class railway."

From the beginning, the railway in Newfoundland was a money loser; the problem was compounded by the construction of hopelessly uneconomical branch lines. There was little or no money available for maintenance or improvements. Breakdowns, washouts and derailments were disturbingly common. The train in its early years was usually behind schedule, sometimes in the winter months arriving at its destination days late. In the winter of 1903 a passenger train was marooned in a fifteen-foot snow drift for an unbelievable seventeen days. At the time, there were no rotary plows available and no money to raise the track way above the level of the advancing snow drifts. The passengers and crew of the unfortunate train were reduced to burning rail ties in order to keep from freezing to death. Conditions reached such an impossible state that the relief train was itself derailed. By the time it got through the drifts, the stranded passengers on the first train were on the verge of starvation. Afterwards, all trains crossing the interior during winter were supplied with additional food stocks. It was about this time that the Newfoundland Railway purchased its first snow plow.

From St. John's, the capital city on the eastern side of Newfoundland, to Port aux Basques, the western terminus, is a distance of some three hundred miles as the crow flies. But the Newfoundland Railway, which rarely traveled in a straight line, switch-backed along a route almost twice that length. From a strictly railroading point of view, of all the routes that could have been chosen the one that was picked was undoubtedly the worst. Quite apart from the extra mileage, the wicked curves, and the brake-squealing gradients, the track went straight through the center of a feature known as the Gaff Topsails Plateau. This area, located in the remote center of the island, has some of the worst weather conditions found anywhere in Canada. The Gaff Topsails is composed of bald exposed rocks and trackless bogs swept by nearly endless winds. In winter, snow-clearing operations were a nightmare. The Topsails, between two hundred and four hundred feet higher than the surrounding plateau, was the highest section of the Newfoundland Railway. Over the years the never-ending battle to keep the track clear proved to be a heavy drain on the railroad's already strained finances.

Of course the Gaff Topsails Plateau was not the only difficult stretch. At a place called Table Mountain and the aptly named Wreckhouse, on the southwest coast of the island, winter winds of one hundred and fifty miles per hour are all too common. Even today it can be an adventure driving the highway through the area. The very ballast could be blown out from underneath the railroad track, causing it to quickly drop as much as two feet. Not so many years ago a "slight" gust blew fourteen freight cars off the track and into a nearby stream. In order to combat this situation, prudent railroaders took to chaining their trains to the track. Heavy links, carried for just this purpose, were wrapped under the rails and hooked onto the underbodies of the cars. Wooden ties and telegraph poles were also brought into play, propping up cars parked on the sidings. These measures usually worked, but once in a while, when a particularly strong wind came whipping around the base of the mountain, a box car or two was still blown over and the track ripped up along with it.

It was no hyperbole to say that the Bullet was not exactly a fast train. At its best — assuming it did not get stuck in the snow or blown off the track — it could be expected to cross Newfoundland in about thirty hours. At an average speed of eighteen or nineteen miles per hour it was not exactly blazing up the track. Toward the end of the Bullet's life, after the Newfoundland Railway had been absorbed by the Canadian National Railways, an experimental train was sent roaring down the rails to see just how fast a train could cross the island. The trip was completed in seventeen hours, but the cars rocked and swayed to such an extent on the hairpin turns of the old trackbed that it was felt that human life would be in jeopardy. It is reported that on more than one occasion paying customers on the branch lines were bitten by curious goats who jumped aboard a slow-moving train to see what all the fuss was about. Timetables kept the printers busy but otherwise, especially in the early days, they were often meaningless.

Nobody really knows for certain where the name "Bullet" came from. It probably originated with some frustrated passenger in a rush to get somewhere. The other possibility, in fact the most likely explanation, is that one of the thousands of American and Canadian servicemen stationed in Newfoundland during World War II became a little sarcastic at the thought of spending most of his precious weekend pass aboard the slow-moving train. Anyway, "Bullet" it was.

The Newfoundland Railway, or the Bullet if you prefer, may not have been a very efficient operation in its early days but it tried hard. And it was so much more than just a train. It was an institution and a way of life. Riding the "Streak of Rust" (another of its nicknames) was a social occasion. The scene in the passenger cars was always lively. Unsophisticated outport folk making the first trip away from their isolated villages considered a trip on the Bullet the grandest of adventures. Strangers became friends on the Bullet, love affairs blossomed. People sang old songs together, fiddled, yarned, played cards, even danced in the aisles. What other train but the Newfie Bullet would stop for everyone to go berry picking?

The *Advocate* says it will never do to send eggs by the coming Railway because they would all hatch themselves out into chickens before they got to their destination. Then they would walk out of the depot with their hands in their pockets, and *without paying their fares*. This would not be *fair* — It would be foul play.... The rolling stone gathers no moss and the rolling stock gathers no money.[7]

What is to become of our picturesque goats if a railway were introduced? They could not be kept off the tracks, and would probably be exterminated.[8]

The projected railway would develop our mineral and agricultural resources, it would elevate and improve the social condition of our people; it would, in a thousand ways, advance the material prosperity of all classes in the community; it would be ... the most potent of all educators.... There must follow immigration with all its attendant advantages: increased revenue and consequently more money to be spent upon public works: increased trade, both import and export; increased employment for the people.[9]

Two

The Battle of Foxtrap

In the early days it could be said, with some understatement, that not everyone in Newfoundland was keen on having a railroad. Some said that the hooting train whistles would scare away the fish. Others declared that the locomotives would run over the cows or that the smoke would poison the air.* And how could a body be expected to get a good night's sleep with some infernal machine racing by outside his bedroom window? In some quarters, a railway proponent faced the risk of physical injury if he so much as dared to speak of the devilish project. Not everyone was sold on the supposed advantages of opening up the interior and starting new industries not based on fishing. The wealthy St. John's merchant class, whose fortunes and place in society depended on maintaining the status quo, were stubbornly opposed to this seemingly revolutionary venture. The merchants saw the coming of the iron horse to the colony as a threat to their power, a challenge to the throttle-hold they held upon the economic life of Newfoundland and the beginning of the long downward slide toward confederation with a remote foreign country known as Canada.

The government of the day was under the venerable "Grand Old Man" of the Liberal Party, Sir William Whiteway. Whiteway was both pro-railway and a closet confederationist. In the heated political climate of Newfoundland, however, he was wise to keep his pro–Canadian sentiments to himself. It was hard enough being a railroad enthusiast without making matters worse. Even most of Whiteway's avowed supporters were not ready to support union with Canada. Whiteway was all too aware of the crushing political defeat suffered by the last pro-confederation government just a decade before. Whiteway and the Liberals represented the up-and-coming middle class and the educated minority of the colony. To their way of thinking a railway would be a much needed breath of fresh air, bringing prosperity to all classes of Newfoundlanders.

Both the Liberals and the Conservatives owned newspapers which, in the true spirit of nineteenth-century journalism, did not even make a pretense of being impartial. Depending on what faction controlled a particular newspaper, railways were depicted in its pages as either devils incarnate or heaven-sent blessings. The papers hammered

---

As a matter of fact, collisions with cows on the branch lines were to become a problem for the railway.

home their message in the crudest sort of purple prose. The Liberal papers were full of glowing accounts of happy Canadian and American railway workers; the speed, efficiency, and comfort of the American Pacific; as well as endless statistics showing the fabulous benefits a railway, any railway, would bring to Newfoundland and its toiling masses.

The St. John's merchants and the Conservative Party had quite a different tale to tell. Their newspapers were full of lurid accounts of American train wrecks, collapsed bridges and mysterious boiler explosions. On the next page would usually be found an account of the misery and near serfdom of the Canadian working class, or an expose of Canadian expansionist plots. A clash between such diametrically opposed factions was inevitable.

The blowup occurred on July 22, 1880, in as unlikely a place as could be imagined, the sleepy little town of Foxtrap, ten miles or so west of St. John's, on the south shore of Conception Bay. Against venomous hostility in the House of Assembly and in the opposition press, Sir William persisted with his plans to get Newfoundland's first railway built as soon as possible. The proposed line was modest enough. It would run from the city of St. John's, around the head of Conception Bay, through Foxtrap, to the town of Harbour Grace, a distance of about eighty-five miles. An American company was contracted to do the construction, but before this could commence, a survey of the projected route was required. To this end a Canadian engineering firm was called in. Fanned by the inflammatory press, feelings in the area around Foxtrap were running at a fever pitch. If we can believe the newspapers, the local people were referring to the surveyors as, "Canadian Comorants [sic] come to pick our bones."

Malicious rumor mills cranked out stories about dark and sinister Canadian plots. No one was bothered by Americans, but crafty-eyed Canadians were soon seen to be lurking behind every fence post and fishing boat. The railway was a fire-breathing monster which would deliver unsuspecting Newfoundlanders into servitude at the hands of the dreaded Mainlanders. People were wide-eyed with fright. They were told that their newborn babies would be rammed down the muzzles of Canadian cannon and they themselves would be left to bleach their bones white on the desert sands of Canada.

One merchant seriously claimed that the Canadians intended to set up a tollgate at the western outskirts of St. John's from which anyone with a horse and cart entering or leaving the city would be forced to pay an outrageous tribute of two shillings and sixpence. The people of Foxtrap believed that they were fighting for their homes and their very existence. Rumors began that once the Canadian surveying team arrived, the land that Newfoundlanders loved and had live on for generations would no longer be theirs. It was claimed that the markers and flags the surveyors used were in fact Canadian flags. Once the flags were in place, the land would irrevocably become Canadian soil from which all Newfoundlanders would be excluded. Both the fisherman and the farmer would, of course, be taxed to the eyeballs by the grasping Canadians.

When the unfortunate Canadian surveyors arrived in Foxtrap, they faced a screaming mob of five hundred people, most of them, to begin with, women. Insult and vituperation were hurled from all sides at the cowering Canadians. The resulting five-day fracas came to be known as the Battle of Foxtrap. Police Inspector Carty, Judge Daniel

Narrow gauge track near Deer Lake (Harvey, 1900).

Woodley Prowse, two mounted constables and nine foot police, hastily assembled in St. John's, comprised the only force that could be mustered to face down an excited mob. The judge, a popular, eccentric and well-known figure in the area, was reluctant to use brute force, especially against women. He knew many of the protesters personally. Judge Prowse sat on a hillside and, with little success, tried to talk some sense into the crowd.

The mob was in no mood for oratory, however. One by one the days passed and the crowd grew larger and uglier. Men returning from the fisheries began to join in. The hundreds of people blocking the surveyors' path loudly swore that the only way any railway was going through the community of Foxtrap was over their dead bodies. The whole area around Foxtrap, from Topsail to Indian Pond, was in a state of agitation.

Narrow gauge track and men on a handcart (Harvey, 1900).

Track hugging the Humber River (Harvey, 1900).

All day and all night the crowd kept close watch over the terrified surveyors and their small band of police protectors. Finally, early on the sixth day, the crowd exploded and stormed the surveyors' camp. The Canadians were pelted with stones and attacked with all manner of kitchen weapons — broom handles, ladles, forks; and by far their most effective weapon, buckets of evil smelling pickle-jar water. The surveyors, wounded more in pride than body, ran for their lives. The crowd surged in and made off with their discarded equipment. This was too much for Judge Prowse. A breach of the peace had been committed under his watch and that could not be tolerated. The judge, marshaling his small force, faced the crowd and, with a show of bravado, promptly arrested the leader — a certain fisherman/farmer by the name of Charley Andrews.

The crowd, momentarily stunned at the judge's audacity, stood still. A voice called out, "Are you going to let them take Charley?" In answer, the crowd rushed the police, but the eleven loaded rifles and the eleven bayonets on those rifles gleamed menacingly in the sunshine. The crowd, cowardly like all mobs without a leader, found that its nerve had suddenly evaporated. Within seconds Charley was safely locked away in a cell. The police guarded their prisoner from the angry crowd, leaving Judge Prowse exposed and alone on the hillside. Judge Prowse, who believed in direct action, wrote,

A tall old man came out with a long gun. He laid his hand on my arm: "You be an unjust judge," he said, "and it would plaze the Lard to shute the likes of you." Now I am a sportsman, and my eye was at once directed to the long blunderbuss; I saw immediately there was no cap in the nipple of his muzzleloader, so before the old chap could defend himself, I gave him a kick in the back, the long gun got between his legs, and down he went. "You old fool," said I, "when you come out to threaten a man's life, get a cap on your gun." A joke always takes with the crowd. My next assailant was a one-armed ruffian who was under bonds at the time to keep the peace. He came along, flourishing a musket also with no cap. I made short work of him by catching the barrel of the gun and smashing it over his back, then ordering him home. The crowd were quite delighted, and cheered when El Manco scuttled off— he presumed that I had not remembered him and his bonds.

After the fuss died down, the survey was completed and the railway to Harbour Grace began operation in 1884. Each man was paid for his land at once. According to Judge Prowse,

Railway track and laborer near Bay of Islands. Note how close the track is to the river bank (Harvey, 1900).

The result was magical; I passed one old fellow sharpening a knife a day before the row. "How are you skipper Abraham?" said I. "Pretty well," he said; "I be getting this yer ready to put into your gizzard when you takes my land." When the cheques began to circulate, Father Abraham followed me about to beg the arbitrators to value his bit of rocky field.

The judge was lenient with the accused. Soon the matter was more or less forgotten. People in Foxtrap began to think that maybe the railroad, if it could put a few coins in their pocket, was not such a bad thing after all. Judge Prowse gradually regained his stature as well. But the next year a St. John's clerk cum poet, singer, actor and playwright, Johnnie Burke, achieved a brief moment of fame when he wrote a musical comedy based on the incident. Its topicality, as well as its music, brazenly stolen from the established tunes of the time, were more than enough to ensure that when it opened on February 2, 1881, at the Total Abstinence Hall, *The Battle of Foxtrap* would be a roaring success on the St. John's stage.

Shortly after the battle, two men who had damaged a surveyor's theodolite were brought before Judge Prowse for trial. They were given six-month suspended sentences upon a solemn promise never to interfere with the railway again. No sooner had the

Narrow gauge track and railway worker at Bay of Islands (Harvey, 1900).

judge said his piece and the men agreed to his demand than one of them looked up at him and asked, "Please Your Honour, would yer be interested in buying a quarter side of lamb?" Things had obviously returned to normal in the community of Foxtrap.

About the same time, Judge Prowse received a message from Charley Andrews, leader of the mob, saying that he would like to see him. Going to his cell, the Judge asked in his usual friendly style, "Well Charley, how is every little thing?"

"O Joodge, A'm ever so glad to see ya. A'm all for t'railroad now!" he answered.

The Judge was understandably surprised and enquired as to the cause of Charley's miraculous change of heart.

> Why there was put in the cell with me last night an English sailor feller who was pretty drunk. When he sobers up he spies me sittin' in the corner and ast me what I was in fer. I told him it was fer fightin' agen a railroad. Quick as a flash he turns to me and says, "Why you poor fool, don't you know nothin'? Why the railway is the poor man's carriage. Ain't no call to go fightin' agen it." Then that sailor man he up and explained to me all about 'em. Well I sure had my eyes opened. He told me that fer just a few coppers I could ride into St. John's like a Lord. Don't make no difference how the wind or tide might be. So now Joodge, A'm all fer t' railroad.

Judge Prowse was more than a little annoyed. After all, he had spent several days and risked life and limb unsuccessfully trying to convince the crowd of that very thing. "Joodge," answered Charley Andrews, "that was different. We all knowed you was paid fer sayin' dem t'ings."

So when all else failed it remained for a drunken English sailor to put an end to the Battle of Foxtrap.[1]

THE "SITUATION" AT FOXTRAP
PEOPLE PREPARING TO DEFEND THEIR PROPERTY

By late advices from Foxtrap we learn that intense excitement prevails there in consequence of the arbitrary and high-handed conduct of the Gov't & their servants, the Railway surveyors. It seems that the people are determined to resist any further invasion of their rights. They say they will not allow their fruit trees to be cut down and their vegetable gardens laid waste, after their toil and trouble in looking after them, and at a time too when they are beginning to reap some benefit from their labours. Yesterday the Gov't surveyors were emphatically given to understand that they should cease operations, and not withstanding the remonstrances of Judge Prowse, backed up by inspector Carty and a large force of the metropolitan police, the people steadily refused to allow the work of invasion & spoliation to go on. Assembling in large force on the bridge they sullenly, but with unmistakable determination prepared to defend their property. Of course Judge Prowse fully realized the importance of the occasion and the weighty responsibility placed upon him by the Gov't in ordering him to enforce what must have been to him an *unjust* and *tyrannical decree*, and very judiciously withdrew his forces leaving the people in possession of the bridge. The opinion prevails all over the district; indeed, we may say, all over the country that this Railway business is a huge fraud, with self-interest running all through it and Confederation at the bottom. All along the South Shore the people are suspicious, and justly so. They say "We have no confidence in Whiteway and Shea. We believe that they want to get us into Confederation; and we will never consent to that!" One arrest was made yesterday and the prisoner brought on to St. John's but under what *act* we are not in a position to say. At present the popular feeling is decidedly against the Gov't, and we believe, if an election were held tomorrow, *very few* of the Whiteway-Shea party would be returned to the House of Assembly.[2]

Three

The Great American and Shortline Railway

In 1865, the same year as Dr. Stabb of the Mental Asylum proposed a trans-island railway, the great Scots-Canadian railway engineer Sir Sandford Fleming fixed his steely-eyed gaze upon Newfoundland's jagged contours. The British Empire was at its height. The red blotches of Queen Victoria's colonies and dominions stretched across the map of the world. As for Newfoundland, what everyone else saw as a remote and backward island lost in the north Atlantic fog Fleming envisioned as the center of a vast system of imperial communications. He called his grandiose scheme the All-Red-Route.

During the previous decade Fleming had been hard at work building the Intercolonial Railway in the Maritime Provinces of eastern Canada. For most men, this task, a great work in itself, would have been a sufficient life's goal. But Sandford Fleming was not like most men. His ambition had been barely whetted. He gazed longingly across the Cabot Strait, which separates Newfoundland from Nova Scotia. Impatient to extend the Intercolonial Railway to the island, Fleming had noticed an obvious fact: the most direct route between the Old World and the New lay in a straight line between Ireland and Newfoundland. This was obvious to Fleming perhaps, but hardly anyone else thought it worth dwelling on. Newfoundland has been called the closest parish to Ireland and St. John's is approximately one thousand miles further east than New York City. Fleming called this route across the Atlantic the Short Ocean Passage. He planned to build a railway across Newfoundland called the Great American and Short Line. His idea was imaginative and innovative but not quite original. It had derived from an idea proposed in 1850 by John Poor of Portland, Maine to make Halifax, Nova Scotia, a trans-Atlantic terminus for the St. Lawrence and Atlantic Railroad.

Fleming's imagination was fired to a fever pitch. He devised a complex plan that hinged on a perfectly coordinated web of steamships and railways, by which he hoped to make it possible for British subjects, and anyone else who cared to pay the fare, to span the globe at record speed and never once lose the comforting sight of the Union Jack fluttering in the breeze. For fast and efficient service between Europe and North America it was necessary that there be a railway across Newfoundland. In order for a properly built railway to come into being Fleming reasoned that the island would have to become one of the Canadian provinces. If Fleming had had his way, the city of St. John's would have become the cornerstone of imperial communications.

Land travel by rail was much faster and quite a bit safer than a journey by sea. Despite these facts, the existing routes between England and America were entirely seaborne. They deliberately ignored the closest land masses, and Fleming could not understand why that had to be. Steamers between Liverpool and New York City took the long way around and thereby added to the danger and expense of travel. Shipping detoured around Ireland, crossed the North Atlantic Ocean, made a wide pass to the south of Newfoundland, and entirely ignored the Maritimes of Canada. This was inefficient, and if there was one thing that Sandford Fleming could not stand it was inefficiency. By existing means, and utilizing the fastest ships, it might take a traveler as much as three hundred and twenty hours (almost two weeks) to journey from London to New York. By maximizing the land travel and minimizing the sea voyage, Fleming hoped to halve the elapsed time. Forget about New York, Fleming calculated that he could deliver mail from London to as far as New Orleans in only two hundred and sixteen hours.

The All-Red-Route would take a traveler from London to New York City, by way of Newfoundland, in only 171 hours (approximately one week). It would go like this: An English traveler would leave London on a fast express train. Reaching Liverpool, or some other port on the west coast of England, the traveler would make a short hop across the Irish Sea aboard a sleek mail packet built for speed. The passenger would then continue across Ireland by rail, reaching the port of Valentia at the southwestern tip of that country. At Valentia an ocean-going steamship would be waiting for the traveler. The ship would cross the Atlantic Ocean at the narrowest point, which could only mean a landfall at St. John's, Newfoundland. Upon disembarking at St. John's the traveler would be entrained and then sped across the island, with the greatest comfort and ease, to the western side at St. George's Bay. From there a fast sloop would connect with Shippigan, New Brunswick, at the mouth of Chaleur Bay. At this point a spur line of the Intercolonial Railway would connect to the railway systems of Canada and the United States. Fleming estimated that the British and Irish rail systems could be traversed at an average speed of forty miles per hour, and the Irish sea, allowing time for transshipment of freight, at sixteen miles per hour. The Atlantic Ocean and the Gulf of St. Lawrence could be crossed at an average speed of sixteen and one-half miles per hour. (Why the ocean passage should be one-half a mile per hour faster than the Irish Sea is a slight puzzle, but no matter.) Fleming was confident that the North American railway grid would be traversed at a respectable rate of thirty miles per hour.

But from the start Fleming seriously underestimated the Newfoundland section of his scheme. He blithely assumed that a railroad across Newfoundland could be operated at the normal North American speed. One hundred and four years later, when the Bullet was making its last run, the average speed was only twenty-four miles per hour. Here is how Fleming figured it would all work out.

London to Valentia, Ireland	16 hours
Valentia to St. John's	100 hours
St. John's to St. George's Bay	8½ hours
St. George's Bay to Shippigan	15½ hours
Shippigan to New York City	31 hours
Total	171 hours

But of course Fleming argued that his estimate was only the unimproved speed. Fleming was confident that once the system was in operation he could cut the total time even further. He had plans to greatly increase the speed of oceangoing vessels by specifically designing them for express purposes. Fleming predicted that specially designed express vessels, carrying only passengers, their personal effects, and the mail, could achieve a markedly higher rate of speed than existing steamers. Carrying the All-Red-Route to its logical conclusion, Fleming envisioned travelers from as far afield as San Francisco and Vancouver journeying by rail to St. John's, then by sea to Europe and then by rail again to India and even Africa. In all of this Newfoundland was at the center.

Unfortunately, there was one unbreachable snag in Fleming's great plan. No consortium of financiers or governments was willing to finance the Great American and Short Line Railway across the nearly unexplored interior of Newfoundland. Sandford Fleming was a wealthy man but this was a very ambitious project. He still needed backers and these he could not find in sufficient quantities. There were too many unknowns in Newfoundland. The interior was desolate wilderness, unmapped and unsurveyed. Even the government of Newfoundland turned a deaf ear. Assuming that the politicians in Newfoundland were unanimously behind the project, and they certainly were not, there was little likelihood that tiny Newfoundland, even in times of prosperity, could hope to finance a railway on its own without going head over heels in debt. Canada was Fleming's last hope.

Fleming approached the prime minister of Canada, Sir John A. Macdonald, to see what could be done. Macdonald promised generous Canadian participation but only on one condition: Newfoundland must become a province of Canada. This the proud islanders had always stubbornly refused to accept. All along they had suspected that Fleming's wild scheme was merely a ploy to lure them into confederation. Faced with rocklike intransigence in St. John's, Fleming's great plan ground to a halt.

The All-Red-Route was a visionary idea for the 1860s. Had it come to pass, what a different place Newfoundland would have become! For the next fifty years most of the freight, mails and passenger traffic of the mighty British Empire would have been routed through St. John's. But it was not to be. Newfoundland was destined to slumber in obscurity for many more years. Political indifference and money problems made the plan unworkable. Sandford Fleming, though he never completely gave up on the scheme and continued to dabble in Newfoundland affairs, turned the main force of his active imagination to other tasks — the epic struggle to build the Canadian Pacific Railway, inventing Standard Time, designing Canada's first postage stamp, writing books, traveling, and laying a submarine cable to Australia.[1]

Four

The Surveys

The Survey of 1868

Five years before Canada's confederation in 1867, Sandford Fleming provided the government of the colony of Canada with a marvelously detailed plan for the construction of a railway to the Pacific coast. The idea was to link British Columbia and Vancouver Island with the rest of the country. This was the genesis of a project which would occupy the lion's share of Fleming's time and energy for the next quarter century. A big, bearded man of inexhaustible energy and imposing physical stature, Fleming became chief engineer of both the Canadian Pacific and the Intercolonial Railway. Despite the crushing mental and physical demands placed upon him, Fleming had by no means forgotten the Great American and Short Line Railway, or Newfoundland. The All-Red-Route was still an excitement to his imagination. With the impatience of the visionary he dreamed of funneling trans–Atlantic passengers through Newfoundland and along his "highway to the Pacific."

To further this end, Fleming sent the noted railway surveyor W. G. Bellairs to conduct a preliminary survey of the nearly unknown interior of Newfoundland and to determine the practicality of building a railway. Fleming got no help from the Newfoundland government so he payed for the entire cost of the expedition out of his own pocket.

Fleming had a meticulous mind. No detail was too small or too unimportant to take into consideration. If Fleming could have gone to Newfoundland himself he would have done so. His other responsibilities made that impossible. What he wanted was an exact estimate of every wooden tie, every yard of rail, every workhorse and every dollar needed to construct the railway.

Bellairs had to obtain the most detailed and reliable information possible concerning the location and nature of harbors that might be suitable as transshipment termini for the All-Red-Route. He also had to see if there were any unsurmountable obstacles interfering with a direct overland passage between such ports, and to make decisions on the proposed railway's mileage and general direction. Bellairs had a big job ahead of him.

Most of the terrain Bellairs would have to travel through was unexplored wilderness. Such information as was available came from Alexander Murray, a Canadian, appointed head of the recently formed Geological Survey of Newfoundland. Murray provided all the help he could, but most of the information and maps he had were, through no fault of his own, old, badly drawn and of dubious accuracy.

But Bellairs, like most surveyors of his day, was a courageous, hardy and determined man. He had a job to do and he was impatient to get on with it. Insects, frostbite, exhaustion, starvation, injury and a minimal wage were all part of the pioneer surveyor's profession. Though a veteran of many rugged expeditions, and a longtime associate of the demanding Sandford Fleming, this was to be Bellairs' supreme test. What Fleming was asking his man to do was to spend weeks and weeks alone, far from sight of civilization and rescue, hacking and slogging his way through a trackless wilderness. That he survived, let alone succeeded in his task, is a tribute to his endurance as much as his skill.

As a result of his feat, Bellairs became only the second white man to traverse the interior of Newfoundland and live to tell the tale. The first had been William Epps Cormack in 1822. Cormack had walked across Newfoundland, east to west, from Trinity Bay to St. George's Bay, crossing the center of the island in a futile attempt to make contact with the last surviving members of the Beothuck Indians — if there were any. Cormack had a fine chance to observe the countryside and its potential. His journal is full of idyllic accounts of what he saw.

> In the westward, to our inexpressible delight the interior broke in sublimity before us. What a contrast did this present to the conjectures entertained of Newfoundland! The hitherto mysterious interior lay unfolded upon us, a boundless scene, emerald surface, a vast basin. The eye strides again and again over a succession of northerly and southerly ranges of green plains, marbled with woods and lakes of every form and extent a picture of all the luxurious scenes of national cultivation receding into invisibleness.... Overland communication between the bays of the east, north and south Coasts, it appears, might easily be established.[1]

Prior to his expedition in 1822, Cormack had found that the inhabitants of the Newfoundland coast knew very little about the interior, having rarely if every left sight of the salt water. Cormack had been warned that his journey would end in disaster and that he was mad to even think of attempting it. The local people believed their own lurid stories when they told Cormack that he would either be torn apart by wolves or eaten alive by tribes of Indian cannibals. More than forty years later, Bellairs heard the same stories and was given the same warnings. For want of any more up-to-date information, or any reliable information at all, Bellairs decided to follow Cormack's general line of march and ignore the doomsayers. What he reported is quite different from what Cormack had seen.

> After leaving the peninsula of Avalon ... a dreary waste of alternating rocky hills and ridges, with wide spread barriers and marshes intersected by innumerable foaming torrents which rush through deep-cut precipitous gorges, flow tumultuously into the many fiords and inlets which indent the southern shore.[2]

Cormack seems to have been something of a romantic. Bellairs was a hard-nosed surveyor who had a railway to construct. Where one man sees "magnificent natural deer parks adorned with wood and water," another man sees only trestles to be built, ballast, steel rails, spikes, and boulders to be blasted.

Despite the considerable difficulties he saw and the hardships he experienced, Bellairs ended his journey on a note of cautious optimism. It would take a great deal of engineering skill but there were no serious obstacles that could not be overcome. In his final report to the delighted Sandford Fleming, Bellairs stated that there was no reason why a railroad could not be constructed across the island of Newfoundland and successfully operated.

The 1875 Survey

Cormack and Bellairs had prepared the groundwork. A railway could be built — in theory. But in order to turn the theory into practice, a more detailed assessment of the terrain and its difficulties was still needed. Only a precise instrument survey would be able to accurately predict the engineering problems to be faced, the miles of track to be built, rivers which needed bridges, the economic potential of the countryside and the exact routing of the line. This step was taken in 1875. Sir Stephen Hill, the governor of Newfoundland at the time, set the ball rolling. At the opening of the Legislature he said:

> The period appears to have arrived when a question which has for some time engaged public discussion, viz., the construction of a railway across the Island to St. George's Bay, should receive a practical solution.... As a preliminary to this object, a proposition will be submitted to you for a thorough survey to ascertain the most eligible line, and with a view to the further inquiry whether the Colony does not possess within itself the means of inducing capitalists to undertake this great enterprise of progress.[3]

In the seven years since Bellairs had made his survey the government of Newfoundland had become much more favorably disposed to the notion of a trans-island rail line. Public opinion had begun to shift and the politicians in St. John's thought it wise to shift with it. A money grant was provided for the new survey and Sandford Fleming was officially invited to take charge. Owing to the pressures of his work on the Canadian Pacific, Fleming was forced to decline the invitation. However, still mindful of the All-Red-Route, Fleming did accept the position of consulting engineer. In this capacity he organized a number of his associates from the Intercolonial Railway to take his place. In May of 1875 Fleming's engineering party, under the command of A. L. Light, left Québec City. Ice conditions on the Newfoundland coast were unusually severe that year, and it took the party two weeks of treacherous sailing just to make port in St. John's. This proved to be a small foretaste of the difficulties that lay ahead. Although Fleming must have been aware of how long it had taken to get to Newfoundland from Canada there is no indication that he ever reconsidered the viability of the transoceanic passage.

Bellairs, and Cormack before him, had travelled fast and light, essentially living off the land. Though their experience had shown that it would be difficult to bring up supplies in even the best of weather conditions, the expedition of 1875 tried to assault the wilderness with brute strength. Nearly one hundred men were scheduled to descend upon the bush, fully equipped with tenting gear, axes, canoes, tools for construction of rafts and boats, three months of food, and the all-important surveying instruments. All of it, bulky and unwieldy, would have to be carried through the wilderness on the backs of the men. No pack horses for them.

The survey was planned for the summer months when the travelling would be easiest. St. John's harbor in the east and St. George's Bay in the west were proposed as the termini. The terrain to be surveyed would be approximately the same as that seen by Cormack and Bellairs. The expedition was divided into three parties. "A," under Thomas Ramsey would handle the western section from St. George's Bay to the head of Red Indian Lake. "B," under W. A. Austin, would deal with the central section, east of Red Indian Lake to Gander River. F. J. Lynch would command "C" and be responsible for the eastern segment of the survey, from Come By Chance at the eastern entrance of the Avalon Peninsula. A. L. Light and Alexander Murray, the government geologist of Newfoundland, organized the engineering teams, planned the objectives and arranged for supplies, relief and transportation to the points of departure. Light was soon called back to Canada to complete other duties, and Murray was left to coordinate things on his own. It was hoped that the survey could be completed in the three months before winter set in. Each of the surveying teams was to consist of about twenty-five to thirty men; chainmen, foremen, locally recruited laborers and Micmac Indian guides. The leader of each party would receive $160 per month and the laborers $1.50 per backbreaking day.

Throughout the hot summer of 1875 these men trekked through the interior, stiff and sore, sweating, baked by the sun and tormented by clouds of relentless insects. Short-tempered, worked like carthorses, their clothing ripped to rags, often short of food, they lugged tons of gear hundreds of miles through nearly unexplored wastes.

"A" Party

"A" party was the first to set out. On June 5, Thomas Ramsey and his men were landed, by the steamer *Hercules*, on the beach at St. George's Bay. On the very first day, the boat containing their tents, provisions and stores was swamped in salt water at a place called "the Gut." After spending a miserable night drying out, "A" party set out for the interior the next morning. Before them lay a maze of lakes, ponds and rivers.

It took a special type of person to work on a nineteenth-century surveying team. Leaders were forever complaining that their men were not dedicated to their task or that they were just not strong enough. Shortly after "A" party's dunking, two of the surveyors became sick from exhaustion and had to be brought back to the coast for evacuation to St. John's.

The team drew its own map as it went. From the first glimmer of dawn the men of "A" party were awake and hard at work, scrambling their way up ridges, down ridges and up still more ridges. They clambered over giant boulders and picked their way through muskeg and matted forests. They forded countless streams and their paddles rippled the glassy surface of ponds which had never known the visit of white men. Whenever they came to a halt, the laborers collapsed in an exhausted heap, cursing their fate and probably their leaders, as the surveyors sized up the landscape with a professional eye. Regardless of the weather — rain, fog or scorching sun — out came the precious instruments, the theodolite to measure the distance they had come and the aneroid barometer to give an approximate altitude above sea level. When the information was duly recorded in the log book, the men were roused and the instruments carefully packed away. Slung on some strong back, the instruments would soon be brought out again on the floor of yet another nameless valley. How the men grew to hate those instruments, coddled and protected as were none of their human bearers.

Though "A" party was depleted by the loss of two of its most experienced surveyors, it was, in the words of Thomas Ramsey, an "admirable gang of men." "A" party reached its destination, at the head of Red Indian Lake, on time. After four months of hard travelling, the men, thoroughly spent but their work completed, were picked up by the *Tiger* and deposited safe and sound on the dockside in St. John's. The expedition of "A" party proved to be the easiest of the three. Ramsey described the country he and his men had passed through as alternating tracts of forest, marsh and barren waste, difficult country but not impassable.

"B" Party

"B" party, under W. A. Austin, left St. John's harbor on June 7, aboard the *Leopard*, a steam-powered sealing barkentine. Austin's instructions were as simple to state as they were to carry out — he was to land with his men on the north coast, travel up the Exploits River to Red Indian Lake, establish a base camp and then work eastward until a linkup could be made with "C" party under Lynch.

Because of unusually severe ice conditions, it took the explorers ten days merely to negotiate a landing at the mouth of the Exploits. It was immediately evident that the light canoes with which they were equipped were unsuited for the task at hand. "B" party had a small mountain of supplies and gear piled on the beach and there was no way that narrow-bottomed canoes would be able to transport it all up the winding expanse of the turbulent Exploits River, at least not in any reasonable length of time. Eight men were put to work for seven days constructing large rafts. In the meantime, the party's Micmac guides paddled the canoes up the river carrying what they could. Even after the rafts were completed, the transport of supplies was still fraught with difficulty. The river was long and there were several sets of rapids to navigate. "B" party's little fleet of boats and rafts was required to ascend and descend the river several times before all the supplies were transported to the base camp on Red Indian Lake. The men of "B" party paddled 2,500 miles up and down the Exploits River before the work of surveying could even be started. The entire length of the Exploits River is only 153 miles. It was not until July 22 that the base camp was established, forty-five days after leaving St. John's!

Working to the eastward, the terrain proved to be very hard going. The party faced alternating patches of dense forest, barrens and rocky outcrops. In parts:

> the surface of the ground [was] strewed with innumerable boulders, many of enormous size, being sometimes observed to reach upwards of forty feet in perpendicular height.[4]

"C" Party

With F. C. Lynch commanding, "C" party left St. John's on June 7 in the schooner *Voyager*. Lynch and his men were put ashore at Bull Arm near Come By Chance on June 10 and immediately headed west through what was probably the most rugged section of the entire survey. Progress was slow and exhausting. The country was a jungle of tangled forests, with an endless number of ponds and lakes, treacherous swamps, hills and steep ridges to be crossed. Incredibly, when the journey of "C" party was being planned, it was equipped with eight tons of supplies and gear but not one canoe for transportation! Every ounce of gear had to be carried through the wilderness on the backs of the men: this through country estimated to be one-third covered with lakes and ponds. As suitable material was unavailable to construct rafts, the men, burdened with huge packs, had to make lengthy detours through extremely rough terrain. So slow was the progress of the expedition that, on average, the line of march had to be halted two days out of seven to allow all hands to be employed packing and bringing forward supplies. So onerous was the advance that men began to collapse from exhaustion and had to be escorted back to the coast and sent home. Evacuating the casualties became a regular duty. The services of four or five men would be lost for days at a time, placing a greater burden on the remainder of the party. More than two months into the survey "C" party began to run seriously short of food. It is easy to imagine how the men must have felt, facing the prospect of starvation deep in the bush. It was estimated that there was enough food left to last but one or two weeks. Alexander Murray wrote, somewhat tersely, in the official report of the survey, that "Mr. Lynch had great difficulty in maintaining subordination among his men."[5] Not surprisingly, the men became sullen and mutinous. They were "only overcome by the personal presence of Mr. Lynch who, by patience and conciliatory measures succeeded in restoring order."[6] Lynch was still game to press forward but prudently established small caches of precious provisions in case a retrograde march became unavoidable. An Indian guide was sent to the telegraph station at Black River with a message to send more supplies as soon as possible. The new supplies were dispatched immediately, but very little that was useful arrived in the bush. The official report said of the relief supplies:

> Owing to some mistakes in the manner in which they were transported and the inefficiency of the men employed to carry them, they were of little avail, a great portion of the much-needed supplement being consumed before reaching camp.[7]

Eventually, Lynch could no longer control his men. He had to turn back. Lynch reached Black River on the evening of September 14 and was joined by the rest of his party, in very bad straits, the next morning. The men then proceeded by boat to Great Placentia and then to St. John's by road, arriving on September 21. It is a credit to Lynch's determination that, despite the privation his men had endured and the formidable nature of the terrain, all but the last fifteen miles of the survey had been completed.

Meanwhile, Austin and "B" party were still hacking their way through the bush of the central section. After almost four months they had received no relief and no extra supplies. "B" party was incommunicado. Despite this, Alexander Murray, who was coordinating the efforts of the three parties from his office in St. John's, had the audacity to request that Austin's party complete the last fifteen miles of Lynch's section. "B" party was so far in the wilderness that it took two relief expeditions just to locate them. The first expedition encountered such bad weather that it had to turn back. It is unrecorded what thoughts these men had about the men still in the bush who could not turn back. The second relief party, under Mr. Costigan, finally intercepted Austin and his men on October 2. By that time they were "shoeless and almost destitute of clothing, with but a limited supply of provisions left."[8] Upon seeing the pitiable condition of Austin's men the relief party immediately evacuated them to St. John's. Weather conditions were such that even this took a further thirteen days of hard traveling.

Except for a single fifteen-mile section, Newfoundland, from the west coast to where the Avalon Peninsula narrows to an isthmus at Come By Chance, had now been surveyed. All that remained was the Avalon Peninsula itself. Supposedly, this would be the easiest section to complete, as the Avalon Peninsula was the most densely populated area of Newfoundland and the closest to St. John's, the capital. But by this time the month of November was upon them. The three parties of exhausted explorers were given a short rest and then sent back into the bush. Murray later noted, "The same tents and other equipment were again used, and every device of economy strictly applied."[9]

Despite this ominous description, enough of the labourers volunteered that another team could be formed. Whatever advantage there was from being close to St. John's and civilization was cancelled out by the fast-approaching winter storms. From the beginning the weather was dreadful.

> Heavy rains, and gales continued in rapid succession till replaced by sleet and snow; fogs were constant and thick and much interfered with the exploration.[10]

The survey of the Avalon Peninsula was finished around Christmas, by which time the men were plowing through waist-deep snowdrifts and suffering badly from frostbite.

In the final report of the survey, Alexander Murray, with admirable restraint, concluded that, "Newfoundland is not by any means, so bad as has been represented."[11] Despite the all too readily experienced difficulties, the surveyors, now that they were safely back in the city of St. John's, waxed enthusiastic about the future — about the interior route, its rich stands of timber, its untapped mineral wealth, even its temperate climate and the possibilities for agriculture. The report advised that a railroad, if constructed, would provide a vital link between St. John's and the west coast of Newfoundland, providing a means for orderly settlement into

> regions which are now only a prey for fire and pillage, and the resort of lawless marauders and smugglers who owe no allegiance nor contribute to any nation or colony.[12]

The railroad, as it was surveyed from St. John's to St. George's Bay, was the shortest line between two points. Some three hundred and sixty miles in length, it cut through the exact center of the island, usually following the high ground. It was estimated that to construct one mile of standard-gauge track along the proposed route would cost the government of Newfoundland $23,589, and to build the entire railway, $8,504,378.[13]

As it turned out, after all the effort expended on the surveys, the railway, when construction began a few years later, was second-class, narrow-gauge, much more expensive and followed a more circuitous route. For political reasons, large portions of the line were shifted to link the remote communities of the great bays on the northern coast. This modification resulted in severe snow-clearing problems in winter and a winding roundabout route, which made it impossible to operate the railway on a break-even basis, let alone a profit.

Even so, Cormack, Bellairs, Ramsay, Austin, Lynch, and the nameless men they led had not labored in vain. Attention had been focused on the interior for the first time in Newfoundland's history and it had been concluded that a railway could be built there. There would be difficulties but they could be overcome. There was no reason, in the opinion of the surveyors, why a railway could not be constructed at reasonable cost.

Five

The Harbour Grace Railway

In 1877 the Newfoundland government received a cash payment of $1,000,000 from the United States. This windfall was Newfoundland's share of a successful arbitration of American fishing rights off the island's south coast. The mood in Newfoundland was one of confidence—the economy was good, roads were constructed, social services extended and, with the American money in hand, all eyes turned to the railway. There were many who felt that a railway would lead Newfoundland to a golden future. "Once it is built," commented one observer, "all things are possible. Hail! To the great Hereafter...."[1]

That same year, Sir William Whiteway, who as attorney general, had negotiated the American award, became prime minister of Newfoundland. Whiteway pushed a motion through the House of Assembly calling for the construction of a standard-gauge railway, the equal of anything on the North American mainland, between St. John's and St. George's Bay, along the route surveyed in 1875. The government was willing to offer generous land grants and a yearly subsidy of $120,000 to any group willing to build and operate such a railway. In Whiteway's view, a railway would be an investment in the future that would be well worth the expense. In Whiteway's opinion, the railway was "a development road, a people's road, and not so much an up-to-date line for the benefit of travellers and importers."[2] Besides opening up the interior to much needed development, a railway could be connected by scheduled steamers to the Intercolonial Railway in Canada. Who could tell what would happen then? If the two dominions could be brought into regular communication, it might just be the first step toward full economic and political union.

But this was not to be. Financial support for the direct route was available but political backing was not. The colonial office in London, for reasons of its own, discouraged the idea. Dating from the Treaty of Utrecht in 1713, Britain guaranteed France certain extraterritorial fishing rights and concessions on the west coast of Newfoundland, an area which came to be known as the French Shore. One of the concessions stated that no foreign installation would be constructed within one mile of the shore. The proposed railway, with its western terminus in the French Shore area, was seen by France as a foreign installation. How a railway on land would negatively affect France's fishing rights is murky, but nevertheless the French government objected strongly. The British were not inclined to defend the interests of an obscure and frankly low-status colony at the risk of antagonizing their powerful European neighbor. In any case, it was Britain's official opinion that the railway had no conceivable economic or strategic advantage for the empire as a whole. Newfoundland was compelled to knuckle under. The St. John's to St. George's Bay railway was not built.

Though disappointed, Whiteway and his government were not about to give up so easily. If, for the present, the west coast was closed, the north coast remained open. The French had no fishing rights there so their opinion was of no consequence. Following close upon the heels of the British rejection, Whiteway set up a committee of the Newfoundland government to study all facets of the railway question. The committee's conclusion, issued in a report on April 2, 1880, was well known and foregone before it was officially made public. It recommended that in lieu of a trans-island railway to St. George's Bay, a narrow-gauge line should be put down between St. John's and the recently opened copper mining developments at Hall's Bay. Hall's Bay was not on the French Shore, so construction of a railway to that area would antagonize neither the French nor the British. Counting branch lines to the towns of Brigus and Harbour Grace, the railroad to Hall's Bay was expected to be about three hundred and forty miles in length. By the time the track had been laid as far as Hall's Bay it was hoped that negotiations would have placated the French. The Newfoundland government made it no secret that its ultimate ambition was to run an extension down the west coast to Port aux Basques and upgrade the line to standard-gauge track.

Both the French government and the British colonial office made grumbling noises but there was little they could do. A railway to the north coast, financed locally, ran afoul of neither the Treaty of Utrecht nor Britain's right to handle the island's foreign affairs.

The railway that had originally been planned for St. George's Bay had been envisioned as a standard-gauge line, the same as anything then existing in Canada and the United States. The Newfoundland Railway to Hall's Bay, befitting its role as a stopgap arrangement, would be much humbler. For one thing, the track would be narrow-gauge, only three feet, six inches in width. The railway committee's report stated with unconscious humor, "The railway to be constructed shall not be what is deemed in England or the United States a first class railway."

The railway would serve the local needs of the colony and be built within the means of the colony. The Newfoundland government planned to do the building itself; private and foreign participation was not invited.

The government did not seriously expect to make any money out of the railroad but hoped that it would serve as a pump-primer for the economy as a whole. Newfoundland needed such a venture badly. Though the finances of the island were, for once, in a healthy state, it was becoming increasingly evident that the fishery and sealing industry, virtually the only resources Newfoundland had at the time, could not be expanded indefinitely. The burgeoning population had already outstripped the capacity of the fisheries to keep everyone gainfully employed. The population of Newfoundland increased fivefold during the nineteenth century while cod fishing, the main economic activity, hardly increased at all. The new copper mines at Hall's Bay were seen, with excitement, as hope for the future. A railway would take up the slack from unemployment while opening up more mines, as well as giving access to lands for timbering and farming. For the first time settlements could spread to the great valleys of the interior.

On April 17, 1880, an act was passed in the House of Assembly authorizing the receiver-general of the colony to raise a maximum of $5,000,000 to be used for railway construction. The passage of this act by no means ended the opposition to the project. Opposition in foreign capitals had been more or less mollified but the home-grown variety actually intensified. The Conservatives or Tories were the opposition party, and the newspapers they controlled were virulent in their opposition to anything and anyone even remotely connected to the railway project. Of course this was before the Conservative Party discovered that railways could be vote getters. In 1880 the Tories thought it sheer insanity for a maritime people to build a railway across an unknown interior on the mere speculation of discovering hidden riches. In their view, the railway was an expensive toy that would ruin the colony forever, and the Liberal politicians who dared suggest its construction were the worst kind of criminals: demented criminals. If the railway were built, Newfoundland would be drowned in debt and driven into the waiting arms of Canada. As it turned out, they were correct about the debt but wrong about Canada. In later years, when confederation sentiment had grown in Newfoundland, the debt-ridden railway made Canada think twice about inviting its poor eastern neighbor to become a province.

Journalism in nineteenth-century Newfoundland was not exactly subtle. There were sixteen newspapers being published, and in order to survive, each of them vied with the others to produce the day's most outrageous headlines. The papers did not pretend to be bipartisan. A casual glance would leave the reader with no doubt as to which side a newspaper was on and which political party it was affiliated with. In accordance with the tastes of the time, the newspapers were full of wild exaggeration, extremity and mudslinging, therefore a delight to read. The opposition press was particularly skilled in this regard. The St. John's *Evening Telegram* was the principal organ of the opposition. Its columns almost shook with rage and righteous indignation at the mention of the railway—"that infernal project." The railway

> seems a cast of the dice in the dark: an inauguration of the era of artificial Progress, whose issue shall finally determine the fate, for weal or woe, of "this Newfoundland of Ours."[3]

With generous use of capital letters and underlining, the *Evening Telegram* branded anyone who supported the railway the lowest sort of scoundrel, thief, blackguard, vulgarian and human skunk imaginable. The insults flew fast and furious, and were often quite creative. On one occasion Prime Minister Whiteway was described as a "Necromancer-General." In opposition to the *Telegram*, another newspaper darkly suspected that the St. John's merchant class, or that "Fishocratic ring," was behind all things anti-railroad.[4]

The *Evening Telegram* in one of its more moderate editorials stated that:

> In common with most natives I consider the Railway a farce, or perhaps a political dodge with the design of getting us into Confederation.

The article concluded with the ringing patriotic call of "Newfoundland for the Newfoundlanders."[5]

The months immediately following the introduction of the Railway Act were spent on yet another detailed railway survey. It had been decided to build the first section of the railroad to the large town of Harbour Grace on the western arm of Conception Bay. To conduct the survey the Newfoundland government made an offer to the man who had organized the 1875 survey, A. L. Light. Mr. Light proved unable or unwilling to accept the task, so the contract was awarded to a firm of Canadian engineers — Knipple and Morris of Greenock, New Brunswick. The firm's suitability for the job was hotly debated, as its previous claim to fame had been the design of a drainage system for the Sewerage Committee of Saint John, New Brunswick. Morris, of Knipple and

Newfoundland Railway bridge (Harvey, 1900).

Morris, just happened to be visiting St. John's when the Newfoundland government announced that it was in the market for qualified surveyors. Mr. Morris was only too happy to organize a team of engineers. The opposition papers commented darkly on how very kind it was of "Mr. Morris to be obligingly handy on the spot."[6]

Early in July the surveying personnel started to arrive. The *Evening Telegram*, under the headline THE CONFEDERATION ADVANCE GUARD reported that:

> Another Canadian engineer is expected here by Thursday's steamer to fatten on the *Newfoundland Railway* and help us spend the fishery money. No doubt we'll have all the tramps in the Dominion down here when they hear of all the "givin's out."[7]

Shortly thereafter, nineteen surveyors arrived in the harbor of St. John's aboard the SS *Nova Scotia*. Even the name of the ship was suspect. The reception the surveyors received was mixed, although probably not so bad as the *Evening Telegram* would have had its readers believe: "The expression of indignation which greeted the invasion of Terra Nova by the nineteen Canadian engineers yesterday was loud and deep."[8]

The nineteen engineers were referred to as "a covy of Canadian comorants [sic]," swooping down upon the unsuspecting islanders to "gobble up the 'unsquandered balance' of the Fishery Award." According to the Tories the government had instructed the predators "not to leave their prey until the *bones of our exchequer are picked clean.*"[9]

Accommodation for the men, at one of the better hotels in St. John's, was paid courtesy of the government of Newfoundland. The *Evening Telegram* was not shy about complaining:

THE CANADIAN COMORANTS "PUTTING ON AIRS"

> Before the arrival of the Canadian Comorants the Government it seems, made arrangements with the proprietors of several private boarding houses for the accommodation of the *precious nineteen*, the charge for *feeding* and *roosting* to be *eight shillings* per day. On their arrival, however, they decided to make their own arrangements to be put up at the best hotels as a much greater cost to the colony. Now, we believe, it is the intension of the proprietors to whom we refer to claim from our bungling government compensation for the expense incurred in fitting up and furnishing rooms for these Canadian railway adventurers. Surely the claim is a righteous one.[10]

Rousing his men from their hotel rooms, Mr. Morris organized them into five parties and work began. Their task was to reconnoiter the eighty-five-mile route from St. John's to Harbour Grace. Except for "The Battle of Foxtrap," detailed in Chapter Two, the survey itself proceeded quite smoothly.

Despite their celebrated hotel bills the "Canadian Comorants" had spent only $36,000 — an amount $14,000 less than had been budgeted! Mr. Morris, smarting under the criticism of the press, was anxious to prove that his firm could do more than build drains and sewers in New Brunswick. Given that iron rail was selling for $37 a ton at the time, Morris and Knipple estimated that it would take $1,250,000 to construct a narrow-gauge railway to Hall's Bay. The estimate proved to be conservative in the extreme. The final bill would be almost five times that amount and the island virtually bankrupted. The surveyors recommended that for safety and efficiency only rail weighing fifty ponds a linear yard be used. As an economy measure the Newfoundland government hoped to make do with forty-two-pound tracks. When construction commenced, cheaper thirty-five-pound rail was used.

The government of Newfoundland had originally planned on constructing the railroad all by itself, raising the necessary funds on credit, but when the House of Assembly met in February 1881 it found itself presented with several interesting commercial proposals. This seemed too good to be true. Here were private investors competing with each other to relieve the government of a costly debt to build and operate the railway. It did not take the Newfoundland government long to decide that the railway to Hall's Bay could be built and run much more efficiently by contract and private enterprise.

E. W. Plunkett and Associates offered to build a standard-gauge railway for cost plus five percent, operating it on an annual subsidy of $1,000 per mile. The company refused to build a narrow-gauge railway because in their judgment, "The cost of operating it in the climate of Newfoundland would be so great as to deter practical railway men from undertaking it."[11]

The Newfoundland government disagreed, still feeling a standard-gauge railway was too rich for its blood.

J. N. Greene and Associates of Saint John, New Brunswick, were of a more adventurous breed. Holding no reservations about the rigors of the climate, they offered to build a narrower railway of only three feet in width for a $246,000 annual subsidy and a thousand acres of land for each mile of completed track. The offer sounded tempting but in the end it was rejected. The government decided that it was too much money for too little railway. A three-foot gauge was too narrow, even for the government of Newfoundland.

The offer that was accepted came from an American firm headed by A. L. Blackman. Blackman's syndicate planned to raise money against its own credit to build, operate and supply the rolling stock for a three foot, six inch railway to Hall's Bay, the initial stage of which would connect the capital of St. John's with Harbour Grace. In return, the government of Newfoundland agreed to pay the syndicate an annual subsidy of $180,000 in half-yearly installments for a period of thirty-five years. In addition, the Americans would receive five thousand acres of good land for every mile of track they constructed, the land to be allotted in alternating segments one mile along the track and eight miles deep. The railway, when completed, would be the property of the syndicate, with the Newfoundland government holding the option to purchase it after thirty-five years. The contract was signed on April 20, 1881 on the promise that the railway would be in full operation within five years.

After dropping the name "Great American and Short Line Railway Company"— but not Sandford Fleming's vision of a trans–Atlantic shipping route — the Blackman syndicate was incorporated on June 1 as the Newfoundland Railway Company. One hundred thousand dollars in United States treasury bonds was deposited as security for the completion of the project. The southern division of the company, known as the Harbour Grace Railway, was to be built from St. John's to the town of Harbour Grace. The northern division, known as the Placentia Railway, was to be constructed as far as the community of Placentia and later to Hall's Bay. To ease the way, the House of Assembly granted that all materials imported to Newfoundland for the construction and the operation of the railway be duty free.

The government of Newfoundland had just made the first in a series of very bad deals. In its eagerness to obtain a railroad at bargain-basement prices, the government became the heir to a railway built to bargain-basement specifications. Within two years the Blackman group went bankrupt. It had lost interest in Newfoundland, preferring to concentrate its scanty resources on a trans–Atlantic terminus in Nova Scotia. Only sixty miles of ramshackle track had been laid, forcing the government to step in and finish the line to Harbour Grace itself. The government was saddled with heavy debts to the Blackman syndicate's creditors and expensive legal battles which dragged on as far as the privy council in London.

On August 16, 1881, the sod-turning ceremony (delayed from August 9) took place at Oak Farm, near Fort William, at what is now the site of the Fairmont-Newfoundland Hotel, close to St. John's harbour. Under the watchful eye of A. L. Blackman and several government ministers, fifty men set to work with pick and shovel. The St. John's *Newfoundlander*, a paper controlled by the pro-railway Liberal Party, reported that "notwithstanding unpropitious weather the men set to work with vigour and will."[12] The *Evening Telegram* was too grumpy to bother covering the opening ceremony at all. It just sourly remarked, "During the last week a show of commencing work has just been made in the vicinity of the town."[13] Except for a few technicians, local labor was employed wherever possible. The work was done entirely without the aid of cranes, derricks or any large machinery. The construction gang worked with hand tools and a few horses and carts and that was all.

By the end of August the work force had grown to three hundred; by December, more than twelve hundred men were hard at work. It was much-sought-after employment.

> Money it was said, began to fall like the gentle rain from Heaven, its refreshing dews descended alike on the friends and opponents of the new enterprise; its rills trickled into everyone's pockets.[14]

Twenty miles of rail bed had been graded and ten miles of track laid. The pro-government papers crowed with the reports of the unabated energy of the workers, the superior quality of their labors, the beauty of the gleaming steel rails and the immense benefits to be accrued to the country once the project was completed. Aside from a flurry over a brief strike for higher wages (the men were already getting a dollar a day!) the opposition press ignored the whole disagreeable business as best it could.

On October 8, 1881, the *SS Standard* arrived in St. John's with a load of Welsh railway iron and the work of laying the track went ahead immediately. The *Evening*

Telegram was, as could be expected, not very enthusiastic. "This incident," it reported, "will doubtless prove a source of infinite pleasure to *some* of our contemporaries."[15]

Though headed for a terminus in the northwest of Newfoundland, the track left St. John's in an easterly direction. On the outskirts of the city the rails turned counter-clockwise in a great semicircle, making the first of their many sharp curves. Rounding

Sign of the Locomotive (Harvey, 1883).

View of Harbour Grace in 1900, terminus of the Harbour Grace Railway (Harvey, 1900).

the head of St. John's harbour, the rails disappeared westward over the rugged spine of the Avalon Peninsula to descend, by the summer of 1882, to the stony beach at the town of Holyrood on Conception Bay.

On October 31, 1881, tenders were called for locally hewn railway ties, or sleepers, as they were sometimes known. About 200,000 ties would be needed to reach Harbour Grace. A skilled man with an axe could cut at least twenty ties per day and each tie, when delivered, would sell for about twenty cents.

The first steam locomotive earmarked for the Newfoundland Railway met with an untimely fate. It was scheduled to arrive aboard the schooner *Millo* on October 24, 1881, but was lost overboard. The engine had been purchased second-hand from the narrow-gauge Prince Edward Island Railway. Once the locomotive was loaded aboard *Millo* at Halifax, the long and stormy passage to St. John's took thirteen harrowing days! The locomotive, fifteen to twenty tons dead weight, was strapped to the deck, making the schooner dangerously unstable. The sea was violent enough to shift this great bulk over on its side, threatening the schooner with capsizing. In order to save the vessel from sinking and their own lives, the frantic crew cut the restraining ropes on the engine and over it went.[16]

The *Evening Telegram* had a field day with the story, claiming that the crew "must be born under a lucky star" and "one of heavens peculiar favourites." The October 26, 1881, edition was crowned with banner headlines.

MELANCHOLY MARINE CATASTROPHE
SUDDEN LOSS OF "OUR" LOCOMOTIVE
A VALUED FRIEND THROWN OVERBOARD TO FEED THE FISHES!!!

Also, according to the *Evening Telegram*, a small boy came bounding into the editorial office to announce

> ... our locomotive's threw overboard.... Well what an ungrateful government.... What a laugh we had ... the engine, being rigged up in a very rickety sort of way ... soon began to feel the motion of Father Neptune's sea floor, and to rock about in a very ominous manner ... at last after rocking about with more and more alarming declensions from the perpendicular, Old Neptune gave a heavier "kick" than usual to the little craft and with an agonizing groan and a mighty lurch, overboard went the poor locomotive and sank beneath the waves.

Newfoundland being a child of the sea, the *Evening Telegram* felt that, "it is only natural that the first locomotive should go down as a meat offering...." The newspaper concluded by writing, "We are sorry to hear that the last locomotive was uninsured."

A second locomotive was ordered from the same source and it arrived, safe and sound, by the *SS Merlin* from Sydney, Nova Scotia, on December 5. The engine was put to steam and run for the first time on December 13. What the *Newfoundlander* called "boisterous and jubilant"[17] the *Evening Telegram* called run-down and laughable.

RUN FOR THE FIRST TIME
OUR "NEW" LOCOMOTIVE
A GRAND PARADE ON THE RIALTO
"ANYTHING GOOD ENOUGH FOR NEWFOUNDLAND."

> Yesterday, the wheezy, old, second-hand "bulgine" sent down to us by Mr. Blackman was put on parade, and made as much noise, smoke and smell as a heathen volcano. Judging by its continuous "puffing" and "snorting" one would suppose that it had taken something internally that had, "not agreed with it," or that it was not yet acclimatized to the fine air of "our Island-home." Evidently its movements were also of the compound principle, for it backed and butted "wuss than a crazy donkey" — as one of our candid fellow-citizens observed — and emitted such a very *poor* quality of smoke and smell, that even the warmest Blackmanite might be tempted to conclude that these were manufactured from the cheapest coal. We fear "Old Number Ten," as the boys call it, has, like some of the rest of us, "seen its best days."[18]

Despite the strident opposition from some quarters of the population, the project continued to forge ahead. By June of the following year, 1882, regular passenger service had been inaugurated, with trains running to Topsail on Conception Bay; in September service was extended to Holyrood. The fare was two dollars.

Despite its well-known opposition to the railway, the *Evening Telegram* did not hesitate to accept front page ads for railway pleasure excursions. Business was business after all. Under a drawing of a train proudly steaming along the tracks were the headlines:

> Take Notice. You are going to the Engineers and Moulders Great Mamoth [sic] PICNIC EXCURSION to Topsail by rail.... Entertainment to be provided by Professor Bennet's Brass and String Band.[19]

First locomotive in Newfoundland, imported from Prince Edward Island. Landed from the SS *Merlin* on 5 December, 1881, it was one of five purchased from the PEI Railway (also narrow gauge 3' 6"). Built in 1872 by the Hunslet Engine Co., Leeds, England, they were all scrapped by 1897 (Public Domain).

The *Evening Telegram*, however, did send a reporter to observe this so-called pleasure excursion. Their headline left no doubt as to how the reporter felt about the experience.

> THE AGONY OF THAT TRIP TO TOPSAIL
> Travelling Capacity of the "Wealthy Syndicate's Engines."

The Total Abstinence and Benefit Society accompanied by large numbers of other pleasure seekers started on an excursion to Topsail yesterday morning with the expectation of enjoying a pleasant time amid the varied scenery of our popular "watering place"... O the excruciating agony of that trip will never be forgotten, nor will the, "wealthy syndicate" ever be forgotten, nor will the, "wealthy syndicate" ever be able to make amends for the mental suffering they have been instrumental in inflicting upon five or six hundred of our people. For nearly three long hours the Society and their friends were cooped up in the Company's boxes and — like the Children of Israel in the Desert of Sinai — kept moving hither and thither before they were permitted to enter the "Promised Land".... The few hours spent at the pretty little village were as much enjoyed as could have been expected under the circumstances. Of course it is only natural to suppose that the terrifying recollections of what they had just passed through, occasionally obtruded themselves upon the minds of the excursionists and threw a tinge of sadness over the features of young and old.... In due time the party trembling turned their faces towards the Company's horrible cars and after similar vicissitudes to what they experienced on the outward journey, arrived back to town as the clock on the steeple struck nine. One gentleman, on being asked how he enjoyed the trip said "...by the great and immortal Father Matthew, red-hot temperance man as you know me to be, I wouldn't travel on the Company's cars again, even if they gave me as much money as has been squandered by the Whiteway-Shea Government."[20]

Compare that account with the railway excursion of the Sons of St. Andrew to Harbour Grace, as reported in the pro-railway *Times*.

The excursion of yesterday proved so delightful, in every respect, without any drawback, that there is little doubt that they will be steady patrons of the railway in the future.... The iron horse starting at the convenient hour of ten o'clock conveyed them in an hour to their destination passing the most beautiful scenery. The ladies stepped out of the carriages, fresh blooming and beautiful, not a ribbon disordered, not a dress rumpled or a cheek pale, prepared at once to enter upon the business of fascination.... The excursionists reached St. John's soon after eight o'clock after enjoying one of the pleasantest trips which could well be imagined.[21]

The Methodist and Anglican Churches and that intrepid guardian of public morality and decency, the Convention of Sunday Schools, felt compelled to condemn Sunday rail excursions.

That whereas we have the solemn command in God's Word, to remember the Sabbath Day to keep it holy and *Whereas* the managers of the Newfoundland Railway have repeatedly, in opposition to the most enlightened human law, run Excursion Trains on the Lord's Day, very much to the moral detriment of the people, therefore *Resolved* that this Conference hereby enter its SOLEMN PROTEST against this violation of Divine Law.[22]

The first serious railway accident occurred on November 18, 1882. At Indian Pond the train collided with a cow. A group of laborers riding on a flatcar were thrown off by the impact. Three of them fell under the wheels and were killed.

By 1883 bungling and extravagance had squandered the money raised by the Blackman syndicate. After two years of work the coffers were empty and only sixty miles of track had been constructed. The Americans declared bankruptcy and the railway reverted to its English bondholders. Under receivership the last twenty-five miles to Harbour Grace were completed, and scheduled service commenced on November 24. Three trains a week connected St. John's with Conception Bay. The last spike on the "Harbour Grace Railway" was driven by a young midshipman stationed aboard HMS *Canada*, a British corvette which happened to be visiting St. John's. The midshipman was later to become King George V.[23] Curiously, there was another last spike ceremony in October 1884 when the Harbour Grace line was officially opened for business.

Saturday last was indeed a red-letter day in the history of the "oldest colony" beholding as it did the formal opening ceremonies connected with the first Newfoundland Railway.

American "Mogul" type locomotive *St. John's* on the Harbour Grace Railway, 1882. Built by R. W. Hawthorne & Co., Newcastle-on-Tyne, England. It was originally fitted with a spark arrester in the chimney as the railroad station was in a densely populated area (The Rooms Provincial Archives, VA 29-3 / The Engineer).

At 1 P.M. the first train from the Junction arrived at the Engine House near Harvey Street East, in the vicinity of which had congregated a large concourse of the townspeople — some who on special invitation, were about to go out on the Line to witness the ceremony of "driving the last spike;" others who, compelled by curiosity, had assembled to observe the novel and interesting sight of seeing the "iron horse" ploughing his way into the precincts of the "second city." A lavish display of bunting was suspended from and in the immediate vicinity of the Engine House, which, together with the presence on the grounds of a number of horses and carriages, had the effect of imparting quite a gala day appearance to the scene.

As Engine Number 10, with a train and car attached, came rapidly into view, the younger as well as some of the older portion of the spectators gave voice to their feelings of wonderment and delights at beholding for the first time a train careening over "the Newfoundland Railway." After a brief delay, during which all necessary preliminary preparations were made, the party of Harbour Grace excursionists entered the car, and soon were speeding onward in the direction of Tilton. Mile after mile was swiftly traversed. As the passengers gazed out over the rapidly shifting scene, and entered into the full enjoyment of the hour, many an expression of pleasure and approval fell from their lips (indeed, even from those who have not proved themselves the friends of the enterprise), concerning the smoothness and evenness of the Line — a fact rendered all the more striking from the circumstance that the track had not been laid longer than a few days, and that this was the first train which had ever passed over it.

The first five miles of the road was traversed when Tilton was reached, and after five miles more had been equally rapidly gone over, the St. John's train was seen some distance ahead, drawn up close by the place where the last rail was to be laid, and where the ceremony above referred to was to be celebrated. The passengers had disembarked, and were standing in knots on the Line. As the Harbour Grace train drew near, they waved many warm salutes of welcome and congratulations. The whistles of the respective engines also sent forth their shrill shrieks of gratulation. In a moment the friends in the Harbour Grace train had stepped down, and soon were exchanging greetings over the auspicious and notable event.

After the mutual congratulations were over, and the last rail had been laid in its place, the ceremony of driving the spike began. Sir William Whiteway, after a few felicitous remarks, handed a large hammer to His Excellency [the governor, John Hawley Glover] and requested him to "drive the spike." His Excellency did so, giving it three smart blows. Another spike was then driven by the ladies of both parties amidst much merriment. Three cheers were then asked and right heartily given, for St. John's and Harbour Grace; and for Her Majesty's Representative, and Her Majesty's Attorney General and Premier. The ceremony concluded, the two parties re-entered the cars. As some of the St. John's party, however, were anxious to be able to say that they had driven over the first through-train from St. John's to Harbour Grace, it was decided to pay a short visit to the second city. This was accordingly done. When the train arrived at its destination, His Excellency, owing to the indisposition of Lady Glover, deemed it wise to go on to Harbour Grace and proceed to St. John's by the sea route.

After a short delay, the two trains again started, and were soon speeding over the Line on their way to the Junction, distance about 26 and three quarter miles from this town. At half past five the train drew up at the long, commodious erection known as the Davenport Hotel. Here the party stepped down, and entered the building. Therein had been prepared by Colonel Davenport for the entertainment of the visitors a substantial luncheon, of which, with appetites sharpened by the long drive, they partook with keen relish. The lunch over, Sir William in happy and appropriate phrase proposed the first toast — "The Health and Prosperity of Harbour Grace." This was responded by R. S. Munn, Esq., [a leading Harbour Grace businessman] in a neat speech, followed by the Receiver General, who expressed in a few sentences his sense of pleasure at the event that had that day been consummated.... In the course of a few minutes more, the St. John's party embarked for the city amid the loud hurrahs of their Harbour Grace friends. The run into St. John's ... was pleasant and uneventful, the station was reached at 10:45, and the participants of the excursion's pleasures could not but feel that they had been present at a great *"epoch in the history of Newfoundland."* They had, at least, made the longest railroad journey ever taken in this Island, and if they felt disinclined at that time to think more deeply of the subject, they could not avoid laying this flattening unction to their souls.

Shortly after the St. John's train had taken its departure for home, the Harbour Grace train followed its example. The night being dark and the road new, the engineer had instructions to drive slowly and carefully; consequently the return journey occupied a little more time than did the preceding one. The train reached the Engine House at 10:15.[24]

Placed under ruthless economies, the railway actually began to show a marginal profit. But that was not good enough for the bondholders, who wanted to extricate themselves from the whole project. In 1896 they got their wish. The government of Newfoundland agreed to purchase the complete operation for $1,581,666. This was more money than had been originally estimated for the entire three hundred and forty miles of track to Hall's Bay.

Locomotive on a trestle bridge at North Arm, 1880s (The Rooms Provincial Archives, C1-132).

By Rail — St. John's to Harbor Grace in 1900

The distance from St. John's to Carbonear via Brigus Branch is 83¾ miles. The scenery along this line is very attractive and the tourist should not omit to make the excursion. Topsail — 15 miles — is a pretty village on the shore of Conception Bay, with comfortable boarding-houses. It is a favorite summer and bathing resort, and has been somewhat ambitiously styled "The Brighton of Newfoundland." Holyrood — 33 miles — at the head of the bay presents some striking scenery, especially in its sea arms. Indeed, the scenery of the whole bay from Topsail, where it first comes into view, can scarcely be surpassed. The thriving little town of Brigus, picturesquely situated among the rocks, with a population of 1,540, is 55 miles from St. John's. The remaining stations are Clark's Beach, 61 miles; Bay Roberts, 65 miles; Spaniard's Bay, 68 miles; Harbor Grace, 75 miles; Carbonear, 83¾ miles.... A carriage drive of sixteen miles, from Carbonear to Heart's Content on Trinity Bay, will be found enjoyable. This is the western terminus of the Anglo-American Company's cables.*[25]

Anonymous complaint, put to verse by someone on the Trepassey branch line on the death of his razor-back pig under the wheels of Engine #9:

The first trans–Atlantic telegraph cable came ashore at Heart's Content, Newfoundland, on July 27, 1866.

To: Gov't Railway Claims Agent

My razor-back came down the track
A week ago today,
When No. 9 came down the line,
And sniffed its life away.
My little pig, no fault of mine,
Broke down the garden gate,
So please do pen a cheque for ten,
Its life to liquidate.

The claims agent was moved to reply the same way.

Your razor-back came down the track
As everybody knows,
But razor-backs on railway tracks
Are sure to meet their woes.
No swine kind lay on our mind
The day we built for No. 9,
And not for razor-back.[26]

Railway Hotel, St. John's (Harvey, 1900).

Six

The Placentia Railway

When the laborers from the railway gangs returned home with money jingling in their pockets, the people of the outports began to look upon railway construction in a new and more favorable light. In a primitive and cruel economic arrangement that virtually enslaved the outport residents to the credit of the local merchant, railway work was a much-sought-after escape. The truck system dictated that merchants would supply fishermen with gear and provisions on credit. The debt would be paid off with the proceeds of the next fishing season — in theory. In practice many fishermen were never able to escape from their debt load and were kept in thrall to the merchant in perpetuity. For some people the few dollars earned at the backbreaking tasks of chopping down trees, grading smooth the right of way, building trestles and laying track was the first hard cash they or their families had ever held in their hands. The laborers earned seventy-five cents per day and built their own shelters. For the first time, then, there was an alternative to the usurious power of the outport merchants.

Robert Bond, the Liberal honorable member for Fortune Bay, who ten years later would become prime minister, made an impassioned speech about the need for more railways. Unemployment was rampant, the common people were destitute and their children dressed in rags. A railway was portrayed as a ticket to a better future, opening up the interior and giving jobs to thousands — essentially a public works project. Though it had yet to be demonstrated that a railway in Newfoundland could make money — the Harbour Grace Railway once came within $5,548 of breaking even[1]— it was beyond doubt that a railway was beneficial to a great number of average families, at least in the short term. During the building and operation of the Harbour Grace Railway $1,500,000 had flowed into the hands of Newfoundlanders, eighty-five percent into the patched pockets of laborers. Most people thought that if a subsidy was required to keep the trains running, it was worth it.

Railway fever took hold. It spread like the tide to the farthest bays and coves. People who had never even seen an iron horse or heard its whistle blow were bitten by the bug. Before long, every elected official in Newfoundland was besieged with demands for railways. Some communities circulated petitions, signed by every adult resident, demanding that railway construction be commenced immediately. In their eagerness, some communities circulated petitions signed by more than every adult resident! Such a groundswell of popular opinion could hardly be ignored by the members of the House of Assembly in St. John's. Things reached such a state that it did not matter where a man stood on the political spectrum. If a politician did not support railway building, he was anti-progress and, therefore, without a hope of being elected. Though the railway policy had been inaugurated in 1881 by the Liberals, their Conservative successors, led by Richard Thorburn, found it politically expedient to continue the policy. Once the politicians in St. John's got on the bandwagon it made little difference where a railway was located. A railway could begin nowhere and end nowhere. The only important thing was that there were railways, that they passed through their constituencies, and gave employment and money to their voters.

On the afternoon of March 30, 1886, just before the House of Assembly was scheduled to sit, a large crowd of unemployed men and boys descended upon the Colonial Building, the seat of government. They carried with them a huge banner emblazoned in large blue lettering: RAILWAY. The mob was determined to air their grievances before the government. Sweeping past a small detachment of police, they charged into the building.

> Hardly had the Chairman assumed the Chair when a crashing was heard in some part of the building outside the Assembly Chamber. As the sound drew nearer the smashing

Interior of passenger car on the Newfoundland Express (Harvey, 1900).

of glass and doors was distinctly audible, and suddenly, as if the crowd had carried everything before them, a rush was made and, in less than a minute, the House was filled. In rushing through the main hall a gasolier was smashed by the pole to which the banner was attached, and the crowd forced an entrance even inside the Bar of the House. The galleries were packed and groaned with the weight of the people, and the building resounded with shoutings.[2]

Neither the Speaker of the House nor the prime minister could persuade the mob to leave. Only with the promise that public works projects would be started to relieve unemployment did the crowd break up and allow the House of Assembly to adjourn.

Early the next morning the alleged ringleaders, Patrick Dempsey and a man named Earles, were arrested by the police and taken into custody. Word of the arrest quickly spread throughout the city of St. John's and before long another angry mob assembled, this time in front of the courthouse. The authorities were ready with a large force of police, mounted and on foot, armed with revolvers, rifles and bayonets. The crowd demanded that the police arrest them all as they were as guilty as the two men locked up inside. What promised to be an ugly confrontation was swiftly defused when Judge Prowse released Dempsey on the grounds of insufficient evidence.

The following day, a certain Connell, the man who had carried the banner, was arrested. Again a crowd assembled before the courthouse and once again armed police manned their posts. Fearful of what might erupt, Mr. Morris, a member of the House of Assembly, advised the attorney general to release the prisoner on bail. He himself would give a personal guarantee that the prisoner would appear when called to trial. This proved to be unnecessary. As evening wore on, the crowd broke up and went home of its own accord. Earles was discharged a few days later and Connell was given thirty days for assaulting a policeman.[3]

Feelings were running so high that the Thorburn government was forced to construct a railway to stay in power. Later that year, 1886, the government began work on a railway, fiananced by the public purse, that would run from the existing Newfoundland Railway at Whitbourne to the port of Placentia, twenty-six miles distant. It was an indication of the government's true feelings that when the engineers recommended fifty-pound rail be used, the cabinet overruled the advice and insisted on the purchase of cheaper and flimsier thirty-five-pound track.

The Newfoundland government could probably have tossed down a line of track anywhere and it would have sufficed. Later administrations would do exactly that. The reason the government picked the community of Placentia had little to do with economics, communications or sensible planning. The railway to Placentia was built simply because the Conservative Party wanted to remain in power. It was true enough that the construction of the railway would keep a gang of men busily employed for at least two years, but that was strictly an incidental benefit. The main reason for constructing a railway was that it was a vote getter. The main reason for constructing a railway to Placentia was that the Conservatives desperately needed the support of the elected members in the House of Assembly whose constituencies just happened to lie astride the projected route.

The building of the Placentia Railway proceeded under the amusing fiction that it was a road. The Newfoundland government was building a number of access roads to the existing rail line and let on that the work between Whitbourne and Placentia was merely another one of these. Of course everyone knew that the Placentia Road was actually the Placentia Railway. The reason for the deception was that many of the traditional supporters of the Conservative Party — the moneyed classes and the merchants — mindful of the expensive misfortunes of the Harbour Grace Railway a few years before, had remained bitter opponents. They were worried that the country might go bankrupt. They were also concerned that the supply of cheap labor might dry up.

The Act of May 18, 1887, provided for the construction of the "road" from Whitbourne to Placentia. The "road" proved very costly indeed. Five hundred thousand dollars, twice the estimate, for a twenty-six-mile railroad was an enormous sum to spend at the time. There was no chance of the railway to Placentia turning a profit. For one thing the terminal was badly situated. It was on a hill half a mile from shore. In 1889 the government engineer reported that, outside of such traffic as may result from the prosecution of operation on the Hall's Bay Line, there seemed to be no prospect of a healthy increase of business.

The Placentia Railway was built as a spur branching off the existing line to Harbour Grace. This latter railway was still under the control of its English bondholders, and the relationship between the Newfoundland government's railway and the privately-owned

Engine No. 3, Reid Newfoundland Company, c. 1898. Train is negotiating a sharp turn along the Humber River (The Rooms Provincial Archives, B 4-230).

railway had not been ironed out. A rather confused situation resulted. A train heading for Placentia from St. John's would have to travel over the track administered by the English bondholders as far as Whitbourne Station and then on the last twenty-six miles to Placentia on track owned by the government of Newfoundland. The bondholders took legal action to prevent government-owned locomotives from traveling down their track. The case dragged on through every court in the land. Eventually it reached the privy court for arbitration. The matter was settled only after the Newfoundland government, quite disgusted with the whole dispute, agreed to buy out the English investors with $325,000 in government bonds, or "fogs," as they were known.

In 1889, before the dispute with the bondholders had been settled, the government decided to take one more crack at building a railway. It was decided to complete the building of the Hall's Bay Line. Only sixteen miles had been graded when an election was called. The Conservatives were defeated. Whiteway and the Liberals were returned to power under the slogans "Vote for the Friend of the Workingman and the Apostle of Progress" and "Vote for Whiteway and $1.25 a day!" The new government

A train of the Hall's Bay Railroad, which became part of the Newfoundland Railway in 1898. Engine No. 8 was built in 1893 (The Rooms Provincial Archives, A 12-157 / R. E. Holloway).

was determined to make good on its campaign promises, but the outrageous cost of the Placentia Railway convinced Whiteway that the government itself had no business building railways: all future construction would be let out for tender. Along with this decision by the Liberal government a new man came upon the stage — R. G. Reid.

A trip on the Placentia branch line in 1913:

We got away [from Placentia] about 5:30, but did not reach St. John's (80 miles) till 2 A.M. the following morning, a very poor performance. The engine could not pull us up inclines. We made a rush and each time stuck half-way and had to run back a couple of miles to make a fresh try. However, it seemed a usual occurrence, for every one on board took it philosophically, many recounting their reminiscences of when they had to stop all night in the train.[4]

Curses and ghosts?

When an Indian suffered some damage to her baskets, she put a solemn curse on the whole line. That winter they had the worst weather in living memory, and the Newfoundlanders shook their heads knowingly. It is not clear whether the Micmac curse had anything to do with the ghost trains that ran down the track. In 1911 and 1912, freights were solemnly witnessed and reported by the station at Arnold's Cove when everybody knew there was no train within 100 miles.[5]

On the eighty-eight miles of the Bonavista branch it sometimes took fifteen hours or more to make the trip.

It was the practice after the train arrived at the station and the passengers disembarked for it to go up on the Y to turn around. It was a mile return journey and the conductors who were usually kindly souls allowed people to go on the train for the short trip.[6]

St. John's to Placentia by Railway in 1900:

No tourist should fail to pay a visit to Placentia — the old French Capital — one of the most interesting places in the island, not only on account of its historic associations, but for the exquisite beauty of its scenery, especially along the arms of the sea, one of which runs ten miles inland. In July these arms abound in sea trout; and with the salmon and river trout make the place a paradise to the angler. The walks and drives about Placentia are delightful and in its scenic beauty the artist will find much of interest.

The route is the same as to Harbor Grace as far as Whitbourne Junction 57½ miles from St. John's. At Placentia Junction, 64½ miles, the line diverges to the left and runs southwest past Ville Marie, 78½ miles, to Placentia, 84½ miles from St. John's. Board can be had at a moderate rate. The town, 5,362 population, has a quaint appearance, being built along a shingly beach. It was founded and fortified by the French in 1660, and held by them till 1713. The remains of the oldest Protestant Church in the island — Church of England — are here, but in a most delapidated state. To this church belongs a handsome communion service of silver in five pieces, presented by William IV, when as a midship in the "Segasus," he visited Placentia. It is carefully preserved and shown to visitors. It bears the inscription: "Given by His Royal Highness, Prince William Henry, to the Protestant Chapel at Placentia, Newfoundland."[7]

Placentia, the Old French Capital

Placentia is eighty-two miles from St. John's and by starting early Saturday morning we reached Placentia in time for evening meal. The actual running time upon the railroad was eight hours. Perhaps I should speak a little more definitely; we were eight hours on the train before reaching Placentia, but we were waiting some of the time.

We waited a long half-hour at Brigus Junction, and there had bread and tea, for which the women charged us thirty cents apiece. If we consider quality and service, high prices and profiteering have reached Brigus Junction. We waited another half-hour at Placentia Junction. My first plan had been to return on Monday morning to this Junction and wait for the train going west. If the trains were on time this would have made a wait from eight-thirty in the morning until four-thirty in the afternoon, but the trains are rarely on time. When I saw Placentia Junction I was glad that I was following the railway official's kindly advise and was going back to St. John's before starting on my long journey west....

The last five miles before reaching Placentia one forgets the long waits and the uncertain roadbed, for the views of the Arms reaching up from the Bay to the south are very beautiful. Nearly every picture is framed in either fir or spruce. Seen through the tree arches, the shining waters away below are enhanced in beauty. The southeast and northeast arms are respectively five and seven miles long and afford safe boating and good fishing.

The train leaves you on the hill and there is a quarter-mile walk down to the water. Small boys arrive at the train to tote your luggage down the hill to the ferry, of the Gut, as the natives call it. Now, there is only one train a day, and usually there are not enough passengers to go around among the boys, but there is no fighting nor bickering among them ... these little boys of Placentia had the rudiments of politeness. They had been taught not to crowd. They were quiet and soft of speech and they did not forget to say a hearty "Thank you."[8]

Seven

Enter R. G. Reid

In 1890 the Whiteway administration asked for tenders for the construction and maintenance of a railway between a point on the existing Placentia Railway and Hall's Bay. After advertisements were placed in the leading Canadian and American newspapers, a large number of proposals were received and duly considered by the Newfoundland government. The most attractive offer came from two Canadian engineers, Robert Gillespie Reid and George H. Middleton. These two men offered to construct a narrow-gauge railway within five years, as well as operate the Placentia Branch Line. Heavy fifty-pound rails would be used and the cost would be a reasonable $15,600 per mile, payable in terms of Newfoundland's three and one-half percent bonds. In addition, Reid and Middleton would receive five thousand acres of land for every mile of track completed. Land was cheap, and experience on the Placentia Railway had shown that the Newfoundland government could expect to pay in the nature of $28,000 per mile if they tried to build a railway themselves. The government had had its fingers burned by impecunious promoters once before, but a man of wealth and proven ability like Reid seemed a much safer prospect. (After directing the day-to-day work on the Hall's Bay Line, Middleton had a disagreement with Reid and ended the partnership.) Reid agreed to deposit $250,000 of his own money as security for the completion of the project and to pay the government $90,000 for some sixteen miles of grading already completed.

Reid was one of those self-made Scots who did so much for nineteenth-century Canada. He was already a millionaire six times over, and well known for his feats of bridge construction and railway building north of Lake Superior.

An astute businessman like Reid must have been aware of what he was getting into. Newfoundland was saddled with desperate economic problems. The rosy times of the previous few years had been only a bubble, and it had now burst. Once again the world price for fish, the island's primary resource, was low, and once again Newfoundland was finding it hard to make ends meet. It seemed almost impossible to make a railway pay in such a place. Reid must have known that the previous contractors had gone bankrupt and the rail lines to Placentia and Harbour Grace had from their inception been money-losing operations. Reid was gambling for high stakes. Against his colleague's advice he was betting his reputation and his hard-earned fortune against the uncertain possibility that the real estate he would receive could be profitably exploited. Only a man of Reid's ability could do it. Only a man of Reid's daring and breadth of vision would even try to do it. The man loved nothing more than a challenge, to control vast undertakings, to do what had never been done before, and what the "experts" said could not be done. He had done it before, he would do it again! In the end, Reid dissipated his fortune and ruined his health, but he built his railway and nearly succeeded in founding a dynasty.

R. G. Reid, born in Coupar-Angus, Perthshire, Scotland in 1842, was the son of a humble linen miller. He was forty-eight years of age and in the prime of his career when first he landed on the rocky shores of Newfoundland. Forced to leave school at an early age Reid worked in a rock quarry with his uncle, learning the trades of stonemason and builder. Scarcely past his twentieth birthday,

R. G. Reid, the man who built the Newfoundland Railway (Harvey, 1900).

and fired by a white-hot ambition, he emigrated to the gold fields of Australia intent on making a name and a fortune. His prospecting career in the Antipodes was brief and unsuccessful, but he shrewdly observed that the real gold was to be found in the pockets of the miners and not in the ground. He took a small contract to build a bake oven and his career was launched. From this humble beginning he quickly advanced to stone bridges and railway viaducts in the Blue Mountains of New South Wales. From bake ovens to railways in three years was a remarkable feat. Reid was only twenty-five. Returning to Scotland for a time, Reid soon moved to North America, settling in Montréal in 1871. He set to work with a fury. In Ottawa, Canada's capital, he worked on several projects in connection with the Parliament buildings and built a number of bridges between that city and Montréal. Soon after, he won a contract to build the International Bridge over the Niagara River between Buffalo, New York and Fort Erie, Ontario. As his reputation grew, he moved further and further afield. In Texas he built all the bridges on the International Railway between Austin and Laredo. Spanning the Rio Grande, he continued on into Mexico for one hundred and fifty miles.

Many of Reid's undertakings were, for their time, considered remarkable feats of engineering. At Austin, the Colorado River was considered by most knowledgeable builders to be unbreachable. But Reid succeeded where all others had failed. Despite treacherous currents and a constantly shifting river bottom, Reid succeeded in throwing up a bridge of sturdy masonry. He went on to build other bridges across the Delaware River Gap in Pennsylvania, the "Soo" at Sault Ste. Marie, and Grand Narrows in Cape Breton Island. A master of detail and a driving perfectionist, Reid insisted on observing each stage of construction in person. The Grand Narrows Bridge crossed a swirling torrent of 1,735 feet in width, and piles had to be driven seventy-six feet beneath the surface of the water. Standing up to his waist in ice-cold water for hours on end, Reid supervised the placement of each pier. As a result he became seriously ill and never fully recovered his health. Reid would be plagued with rheumatism for the rest of his life. Such was R. G. Reid's reputation that in 1886 the directors of the Canadian Pacific Railway, without calling for tenders, asked Reid to assist in the building of a mammoth bridge, three-quarters of a mile in length, at Lachine, Québec.

Reid had also been busy building railways. Besides his early work in Australia he had laid eighty-six miles of track in connection with the Sault Ste. Marie bridge, as well as a forty-six-mile stretch connected with the Intercolonial Railway and the Grand Narrows Bridge. His crowning railway achievement, before he came to Newfoundland, was blasting a cutting through the Precambrian shield north of Lake Superior, on the heretofore impassable Jackfish Bay section of the Canadian Pacific Railway. As part of this task Reid was required to bore a tunnel four hundred and fifty feet through solid granite.

The pictures we have of Robert Gillespie Reid show a nattily-dressed aristocratic, even autocratic, figure with high cheekbones, a massive pointed mustache and a high forehead. He was a soft-spoken man who made each word mean something. Reid was determined, inflexible, the possessor of an incredible talent for organization and detail, as well as an exaggerated sense of personal honor. Hard driving, as much on himself as on the men he employed, Reid could be ruthless toward any opposition — human or otherwise — which might stand in his way.

The driving forces in Reid's life were his sense of honor and his sense of ambition and accomplishment. When R. G. Reid pledged to do something, one could rest assured that his word was better than any bond. A contract was unnecessary to hold him to an agreement. A simple handshake was sufficient. Once, on the Delaware Water Gap project, his partner, realizing that they would lose money on the job, ran off leaving Reid holding the bag. Though he had signed no contract, originally being just a consultant, and knowing full well that he stood to lose as much as $15,000, Reid's sense of honor obliged him to fulfill the terms of his partner's promise to the letter. The bridge over the Delaware River was built and Reid took a loss, but more importantly, his good name remained intact.

The other side of Reid's character was revealed after he came to Newfoundland in 1890. He set himself up as a virtual princeling whose power threatened to eclipse that of the elected House of Assembly. Controlling one-sixth of the entire land surface of Newfoundland, with vast railroad, shipping and mining holdings, Reid did not hesitate to subvert the government with bales of hard cash. Clearly, Mr. Reid was not a man to be fooled with.

On June 16, 1890, the government of Newfoundland negotiated an agreement with R. G. Reid and his associate to construct and operate a railway to Hall's Bay, a distance of two hundred and sixty-two miles. As part of the agreement Reid was obliged to take over the operation of the ailing Placentia Railway and was given a maximum of five years to complete the project to Hall's Bay. Work began in the autumn. Fifteen hundred men were employed and ten miles of track were laid before the snows of winter closed in. The work started again in the spring of 1891. The labor force swelled to eighteen hundred, and fifty miles of track were completed in difficult conditions.[1]

Eight

Life on the Line

It is hard to imagine a life of harsher toil than that endured by the nameless navvies who built the Hall's Bay Railway. Virtually marooned for weeks at a time in desolate wilderness, far from the comfort of family and friends, the men of the section gangs were overworked and overpaid, at risk of accident and injury, and were held in the thrall of the company. Often the only contact the navvies had with the outside world was along the tracks that they themselves had laid.

After a week of sixty hours of hard labor, a laborer could look forward to a pay packet of only six dollars; six dollars from which he was expected to feed himself and set something aside for his wife and children. Of course, a man received his six dollars only if he was able to work a full six days. If a navvy was ill or if inclement weather prevented construction activities, his pay would be reduced accordingly. Mr. Reid was not running a charity. The Hall's Bay Railway could not be expected to pay a man an honest day's wage if he did not work for it. Similarly, the company was in no position to pay for medical expenses, or even food and shelter. A sum of thirty cents was collected monthly from each man for the provision of medical care. In theory, the men were free to provide for their own sustenance as they saw fit. In practice, this usually meant that food and cooking utensils were purchased at construction headquarters. (Headquarters consisted of several wooden-floored canvas tents which provided quarters for the engineers, foremen and blacksmiths, as well as storage for equipment, supplies and horse feed.) If a man had a run of bad luck, it was quite possible for him to work and lose money at the same time!

Even though there was absolutely no danger of becoming well-off working for the Hall's Bay Railway there was no shortage of recruits. Most of the men were grateful for whatever gainful employment they could secure. There were a few complaints, however.

> Honourable Sir,
> Some of the contractors complain of being hardshipped in having to walk 15 or 17 miles for their provisions and at the same time there are plenty of supplies about 3 miles of where they are working and the Walking Boss of the division refuses to supply them from that store. I consider this matter requires only mentioning it to Mr. Reid

about it to be act right as it is only a fad of the Walking Boss. I have spoken to him about it but cannot move him in any way.[1]

Life on a construction gang in the wild interior of Newfoundland was primitive, to say the least. The men who worked on the Canadian Pacific Railway lived a life of comfort compared to that faced by their counterparts in Newfoundland. In some of the roughest countryside imaginable, R. G. Reid's Hall's Bay Railway could not even provide its navvies with a tent or a horsehair blanket, let alone luxuries like cooks and log bunkhouses. When a man started on the job, he was given a fistful of nails, a roll of felt and told to fend for himself. After his ten hours of work were done, a man would be expected to prepare his own meal over an open fire. Often the only cooking utensil would be a round-top shovel used as a frying pan. Fried dough, known as damper dogs or damper devils, was a staple. As darkness came on, the navvy would hack down a few saplings for tent poles, arrange the felt as best he could, and sleep directly on the hard ground under a crude lean-to. The Sabbath, supposedly a day of rest, was spent sewing patches on torn clothes, mending boots, washing (for those so inclined) and baking bread for the upcoming week in heavy iron pots.

The work on the railway was hard physical labor and often dangerous. Many a finger was crushed between two steel rails that suddenly slipped, and more than one life was taken in a blasting mishap. Tales of the strength and endurance of the men are legendary.

A powerfully-built young section hand arrived for his first day on the job. It was the task of his section to replace a rail that had been damaged. A rail weighed fifty pounds a linear yard. The foreman, speaking in the general direction of the new hand, said, "Go down around the curve and bring up that piece of fifty-pound rail." The boy, eager to please, did exactly as he was told. He picked up a fifteen-foot piece of rail, hefted it without effort to his shoulders and hauled it back for his foreman to see. "Here's your rail sir, but it's more than fifty pounds."[2]

The job these men had to do was immense. Thousands of cubic yards of earth and stone would have to be removed by shovel and cart; every single rail, spike and ounce of food would have to be transported many miles, to that constantly shifting location known as the End of Track. Massive quantities of bridge pilings and trestles had to be cut, assembled and placed, and seven hundred thousand wooden ties had to be produced.

After the route had been agreed upon and the surveyors had located the line by instrument, the laborers, often a thousand strong, spread out over a five- or ten-mile section, chopped a wide swath through tangled forest or drilled and blasted their way through armored expanses of solid rock. Wooden trestles were thrown across fast-flowing streams and the track bed was graded smooth. The grading had to be completed before anything else was done as the right-of-way had to be in a stable condition before track could be laid upon it. Embankments, cuttings and landfill were used only when absolutely necessary. These would take time to settle to a permanent level and were expensive to construct. Wooden ties, or sleepers, would be brought up from the rear and arranged across the grade at exactly two-foot intervals. At the end of the line the laborers would unload the wooden ties from a flatcar and stack them beside the roadbed. The rails would then be transferred to a pushcar and brought as close as possible to where they were needed. The steel rails were then carefully placed on the ties by strong men armed with massive tongs. Then it was time to attach fish plates across the sleepers and securely spike everything in place with sledge hammers. Two bolts would be put in each fish plate lining up and connecting the rails. Another crew then began pounding in the spikes. Two men positioned on either side of the track delivered alternating and perfectly coordinated hammer blows to the spikes. A back-bolter would bring up the rear, pounding in additional bolts. In this fashion the end of track could advance about a mile per day.[4]

Crushed stone, borrowed from blasting sites, was then packed between the sleepers as ballast to keep the track from shifting out of position under the weight of the moving trains. Even then the work was far from completed. Sidings, sheds, station houses, water towers, and branch lines would all have to be added. Sometimes the work went on into the night. If a train had to be fueled, the nearest available laborers were expected to shovel the coal without receiving any extra wages for their troubles. At daybreak the next morning the men would be hard at work laying track as usual. In winter most of the men were laid off, but a few gangs were always kept busy cutting extra timber for sleepers, pilings and telegraph poles. It was a tribute to the endurance of the navvies, as well as an expression of the poverty of the country, that the entire railway was built by hand. Aside from a few wheelbarrows, picks and shovels were the only tools available for construction. It was not until 1915, long after the railway in Newfoundland had been completed, that the first machinery was introduced. In that year the Newfoundland Railway obtained two surplus steam shovels left over from the building of the Panama Canal.

Reid took all the steps in his power to cut expenses. He was not a miser and he was not insensitive to his men, but it was simply that the cost of constructing a railway in Newfoundland was crippling him. Even with all his economies he was spending twice as much money as he was receiving. Most of the men would have given up, but Reid was not most men. He had been contracted to build a railway, and being the kind of man he was, R. G. Reid was determined to do exactly that.

Until the early 1900s a trainman could be obliged to work twenty-four hours straight, or more. A freight train departing the capital at one in the morning might work its crew until 11:30 P.M. (twenty-two hours and thirty minutes). This was considered to be one day's work. A passenger train could depart St. John's at 5:00 P.M. and arrive in Port aux Basques at 11:00 P.M. the next day. The crew would have been on duty for thirty hours without a rest period. This was considered two days' work. The unwritten law was that a crew must take its train all the way to the terminus. If there were washouts, accidents or snow blockages the crew could be on duty for many days without a break. When the trainmen's union was formed in 1919, it won the right to a rest period after twelve hours of duty. Crews were ordinarily scheduled for a nine-hour day. After more than twenty nine-hour days in the course of a month, a trainman was entitled to overtime pay. After Canadian National took over the railway in 1949, eight-hour shifts became the norm. Overtime was earned at hours over that amount.[5]

1948 Salary Scales for the Newfoundland Railway

	Per Month	Per Hour
Locomotive engineer	$180.16	$0.86
Locomotive fireman	$141.68	$0.68
Passenger conductor	$213.00	$1.02
Freight conductor	$168.00	$0.80
Freight brakeman	$148.00	$0.71
Passenger brakeman	$153.00	$0.74
Baggageman	$153.00	$0.74
Expressman	$163.00	$0.78
Station agent	$163.21	$0.78
Clerk	$150.00	
Mechanic (1st class)		$0.99
Locomotive and car repairman		$0.85
Helper		$0.79
Assistant		$0.58
Stationary oiler fireman		$0.64
Section laborer		$0.625[6]

Comparable pay scales on the Canadian National Railways were between thirty and fifty percent higher.

NINE

King Reid

By 1892 End of Track was somewhere north of Gander Lake and the surveying teams had paced off the remaining distance to Hall's Bay. The end was in sight — until the Newfoundland government abruptly cancelled the whole scheme. The politicians still had their hearts set on a trans-island railway. It was decided to reroute the line away from Hall's Bay, extending it along a more or less direct route westward, to what is now the city of Corner Brook on the Bay of Islands. From Corner Brook the new route would travel down the heavily forested west coast, through the verdant Codroy Valley and on to Port aux Basques at the southwestern tip of the island, the closest point to Nova Scotia.

Even after they had announced their intention to connect the mining settlements at Hall's Bay by rail, and even after construction had commenced, the government was still hopeful that the eventual terminus of the railway might be at Port aux Basques. With this aim in mind the government sent a team of surveyors to the west coast in 1889. They concluded that a railway in the area would not be easy to build but it would be possible. They also concluded that a rail line to Port aux Basques would be the most economically viable and the one most likely to open up new lands for settlement and development. What had delayed matters so long and made Hall's Bay the initial terminus were the stubborn objections raised by the French over what they felt were incursions on their extraterritorial fishing and commercial establishments along the west coast. But by 1892 the economic worth of the region was in decline. The French were losing interest as fewer and fewer of their fishermen were visiting Newfoundland waters. It was only because the dispute was drifting to a solution of its own accord that the Newfoundland authorities dared to be so bold. To be sure, the French made some token protests but they did not force the issue. Eventually, the French were persuaded to relinquish all their rights in Newfoundland in exchange for certain territorial adjustments between the West African territories of Senegal and Gambia. When the government of Newfoundland proposed that the railway be shifted westward they were correct in assuming that though both France and the colonial office in London would be obliged to grumble, neither would move seriously to stop them. In any case, the proposed terminus at Port aux Basques would be three miles beyond Cape Ray, the point where the traditional French claims ended.

Railway station, St. John's. Built by R. G. Reid, it now houses the Railway Coastal Museum (Hollis Harding).

Though the direct route to the west coast of Newfoundland had the advantage of saving mileage it had the disadvantage of crossing the bleak Gaff Topsails Plateau. The Topsails is as desolate a tract of land as any to be found in Canada—a howling waste of muskeg, swamp and solitary peaks rarely visited even in the present day. From a distance, the hills looked to a seafaring people like the sails of a square-rigger, giving rise to the names Gaff, Main and Mizzentopsail. Such maps as existed of the area were virtually useless. More in the realm of mythology than cartography, they showed mountains, lakes, streams and rivers that either did not exist or were in the wrong place.

The elevation is nine hundred feet higher than that of the area around Hall's Bay, and the area is subject to weather conditions that can be described with no other term but abysmal. Despite the flurry of mapping that had gone on in the previous few years, the Gaff Topsails Plateau had remained virtually untouched by surveyors. When the time came to lay the track, surveying and construction went on almost simultaneously. In latter years the Newfoundland Railway would pay for this hastiness many times over. It would prove a constant headache and drain on resources to clear away the massive winter snowdrifts that blocked the track, for the roadbed had not even been raised above the level of the snows. It is no accident that the Trans-Canada Highway, which

Statue of "Industry," train station, St. John's. The statue was carved out of a gatepost which had been salvaged from the Anglican cathedral after the Great Fire of 1892. The model was a maid in the household of R. G. Reid (Hollis Harding).

hugs the railway right-of-way through most of Newfoundland, makes a wide sweep to the north to avoid the Gaff Topsails Plateau.

Reid strongly supported the new route to the west coast and probably had a hand in instigating it. Though his surveyors had just handed him a report that was only cautiously favorable with regard to the Hall's Bay route, Reid thought nothing of tackling the even worse conditions to be found on the Gaff Topsails.

Reid's advisors thought he was insane to willingly get himself any deeper involved in Newfoundland. But according to Reid's political supporter Alfred B. Morine, the contractor "regarded the operation as a burden assumed to secure the construction contract, and the losses to be deducted from construction profits, for which reason he had stipulated the shortest operating period the government of the day would agree to."[1] At the time there was a general economic depression throughout North America. Credit was hard to find and Newfoundland, hit harder than most, was staggering toward collapse. It was against this canvas that Reid wanted to build a railway. He was already losing an immense sum of money, and the new plan would only make matters worse by adding on three hundred more miles.

By the end of 1893 the metals had been inched forward to Grand Falls on the edge of the Topsails. A certain Mr. Massey, an engineer on Reid's staff, one of the very few who had any personal knowledge of the west coast and the formidable difficulties it presented, telegraphed Reid in St. John's, in a last-ditch effort urging his employer to have nothing more to do with the railway venture. The man had just survived a howling blizzard in the Topsails, a blizzard which piled up drifts of snow forty feet high! In Mr. Massey's view only a lunatic would try and build a railway across the center of Newfoundland and expect to operate it in the dead of winter. The advice reached Reid too late. The contracts had already been signed. It is unlikely the telegram would have made any difference anyway.

Reid had already given his word and he was determined to fulfill it. What Reid proposed to do — in fact was eager to do — was unprecedented. Against his senior engineer's advice, and contrary to all sane economic advice, Reid was planning to extend a railway which had never earned a cent hundreds of miles across primitively mapped terrain.

The eight years that Reid spent building the railway were among the most disastrous in Newfoundland's long history of disaster. Reid was plagued by a heart-rending series of setbacks that would have made a less determined man give up in disgust. His associate, G. H. Middleton, did give up.

The first disaster was the Great Fire of 1892. About 4:00 P.M. on July 8 a stable hand named Fitzpatrick dropped his pipe into a pile of hay in a barn. It had been a hot dry summer and the wooden walls of St. John's many buildings were like tinder. A fire started in the hay and quickly blazed out of control. High winds spread glowing embers throughout the city. Within hours St. John's was engulfed in a conflagration. Houses, schools, churches, the just-completed Anglican Cathedral, the courthouse, banks, the entire business district, warehouses, wharves, and ships in the harbor were reduced to cinders. Even the fire department's hoses burned. Newfoundland and, by extension, its infant railway had been dealt a staggering blow. But Reid, often dipping into his own pocket, was undaunted and construction of the railway continued.

With the able assistance of his three sons, William Duff Reid, Harry Duff Reid, and Robert Gillespie Reid Jr., End of Track continued to inch further and further across the island. In the year 1892, despite desperate shortages of money and supplies, with investors failing and businesses collapsing all around, Reid's workforce of twenty-two hundred men completed eighty miles of track.

The next setback occurred in 1893, after the Whiteway Liberals had been returned to office in the general election. As a result of the vote, the country became crippled by savage political strife. The losing Tories filed election petitions against seventeen of the twenty-three Liberal members, including Whiteway himself. The Liberals were accused of violating the Corrupt Practices Act. After two Liberals were unseated, the Whiteway administration resigned in the hopes of canceling the proceedings. The governor complicated matters by refusing to accept the resignation, thus causing the Liberals to retaliate by refusing to pass a revenue act! The country was in an uproar. Bitter attacks were made in the press, in the courts, on the floor of the House of Assembly and in the streets of St. John's.

To outsiders, Newfoundland was beginning to look like a bad risk. The country's securities began to sink in value as nervous investors tried to unload them as fast as they could. The $4,000,000 in government bonds with which Reid had been paid were rapidly becoming worthless. Reid was spending his own money to keep the railway afloat while in St. John's the entire financial and governmental structure of Newfoundland was coming unglued.

The final blow came on December 10, 1894 — the bank crash. The Commercial and Union banks folded and thousands of ordinary citizens lost their life savings. Overnight, Newfoundland bank notes became nearly worthless paper; trade was crippled, old established firms went bankrupt and large numbers of working people lost their jobs. Bread riots broke out on the street corners, shops were looted and the military had to be called out to restore order.

> It was Reid who went to Montreal with Robert Bond and introduced him to the financiers who eventually found the money which enabled the colony to avoid default on its debt payments, and the probable loss of responsible government that would have resulted. In giving credit where it is due, it is important to remember that Reid was not acting entirely from altruistic motives; he was being paid in Newfoundland government bonds, and if they were not saleable, then he could be in financial difficulties.[2]

As the Liberals stubbornly refused to pass a revenue act so long as they continued to be accused of improprieties, a truncated parliament and a slapdash administration were formed to run the government. Moneys were collected without benefit of law but with the benefit of a British warship's guns. Eventually, in order to restore some semblance of peace, an act was passed allowing the discredited members of the House of Assembly to resume their seats. Things calmed down, and by February 1895 William Whiteway was once again the prime minister of Newfoundland and the Liberal Party once again formed the island's government.

Given the conditions he had to face, both the physical uncertainties in front of him and the economic and political upheavals behind him, it is not surprising that R. G. Reid ended up building a most rudimentary sort of railway. It was a genuine accomplishment to be building anything at all. Reid had little alternative but to build the railroad piecemeal, out of the cheapest scraps available. Rolling stock consisted of three second-hand locomotives from Prince Edward Island, forty flatcars, ten boxcars and one club car. During the winter much of the track was impassable and there was no money for improvements. Right up until the takeover of the Newfoundland Railway by Canadian National in 1949, trains were sometimes marooned in snow for days at a time.

Until 1904, when the first steel rotary plow was acquired, snow clearance equipment consisted of a few wooden push plows and gangs of strong men shoveling by hand. As the men shoveled their way through drifts, they piled up banks of snow so high that the width of loads on the flatcars had to be sharply reduced in order to pass between them. Trains still got stuck but the rotary plows, once they had been acquired, certainly made life easier. Shoved along the track by a locomotive, one plow could do the work of a whole crew of shovelers. Two more rotary plows were acquired in 1905. A battery of steel cutting blades spinning at very high speed could eat its way through a drift and blow the powdered snow one hundred feet out a funnel to clear the right-of-way.

Snow-fighting was a daily struggle for four or five months every year. The track was so close to the ground that the first snowfall covered it over. Every pass of a plow would build snow cuts higher. By the end of winter there would be walls of snow twelve to fifteen feet high. Drifting snow could quickly fill in the cuts.

A rotary plow was usually pushed through the snow by two locomotives with a cook car, rest car and a crew of thirteen. Plowing was a difficult and disagreeable duty. As the windows of the cabs could not be opened due to the flying snow, the pusher locomotives could become roasting hot. Snow would still break into the cab and create an unpleasant Turkish bath effect. Sometimes, the mountains of hard packed snow became too much for the plows and they jammed. Running them in reverse and using a steam thawing hose would get the plows back in operation. Apart from the huge amounts of snow to be moved, plowing was a slow operation because large quantities of water had to be frequently replenished to keep up the steam.[3]

Of course winter was not the only season with bad weather conditions. The road bed was subjected to all kinds of calamities the year round, and it was virtually unprotected from any of them. High winds strong enough to blow a loaded boxcar on its side, washouts, floods, forest fires, and slippage from lack of ballasting were constant problems. As the line advanced down the west coast, the coastal range of mountains forced the track to hug the shoreline. At times the seas were so rough that waves washed over the tracks and ripped them apart. Sometimes salt spray would cling to the rails and freeze. This made the tracks so slippery that the tired old locomotives could hardly move forward, or stop once they were moving. In order to get around this problem the train crews, using a trick known as "rocking up the grade," sprinkled small stones and gravel on the rails.[4] It was unorthodox but it worked.

Bridges were another problem. On the main line there were one hundred and fifty bridges, an average of one every four miles. Even the biggest bridge could be knocked out of commission by a sudden washout or a heavy flow of melting spring ice. In March 1897, a six-hundred-and-ten-foot bridge, built in five steel spans, was completely destroyed by ice conditions on the Exploits River. At great expense it was replaced by an all-new steel bridge the next year. Exactly three years after the first bridge was destroyed, in March of 1900, ice destroyed the new bridge. A new site on the Exploits was chosen, and a third steel bridge was proposed. This one would be nine hundred and twenty-seven feet long. Only two spans of the bridge and a temporary wooden trestle were constructed before the ice did its work again. It was not until 1901 that the Exploits River Bridge was completed and stayed completed.

When a bridge piling collapsed or a section of track was damaged, a special work train consisting of a locomotive and a few flatcars scooted up and down the line hurriedly pressing into service any workers it passed. The navvies were expected to come at a moment's notice. The men grabbed hold of their picks and their shovels and went exactly as they were — no food, no blankets, not even rolls of felt for a tent. They could be gone for a few hours or a few days. Either way, the men would not return until the job was done. There were no cabooses to provide shelter and the workers had to eat whatever and sleep wherever they could. If the weather was warm and dry so much the better — if not, so much the worse.

On a rail line built to such economical standards, it was much too expensive to dig tunnels (in the entire line there was not even one) or to flatten out obstacles. The only solution to the problem of physical obstacles was to go around them or over them. As a result the track turned and twisted like a bucking bronco. Steep grades and wicked curves would plague the railway and its passengers throughout its days. For safety's sake, the top speed was originally restricted to a sedate five miles per hour. Once, an engineer was fired from his job for speeding along the track at sixty miles per hour. A worker had been killed in a blasting accident and the construction supervisor, Reid's son William, had lost an eye. A work train was detailed to bring William Reid to medical attention. After his recovery it was William himself who suspended the engineer. Better to lose an eye than your life.

It had been specified that all train cars on the Newfoundland system should have automatic air brakes. This meant that if a car became uncoupled inadvertently, the entire train, as well as the breakaway car, would be stopped automatically. However, as late as 1916 there were still cars operating which were not so equipped. These cars had to be coupled by hand with a linch pin — a source of many mangled fingers among old-time railroaders. If the pin broke on a grade, the escaped car might race off by itself at a frantic pace. It was not unknown for a runaway car to go sailing off the wharf at Heart's Content or some other wayside station.

On May 16, 1893, Reid signed a new contract on the same terms as the first one. In this agreement he promised to continue the railway down the west coast to Port aux Basques, operate it for ten years, and accompany it with a telegraph line. On the same day he signed another contract agreeing to take over operation of the Placentia Branch Line. The entire operation was to be known as the Newfoundland Northern and Western Railway.

The government was beginning to think of the railway as an expensive white elephant. They were still anxious to have it span the island but they were only too happy to hand the whole bag of problems over to Mr. Reid. Reid had now become the biggest capitalist and the biggest landowner in Newfoundland's history, controlling almost three million acres of land. Unnoticed, Robert Gillespie Reid was becoming more than just a contractor of the government. He was becoming the power behind the government. Increasingly, the Newfoundland government was turning to Reid for financial advice and emergency loans. It was only Reid's personal presence which had staved off certain disaster after the 1894 bank crash. It was Reid's influence with the Bank of Montréal which was responsible for the bank deciding to open a branch office in St. John's. This brought much needed Canadian currency into Newfoundland at a time when there was no negotiable currency in circulation.

In 1895 a delegation was sent to Ottawa, cap in hand. Things had reached such a state that even the greatest taboo—confederation with Canada—was being considered. When the negotiators from Newfoundland arrived in Ottawa to discuss the terms of union, R. G. Reid was close by their side. Reid did everything he could to drum up support for Newfoundland among his influential Canadian friends. Both Reid and the Newfoundland delegation were confident that their railway was a valuable asset which Canada would be pleased to acquire. They were shocked and dismayed by the reaction of the Canadians. As far as the government of Canada was concerned, the Newfoundland Railway was an obstacle to union, not an encouragement. In their opinion, the railway being built in Newfoundland was a second-class "streak of rust" and a certain money loser. They wanted no part of it. At the time of the conference three hundred and seventy-four miles of track had been laid at a cost of $6,000,000. It was estimated that a further $4,000,000 would be required to complete the line to Port aux Basques. That figure did not include the cost of rolling stock, terminal wharves, feeder lines and various other paraphernalia. Canada, too, had been sent reeling by the depression. A total debt of at least $10,000,000, a huge sum in those days, was more than Canada was willing or able to assume. With Canada's refusal to accept the country's debt, Newfoundland refused to join Canada. The conference ended in failure and Newfoundland was fated to remain on its own for another fifty-four years. It is an irony that during the ten years prior to the conference, Canada had offered several times to provide financial assistance to the Newfoundland Railway but the gesture was rejected by Newfoundland.

After the unsuccessful mission to Ottawa, another more successful delegation was formed. Accompanied by Reid, the delegation traveled to Montréal and London in a desperate attempt to borrow money. In Montréal, Reid introduced the delegation to a firm of influential financiers and enough money was raised to keep Newfoundland solvent, at least for the time being.

The borrowed money was only a stopgap at best. The economy of Newfoundland remained weak, and in order to alleviate the general state of distress, the government in London was forced to set up a relief fund. The destitute were hired at the wage of fifty cents per day to labor on public works projects.

A prestigious firm of London financiers reneged on an agreement with Reid to purchase some of his Newfoundland government bonds. It is illustrative of Reid's stiff character that later, when the financial crises in Newfoundland had eased, and the same London financiers apologized and once more agreed to purchase Reid's securities, at generous terms, he haughtily refused. Reid is quoted as saying, somewhat primly: "No, you have broken your word and gone back on your bargain; I will not give you these bonds now."[5]

Even in the unfettered world of nineteenth-century capitalism, Reid's sense of honor would not be compromised.

The rigors of the terrain, the inclemency and dampness of the climate, the political pressures, the financial responsibilities he shouldered, and the long hours at his desk were beginning to have a telling effect of Reid's health. He was forced to take a vacation in Egypt for a complete rest and in hope that the warm dry climate, so different from that of Newfoundland, would bring him relief from his rheumatic condition. Yet despite the strains and Reid's enforced absences from Newfoundland, the work continued onward. Each year, come what may, the navvies in Reid's work gangs pushed the End of Track another seventy-five or eighty miles further on. In 1895 Corner Brook was reached. It would take another two years to complete the remaining two hundred and fifty miles down the west coast, creeping mile by mile through the Long Range Mountains. Finally, in the spring of 1898, the work was done — Port aux Basques was reached. Twin ribbons of steel, forty-two inches apart, crossed Newfoundland from coast to coast. At 7:20 A.M. on Wednesday, June 29, 1898, the first trans-island Express — baggage car, day coach, dining car and two sleepers — pulled by two ribbon-bedecked locomotives, puffed out of the Fort William station in St. John's, heading west for Port aux Basques.

A man from Mars lands in Newfoundland where he met a citizen of St. John's whose face was very sad.

"Mornin'" said the Martian.

"Mornin'"

"What's the matter?"

"Hungry."

"Why don't you eat?"

"No money."

"Work and get some."

"Can't get none."
"Work on this great tract of land and dig out the iron, coal and all such things, see?"
"The owner wouldn't hire me."
"The WHAT?"
"Owner won't hire me."
"What's the owner?"
"Why them that owns it."
"Does one man own this island?"
"Of course."
"Well I'll be blo___ Say, didn't God make this island?"
"I heard so."
"Didn't He make it for all His children that they might live?"
"I — I've heard so — I guess so — I dunno."
"How does it happen that one man owns it all?"
"Why the law gives it to him of course."
"Who made the law?"
"We do, of course."
"Who's we?"
"Why, the voters; me and the rest of use — the sovereign people."
"And you make laws giving one man a great and valuable island like this, which he can let lie idle if he chooses, while you beg for work and starve for food?"
"Ye-es."
"Would you kindly take off your hat and let me see the shape of your head."
And the gentleman from Mars cut the anchor of his airship and sailed away repeating "What fools these mortals be!"[6]

Ten

The Contract of 1898

> The Railway, it must be remembered, will not for years pay for the grease to the wheels.
>
> Colonial Office memo of March 1, 1898

It was 1898. After all the toil and the sweat, Newfoundland finally had her railway. But what had she received for her effort? The rails had already begun to rust. When that first cross-country Express puffed into the depot at Port aux Basques, did it bring with it prosperity? No, it did not! Easy times, jobs for everyone? Unfortunately, the opposite was closer to the truth. During the years while the railway was being constructed, there had been some glimmer of prosperity. But now that the metals had been laid, even that had gone. The work crews, some three thousand people, suddenly found themselves without jobs. After the Bank Crash of 1894, Newfoundland was an economic basket case. Cast aside by Canada as a bad risk, the country's money was nearly worthless, and the national debt, aggravated by the cost of the railway, unmanageable. With the new century fast approaching, aside from the sound of an occasional train whistle Newfoundland seemed to remain much as it had long been, a slow-moving rural backwater of some two hundred thousand souls.

But there was one significant change. For the first time in history, money could be obtained from a source that did not involve fishing, and even more importantly, political patronage could come from a source other than the merchant elite in St. John's. R. G. Reid was this source. The arrival of a fire-breathing capitalist from "Away," the word Newfoundlanders used for every place in the world that was not their beloved island home, would prove to be more than Newfoundland could survive.

Reid was one of the wealthiest individuals in the Dominion of Canada, at a time when the rich paid no personal income tax. His fortune has been estimated to have been more than $40,000,000 in today's terms. It is a universal truth that he who has money soon has power. Reid had the money; Newfoundland not only gave him the power but begged him to take it. In the space of five short years Reid had risen from the status of a builder, working on a contract for the government of Newfoundland, to a point where he was virtually dictating the government's policy. Reid was the biggest landowner, the biggest employer and the island's principal financial advisor and supporter. By virtue of pumping vast quantities of money into what had been, to some extent, a barter economy, Reid exerted a force that was arguably more powerful than that of the elected government.

The Conservative Party, under James Winter and his unscrupulous lieutenant A. B. Morine, came to power in the election of 1897. Winter saw Reid as the solution to the economic doldrums he faced. The railway was simply too expensive to keep. The government had to get rid of it but not close it. With this aim in mind, Morine, acting in his capacity as minister of finance, negotiated a contract with the Reid interests that was so astonishing in its implications that it is still a controversial matter today.

The governor, Sir Hubert Murray, had no delusions as to the competence or even the honesty of the Winter administration. He confided in strong terms to the colonial secretary:

> We must, if we help the colony, have control of the administration as there is no party or minister in Newfoundland under its present constitution whom we can trust with money.[1]

The governor's worst suspicions were confirmed when Winter tabled a document in the House of Assembly which promised to sell the railway to Reid for the absurdly low sum of $1,000,000. As part of the deal, Reid would agree to operate the railway for fifty years in return for a vast increase in his land holdings.

Like the parents of a half-grown child who refuses to listen to reason, the governor of the island and the colonial secretary in London were exasperated by the Newfoundland government's reckless behavior. They were frustrated by the fact that constitutionally there was nothing they could do about it. Wrote the colonial secretary:

> Practically it seems that the Ministry are going to sell the Colony to a contractor, a rather novel proceeding and a questionable result of self-government. We cannot prevent them — but we might at least wash our hands of the business.[2]

What Prime Minister Winter and A. B. Morine were doing was giving one man title to a parcel of land equivalent to half the size of Belgium and selling that same man six hundred miles of railroad, the fruits of seventeen years of hard labor, at a price that would not have built the first sixty miles! As one bitter Colonial Office dispatch put it, "The sale of Esau's birthright was a joke compared to this transaction."[3]

The government was not concerned that the entire communications system of Newfoundland and the best stands of virgin timber on the island were about to pass from Crown control and into the hands of the Reid family. government members were actually worried that the deal was not generous enough! According to the agreement signed in 1893, Reid was obliged to operate the railway for another five years and then turn it over to the control of the government. If only Reid would run the railway indefinitely, all our problems would be over, thought the government members.

The government approached Reid like a beggar, never a good negotiating position. The builder was only too happy to expand his empire but complained that it would not be practical for him to operate the Newfoundland Railway unless the Placentia and Harbour Grace divisions were also consolidated under his control. Of course, in order to make the railway pay he would have to have certain concessions and properties transferred to him. As the government was hard pressed to meet the interest payments on its loans, there was little likelihood that Reid would be refused.

For health reasons Reid journeyed to California, giving his sons William and Harry full power of attorney to carry on in his absence. The contract signed on March 15, 1898, to operate the railway as part of the Reid Newfoundland Company, was one of the most incredible legal documents ever put into force. It was more of a sell-out than the Colonial Office had feared. Exasperated and frustrated, the Colonial Office wrote: "This transfer to a contractor of the most important functions of government in a self-governing Colony cannot be viewed as anything else but a confession of incompetence."[4]

For the $1,000,000 he gave the government, Reid would operate the railway for fifty years and then have ownership pass to him. He was to receive huge chunks of additional land and exclusive mining rights on all his properties, including a land grant in an area known to have valuable coal deposits. Reid's land holdings were now in excess of six thousand square miles. For a further sum of $325,000 Reid bought the government dry dock at St. John's, intending to use it as a deepwater terminus for his railway. Reid planned to build seven miles of track through the west end of St. John's to connect it with the main line. The dry dock, one of the biggest installations of its kind in the world, was six hundred feet long and had cost the government $550,000 to build fourteen years before.

There was more! For $125,000 Reid gained control of the island's entire telegraph network, more than one thousand miles in length. He promised to reduce the rates charged to the public by fifty percent.

Reid also engineered a monopoly on coastal passenger and mail service for a period of thirty years. For his pains, he received an annual subsidy of $92,000. Under the terms of this agreement he pledged to build eight new steamships on the River Clyde in Scotland and sail them to Newfoundland. The *Bruce*, which plied between Port aux Basques and Sydney, Nova Scotia, was built for $250,000. Seven other vessels which traveled around the shores of the island and along the coast of Labrador were constructed for $100,000 each.

As part of this and related contracts, Reid built a $125,000 railway station in St. John's. (The terminal burned down on March 31, 1900. A second terminal was built in the west end of the city, opening in January 1903.) Reid encouraged tourism, built a skating rink, constructed the tram system in St. John's and for $150,000 paved the main streets with granite supplied by his own quarries. Still not finished, he agreed to illuminate the city of St. John's with electric light. At a cost of $750,000 he dammed ponds and installed a hydroelectric generating station capable of producing 36,000 horsepower.

In addition to its "give-away" provisions, the contract of 1898 was not an example of a good legal document. The obligations of each party with respect to the other were often unstated or open to various interpretations. In one clause Reid agreed to pay a sum of money to the government which, in another clause, the government agreed to pay to Reid. But whether or not it was confusing, the agreement was binding. With the contract of 1898 tucked in his pocket, Robert Gillespie Reid controlled the government, the railroad, mail delivery, coastal shipping, telegraph lines, hydroelectric power, a large dry dock, and 6,320 square miles of land with complete mineral and timber rights. In an unparalleled action, Newfoundland had willingly abdicated all power for influencing its own economic future. Nowhere in the contract's clauses was it stated that Reid had to develop his empire in any way that would benefit the people of Newfoundland. It was not even stated that he had to develop his land at all. It was just assumed that he would, and it was just assumed that jobs and prosperity for Newfoundland would result when he did so. The contract served "to convert the State into Man." No one was quite sure "as to whether the Man should be looked upon as incarnate Atlas or Leviathan."

Even a Central American banana republic was capable of negotiating a better deal for itself than Newfoundland. The *Evening Telegram* unfavorably compared the Reid Deal, as it came to be known, with a contemporary contract made between the government of Honduras and a syndicate of New York investors headed by Jacob Astor. Instead of a one-time payment, the Americans agreed to pay Honduras $1,000,000 a year for twenty years. For this money they would have a franchise to construct and operate a string of lighthouses, found a national bank and extend the Honduran railway to the Pacific coast. After the twenty years had elapsed, ownership would revert to Honduras.[5]

If only Newfoundland could have had the foresight of Honduras! Once the news of the Reid Deal got out, however, the people of Newfoundland were in a state of outrage. They saw the contract with Reid as nothing less than a sellout of their country's sovereignty and future. When the negotiations were underway, the electorate was not informed. Winter had a solid majority in the legislature and could afford to be arrogant. With the backing of his Conservative yes-men, the bill authorizing the deal passed easily. The government was then free to give away some of the most valuable assets of the island for one-seventeenth of their face value. The anti-government newspapers exploded with a wave of angry editorials. One newspaper deplored the fact that Newfoundlanders were now little better than Russian serfs, screaming "Are we to be bound hand and foot forever?"

> Are our Dock, our Coal Mines, our Municipal Basin, the Marine promenade, the most valuable water power ... to go *for ever, for ever, for ever,* after a few days talk in the House of Assembly and by the vote of a majority composed of men who, taking them as a whole are utterly worthless....[6]

From his vantage point in government House in St. John's, Governor Murray was so appalled by what had happened that he wanted to refuse royal assent for the bill. In

London Joseph Chamberlain, the secretary for colonies, was equally disgusted, but his hands were constitutionally tied. This was a matter of local finance and therefore neither he nor the governor had the right to interfere. Though the colonial secretary was supposed to remain above local politics, Chamberlain took the unprecedented step of issuing a public statement denouncing the contract. Chamberlain bitterly complained that: "Such an abdication by a government of some of its most important functions is without parallel."[7]

Despite the intervention of the colonial secretary and spirited protestations by Governor Murray in St. John's, the Reid deal went through just as planned. The legislation finalizing the contract was rammed through the House of Assembly in barely thirty minutes, with all but five members of the opposition voting in favor of it. What debate did occur was spirited. The *Daily News* reported that Mr. Bond, leader of the anti–Reid faction,

> was most insulting at the House of Assembly last night during the delivery of Sir James Winter's speech. He should modify his expressions in the presence of ladies.[8]

The politicians in the Conservative Party were, for the most part, simply mouthpieces for R. G. Reid. But when even the staid *Methodist Monthly Greeting* denounced the contract, what hope could there be for popular support? "Will not future generations," wrote the *Greeting*,

> curse the unnatural sons of the present time for their utter imbecility or perfidy if such an offer be accepted. [If only there were] men who can't be bought, coerced or deceived by smooth speech.[9]

Owing to the infrequency of contact between many isolated communities and the capital, and the deliberate and outrageous attempt by the government to stifle debate, it was not until late summer that the average resident of the remote outports began to realize the enormity of what had occurred. When they did, they were furious and felt betrayed. The newspapers and broadsheets that had trickled down to them were full of scandal-mongering headlines; "Reid the Monopolist," "Boss Morine," "Tyranny and Terrorism," "Coercion Rampant," "Slavery and Starvation."

What made the contract even more morally bankrupt was that the Conservative Party had been elected a few months previous on a platform which had explicitly condemned the Reid contract of 1893.

Such a wave of angry petitions flooded into St. John's that it was said with some measure of truth that "the islanders stopped fishing and turned to petitions."[10] By the end of 1898 petitions denouncing the contract had allegedly been signed by more than 40 percent of the eligible voters in Newfoundland.

The British authorities were so dismayed by the contract that they actually considered having Queen Victoria revoke the Newfoundland Act, under which the country had been given the authority to manage its own internal affairs.

Ten. The Contract of 1898

By this time, October 1898, it was too late to turn back the clock. The contract had been signed and Reid was already well on his way to fulfilling his side of the bargain. Five hundred thousand dollars of the $1,000,000 owed to the government had already been paid by the contractor, and Reid's crews were busy relaying the track with new fifty-pound rail. Reid had commissioned the construction of a fleet of coastal ships and had formed the St. John's Street Railway Company and the St. John's Light and Power Company. The Colonial Office regrettably concluded that it had no constitutional grounds to intervene in the financial affairs of the country.

At this time there were thirty-one members in the House of Assembly. The Conservatives under Winter, with eighteen seats, had a clear majority of five. The thirteen opposition members were about equally divided. A group of six, led by Edward Morris, supported the contract and the remaining seven members, under the leadership of Robert Bond, did not. As popular discontent grew, Winter's parliamentary support began to erode. Bond charged that Winter had made Reid the uncrowned czar of Newfoundland. Winter replied that all the lands and properties Reid were administering would never make him a dime of profit unless he invested a large amount of money in them. The contract with Reid had freed the government from operating the railroad, the telegraphs, the dry dock and the steamship service, all of which were heavy money losers. Reid would be forced to invest heavily in his land holdings just to break even.

But before any new industries could be opened, a scandal erupted. In November, it was discovered that James Winter's finance minister, Alfred B. Morine, the man most responsible for the signing of the infamous contract and its most vociferous defender in the House of Assembly, was also R. G. Reid's personal attorney. The services he rendered to Reid in this capacity were unclear, but it was clear was that Morine was receiving a juicy stipend of $5,000 a year. Governor Murray, who already considered Morine to be little better than a common crook, was delighted to ask for Morine's resignation. Morine duly resigned and, of course, denied any knowledge of wrongdoing.

The Morine scandal did nothing to enhance the image of the Conservative Party. Opposition in the House of Assembly had turned from tame to violent. But despite the pressure, Winter refused to call an election, staying in office throughout 1899. On March 5 of that year Reid was granted an additional 3,345,948 acres of land as promised by the contract. The way the land had been doled out, in the form of blanket grants, could not have been more insensitive. Even more people became antagonized. The land that Reid was slated to receive included sections upon which families were already living. The burden and expense of proving ownership fell on the heads of these people. As maps and boundaries were inaccurate and deeds frequently nonexistent, residents had a hard time proving their cases.

By 1900 Governor Murray had left Newfoundland and his replacement, Henry McCallum, had arrived. Morine wasted no time before he approached the new governor. He convinced McCallum to reinstate him to public office on the sworn promise that he would irrevocably sever all public and professional ties with Robert Gillespie Reid. Before long, Morine resumed his place of honor in the Conservative cabinet!

Winter left for England on a business trip and Morine was appointed acting prime minister in his absence. It was during the four or five months of this stewardship that Morine showed his true colors. He bungled the administration of the government to such an extent that Winter, upon his return from England, angrily demanded that Morine resign. This earned Morine the somewhat dubious honor of being publicly disgraced twice in one year. Winter went so far as to describe his erstwhile lieutenant as "the greatest scoundrel who ever entered the Narrows [the entrance to St. John's Harbour]."[11]

The end was in sight for the Winter government. The faction in the opposition led by Edward Morris changed sides and joined Bond in condemning the contract and the irresponsible government which had negotiated it. Eventually, bowing to the rush of popular opinion, a few of Winter's own Conservatives defected to the opposition. Winter lost a non-confidence motion; an election was held, and Winter went down to defeat. On March 7, 1900, Robert Bond, who had won the election under the slogan "Reid even owns our graveyards,"[12] was called upon to form a minority government.

Meanwhile Reid had gone to London with the intention of borrowing $5,000,000. But the London financiers felt uneasy that his vast empire was held entirely under Reid's own name. They were willing to lend Reid the $5,000,000 but only on the condition that his properties be administered by a limited liability company.

Reid returned to Newfoundland with a plan to convert his holdings into a limited corporation with an initial capitalization of $25,000,000, entirely controlled by himself and his three sons. Robert Bond was determined to bargain toughly and force Reid to modify the deal of 1898. By some miracle of foresight, there was a clause in the 1898 contract which stated that Reid could not transfer his rights and obligations without government approval. Even though the stock of the proposed company would be held entirely by the Reid family, it was technically a transfer and therefore fell under the terms of the contract. Bond, who realized that he was in a strong position, refused to allow Reid to incorporate himself unless he gave up ownership of the railway and the telegraphs, and to make modifications in his land claims in favor of existing residents. Reid, who was unaccustomed to being dictated to, felt sufficiently sure of his position to defy the government. Turmoil ensued, and for the second time in 1900 Newfoundland was embroiled in an election battle. There was only one issue, the Contract of 1898.

Reid was angry. He threw the entire might of his empire into the fray, backing the Conservative Party to the hilt. With the defeat of James Winter and his retirement from political life, the irrepressible A. B. Morine returned to the stage, becoming the new Conservative leader. Morine dropped all pretense. His recent promises to Governor McCallum to have nothing more to do with Reid were completely forgotten, and Morine fought the election against Bond as nothing more than a stand-in for R. G. Reid himself. Reid's influence in the election was so blatant that a correspondent for the *Times* of London reported,

> One of Mr. Reid's sons has been accompanying him throughout his constituency and is mooted as a candidate. Two captains of Reid's bay steamers are running for other seats. The clothier who supplied the uniforms for Reid's officials is another, and a shipmaster,

until recently ship's husband for the Reid steamers, is another. His successor, who is a member of the Upper House, has issued a letter warmly endorsing Mr. Morine's policy, and it is now said that one of Reid's surveying staff will be nominated for another constituency.[13]

The ships and trains of the Reid empire sported Tory colors. As the organ for his interests, Reid had surreptitiously purchased the St. John's *Daily News* in 1899. For appearance's sake the paper was placed in Morine's hands, with the understanding that Reid would retain ownership.

However, Reid and Morine had seriously misjudged the mood of the voters. The electorate was in a state of outrage that no amount of money or propaganda could smother. Bond shrewdly turned the high feelings of the voters to the Liberal Party's advantage. Unlike the Conservatives, the Liberals had grassroots support with a strong moral case to present. The result of the election was really a foregone conclusion. The Reid interests went down to a shattering defeat. If the Conservatives had won, Reid would have truly been able to say, "L'état, c'est moi."

It was almost a clean sweep for the Liberals. They won thirty-two out of a possible thirty-six seats. Morine (a cat with nine lives if there ever was one) was handily reelected in his own riding of Bonavista and retained claim to the title of Leader of the Opposition. Robert Bond, the new prime minister, finally had a majority sufficiently powerful to challenge Reid. By August 1901 the Liberals passed a bill through the House of Assembly entitled the Railway (Amendment) Act. Under the terms of this act, Reid would be able to incorporate himself just as he wanted. In return, the 1898 contract would be invalidated and a new one, more favorable to the interests of Newfoundlanders, drawn up. The new corporation would be called the Reid Newfoundland Company and have a share value of $25,000,000. The new contract was signed on August 2, 1901. Reid agreed to surrender ownership of the railway upon repayment of the $1,000,000 he had paid for it, and 6 per cent interest for the time the government had held the money. When 2,550,000 acres of land were returned to the Crown, the government purchased them at the going rate of thirty-three cents each. Reid returned the telegraph system as well as all rolling stock and equipment associated with the railway. It was understood that, subject to the assessment of an arbitration board, Reid would be reimbursed for all losses and improvements that he had made.

Despite the huge majority he held in the House of Assembly and the hostility Reid had displayed against him during the election campaign, Bond was scrupulously fair, even lenient, with the contractor. In the end, the government of Newfoundland paid some $2,500,000 for the return of assets which the majority of Newfoundlanders felt never should have been surrendered in the first place. With the decision of the arbitration board, it was announced that Reid would receive a further award of $2,000,000. While Reid had been stripped of the grosser vestments of power, he was hardly pauperized.

Reid could no longer be called the "Nabob of Newfoundland," but he was still immensely wealthy, and was undoubtedly the island's most influential private citizen.

He still owned nearly four thousand square miles of land and was the biggest employer in Newfoundland. Reid's territories were rich in silver, copper, iron pyrites, lead and slate. The Reid finger was in seemingly every pie: fishing, sealing, saw milling, quarrying, pulp and paper, timber, flour mills, cold storage, hotels and "sportsmen's holidays." Reid was still involved with the railway, the telegraph system, the coastal shipping service, the tramway and hydroelectric companies. No matter what the Liberals thought of R. G. Reid, his railroading experience and organizational knowledge were irreplaceable. In some respects the new contract resembled the original contract of 1890; Reid would continue to operate virtually all the public utilities but only as a contractor. The proprietorship would be exclusively reserved for the government of Newfoundland.

Meanwhile, Reid and his former lieutenant Alfred B. Morine had a falling out. Morine had begun to grow tired of the world of politics and decided that he would have a more promising career in the newspaper business. With this aim in mind he decided to take over the St. John's *Daily News*, which Reid had placed under his nominal control prior to the 1898 election. A very ugly court battle ensued. In the course of the suit it came out that Morine not only received a $5,000 yearly payment from Reid when he was the minister of finance but continued to receive payments after his first resignation from office. At the time of his promise to Governor McCallum to sever all business arrangement with the Reid family, Morine not only continued to enjoy his retainer but had the amount raised to $8,000 a year. After the 1900 election it was increased to $10,000.

The consequences of the court action, by this time, must have been second nature to A. B. Morine. For the third time he was publicly disgraced. It was judged that Morine only held the newspaper in a trust capacity. The *Daily News* had to be returned to R. G. Reid. Morine felt compelled to flee to Canada. He continued to receive a $10,000 a year payment from Reid but only on condition that he never again show his face in the city of St. John's and never return to any other place in Newfoundland except during the summer trout-fishing season.

A. B. Morine was one of the most thoroughly unscrupulous opportunists to have ever disgraced a public office. It is interesting to note that after his banishment from Newfoundland he went on to a very "successful" career with the government of Canada, becoming head of the Public Service Commission and Minister of Justice. Returning to Newfoundland in 1919 he became attorney general, and Morine even received a knighthood in 1928!

After the contract of 1901 had been signed and Morine had fled the scene, the Reid Newfoundland Company went on to open its lands to industry, provide many jobs, build more branch railway lines, and lose more money. Though Reid was one of Canada's richest men, Newfoundland had proven to be a bottomless pit. After coming within an ace of founding a dynasty he ended up losing more than $6,000,000. But Reid was always the optimist. Though he never made a cent of profit in his Newfoundland ventures, he never lost faith that someday his real estate, his railway, his steamships and his varied other interests would pay off. The only payoff was to the long-suffering people of Newfoundland. Despite the corruption, incompetence and scandal, Newfoundland and her people were dragged kicking and screaming into the twentieth century. Deep bays and remote coves had been linked together by twin ribbons of steel. Mines, farms, quarries, paper mills and settlements had come into existence where before there had been nothing. No longer would Newfoundland be just an unsinkable fishing platform. Life would never be the same again.

Reid was to live seven more years. During this time he was appointed to directorships with the Canadian Pacific Railway and the Bank of Montréal and, because of his wide-ranging philanthropic activities, was named director of the Montréal General Hospital. In 1907, in recognition of his services to the Empire, he was created *Sir* Robert Gillespie Reid. But the driving pace of his ambition and the problems he faced in Newfoundland were finally beginning to catch up with him. His arthritic limbs grew so stiff and painful that he was able to spend only his summers in Newfoundland.

At 10 A.M. on the first of June 1908 a special train left the station in St. John's and raced along the five hundred and forty-eight miles of track to Port aux Basques. On board was William Reid and his wife. On Reid trains and Reid steamships they hoped to reach Montréal by noon on the fourth. They were too late. Sir Robert Gillespie Reid lay dead, carried off by pneumonia. He was sixty-eight years old. In Newfoundland, the *Evening Telegram* carried a tribute one column in length, as church bells pealed and a vast empire of locomotives, street cars, steamships, mines and factories stood silent in tribute.

Eleven

The Cross-Country Express

In the early days of the twentieth century the Reid Newfoundland Company operated a fiercely individualistic trans-island train called the Cross-Country Express. According to the Reid Company's promotional literature, the individual lucky enough to be a passenger could expect to be whisked effortlessly down the rails from St. John's to Port aux Basques to arrive refreshed, well fed, without a care or a worry, about twenty-five hours later. Officially the Express ran three times a week in summer and, weather permitting, twice a week during the winter months. With disturbing regularity, however, bridges were washed out, trains were derailed, locomotives buried in snowdrifts and boxcars blown off the track by powerful winds. The rocky roadbed looked ominously temporary, its track went straight up the sides of hills, down slopes and madly zigzagged through a maze of ponds and bogs. Embankments were often too steep for safety and the cuttings beside streams too narrow.

Most Newfoundlanders, unfamiliar with anything else, thought the little train, as it chugged out of the station, to be just about the most marvelous thing they had ever seen. To a traveler from "Up Along," used to the relative luxury of the mainland of Canada or the United States, a Newfoundland train must have been a thing of wonder—or perhaps trepidation.

At a place called Trinity Harbour the distance between the hilltops and the shoreline was so short that the gradient between the two was considered suicidal. There was only one valley suitable to grade down through but it was not long enough. To build a tunnel would be too expensive. The obvious solution was to build more curves, in fact a loop. The Canadian Pacific Railway maintains spiral tunnels, but the loop near Trinity was the only one of its kind. At the valley's narrowest point a trestle bridge was constructed. The track was routed across it and then gradually wound its way downward in a brake-screaming incline until it reached the floor of the valley, circled under the bridge and exited at the shoreline.

More than one foreign traveler took his revenge in print about the battering he had endured on the Newfoundland train.

> ... how we did bump over that line; whether it was the fault of the laying of the permanent way or the driving I cannot say, but in a long experience of railway travelling I

Eleven. The Cross-Country Express

Mixed train crossing a wooden trestle at Codroy (The Rooms Provincial Archives, A1-34 / R. E. Holloway).

have never been so jolted, the driver seeming to take a special pleasure in pulling up with a jerk sufficient to knock over any one standing up, and then start, if possible in a rougher manner. However, no one seemed to mind....[1]

In Newfoundland the Express was celebrated in story and song. To quote an anonymous Corner Brook poet:

> The trains on their schedule triweekly depart,
> But seldom exhibit a hurry to start;
> Port aux Basques is the place where they linger awhile,
> Awaiting in patience some news of the Kyle. [One of the Reid Company's steamships. Brought to Newfoundland in 1913 she remained in service on the Labrador coast until the late 1950s.]
>
> Then over loose sleepers they rattle and swerve
> For this railway has many a serpentine curve;
> When a roadbed is laid in this torturous style
> The cost is quite heavy when based on the mile!

> The gauge is so narrow that people complain
> Restriction of space is a positive strain;
> For a seat that fits one it is certainly true
> In modified comfort will never hold two.
>
> The engine may stop and pass out of control
> In absence of water or shortage of coal;
> Or a train at a station may loiter a day
> For another to pass the opposite way.
>
> The reason they wait I had better define,
> For on this particular Government Line
> Officials are strict and consider it slack
> If trains try to cross when upon the same track.
>
> Now over the Topsails where hurricanes blow -
> Through valleys where cuttings are buried in snow -
> Though passengers fume, yet the dutiful crew
> With zeal and with shovels a passage cut through.
>
> When sometimes you wait at a station all night
> For a train that's supposed to be coming in sight,
> You can hope for the best and prepare for the worst
> For daylight will probably welcome you first.[2]

The poet was exaggerating, of course, but Newfoundlanders were used to their train's peculiarities, even proud of them. For most of them a ride on the Cross-Country Express was a special event; a festive occasion. Stuffed in like salt fish in a barrel, the passengers would read, play cards, tell stories, sing old songs, play fiddles. At regular intervals the train would hiss to a stop at a water tower and everyone would get out for a few minutes and have a stretch. Depending on the time of year, the passengers would loaf in the sun, drop a line in a nearby brook for a trout or salmon, have a snowball fight or gather a few pails of fresh partridgeberries. But whatever the season, once that big bell on the locomotive began clanging, everyone would rush back to the train, laughing and jostling one another, as they scrambled up the high steps of the cars.

As night came on, those who had paid for a berth retired to the sleeping car. At the best of times it can be a tricky operation dressing and undressing in the confines of a narrow berth, but with the rocking and rolling on the Newfoundland Express some passengers thought it was virtually impossible. It was downright laughable to watch a tired commercial traveler shyly peeping through the curtains to determine if there was a stretch of straight track up ahead. If there was, he would leap into the aisle in a mad attempt to change his clothes before he fell over on the floor.

The end of each sleeping car was reserved for washing. This, too, required considerable practice. If the train took a sudden sharp turn, as it was in the habit of doing, a passenger was liable to smash his skull into the mirror over the washstand, or if the train pulled up with a jolt, several passengers were likely to be thrown on top of each other while washing their hands. Shaving was the hardest art of all to perfect. It was not unusual to see the faces of male passengers covered with bandages by the time they reached their destinations.

The next morning as the Express approached Port aux Basques it might have to make an unscheduled stop of several hours. The problem was the wind. It often whipped in off the sea and whistled around the base of Table Mountain at a speed of one hundred and fifty miles per hour, quite enough to tip a train car off the track and into a stream. If the wind subsided to their liking, the trainmen would guide their charge through a swamp, over a viaduct and into the terminal at Port aux Basques. Canada-bound passengers would hurry off to the dock to get aboard the railway steamship, the *Bruce*. Eight hours later they would be in North Sydney, Nova Scotia.

It may be hard to believe, but the Cross-Country Express was considered to be the luxury train. The really adventurous traveler would buy a ticket on the Accommodation Train. The Accommodation Train was a freight with a few passenger cars and a caboose hitched on behind. Who it accommodated was never made clear: certainly not the passengers.

In 1907 English sportsman by the name of J. G. Millais published a delightfully catty book, entitled *Newfoundland and its Untrodden Ways*, leaving us with an only slightly hyperbolic account of the Accommodation Train.

> The people of the island regard the "accommodation train" with dread; strangers suffering a single journey resolve never to repeat the experiment. But the "accommodation train" must accommodate somebody — perhaps it is the Old Gentleman himself! Every second day that passes, Satan must bless the island's government for running such a show entirely for his benefit. Could the walls of those "First Class" carriages speak, what a tale of wicked thought and wickeder language they could tell, and how oft had the nature of the most gentle of men been turned to acid and gall through the bitter experience of a night's travel![3]

Millais went on to say that it was once his great misfortune to be waiting for the Accommodation Train in the tiny wayside station of Glenwood (the train was a mere six hours late at the time) and the stationmaster, an eleven-year-old boy, told him a story. One day the boy saw a big black bear approach the station.

> He warn't walking away either, he come straight towards me ... I stopped right still, and as I hadn't no gun I jes' said somethin' that I knew would scare him proper ... I ses quit like, "Go way, you black devil, or I'll send you to St. John's by the 'accommodation train,' and you should ha' seen him scoot." (4)

The long-suffering Mr. Millais was scheduled to leave Glenwood station at 7 P.M. Punctually at 1 A.M. the train arrived.

> Far away, out in the darkness, overhanging a pool of water, was the passenger coach, on which was printed the curious legend "First Class." The train was designated as

> "mixed," not out of a compliment to the passengers, but to individualize its component parts. It is really a baggage train, with a coach sandwiched between the trucks, so that the passengers may experience the full joys of shunting, which takes place at every heap of lumber piled beside the track between the Bay of Islands and St. John's, a distance of five hundred miles. This journey is variously performed in two days, or, with the help of a snow storm or a spring wash-out, in a week.
>
> I opened the door of the "First Class" carriage, and was at once greeted with a terrible atmosphere. There were eight hard benches, capable of holding two passengers each, and occupied by twelve men, four women, and three children. Of course there was no seat to be had, so I sat on a biscuit box and allowed the door to stand open a minute although it was freezing slightly. Soon a man from outside came and shut it. Then I opened it again, and then a passenger shivered, shook himself, got up and shut it. This went on for some time until there really was a little fresh air in the car, and I tried to get asleep sitting on my biscuit tin.[5]

The train was already six hours behind schedule and would spend another four hours sitting at the station before getting under way. An engine was coupled on with enough force to throw the poor passengers end over end.

> All the men in the carriage woke up and swore. Then another fearful jolt, which put out the light and sent me into the arms of a perfectly innocent old lady, and off we went. These fearful shocks are caused by the engine's playful way of coupling on; this is effected apparently by adhesion, and it has to make a run at the train to make sure of sticking. This happened whenever the engine was required to detach for wood, coal or water, or the driver went to gossip with the section man or the stationmaster.
>
> After winging, creaking, and swaying round the marvellous curves of the line I became sleepy, and so spread two weekly editions of the *Times* on the floor of the carriage, placed my ulster above these, and, lying flat out, had a very nice nap for several hours. When I woke up, it was broad daylight, and somehow I had imagined we had got on splendidly and were nearly at Port Blandford. I said as much to a pleasant looking man sitting close to me, and the humour of the remark, quite unintentional, was received with roars of laughter by all the other men in the carriage.
>
> "Why, we're nowhere near Gambo [about thirty-six miles from Glenwood] yet."[6]

One good thing you could say about the Cross-Country Express was that the food was good and there was plenty of it. A passenger on the Accommodation Train would soon find out that food was nonexistent.

> Quite as tiresome a feature as the train itself was the fact that it was well nigh impossible to get any provisions en route. Except at Whitburn [sic] (eight or nine hours out of St. John's), where it is possible to obtain a slice of corned beef and a cup of tea—that is, if the train will wait for you—there is no other halting place where food can be obtained. My friends in the train had telegraphed on to Gambo to have a breakfast ready at the hotel [sic]. When we got there the "lady" in charge said, she did not make breakfasts for travellers, but that we could have "a glass of whisky" apiece at an exorbitant price. At Gambo I managed to steal two pints of hot water out of a section man's house which I invaded, and so got enough to give the tired looking women and children some tea. I also had a small supply of biscuits and cooked caribou meat, and this was all most of these unfortunate passengers had in thirty-six hours of travel.[7]

Turning the first sod on the Trepassey branch line, 9 May, 1911. The ceremonial shovel bore a silver plate and was decorated with ribbons (The Rooms Provincial Archives, B1-99 / Vey).

The food and shelter at some of the local hostelries were not much better than that on the train. There would seldom be rooms for everyone, so many of the travelers would be forced to sit up all night. Those unwise enough not to bring their lunches might have to survive on a humble diet of tepid tea and lemon-creme biscuits.

Near Terra Nova the train stopped for a couple of hours. Millais and some of the hungrier and more impatient passengers volunteered to load lumber from a pile beside the track in the vain hope that the journey would be that much speeded up.

The remainder of the trip to St. John's was quiet, except for when they pulled into Whitbourne Station and the train jumped the track, plowing up the right of way for two hundred yards. A little farther on at Avondale, the locomotive blew a cylinder head and this gave the passengers time to pick blueberries and make snide comments. Eventually though, the travelers did arrive in St. John's, and what is more, they reached the city "within a day of the advertised time, which is considered pretty good traveling time in Newfoundland."[8]

The main track was nearly five hundred and fifty miles in length. Branching out from it were a number of secondary lines totaling three hundred and seventy-five miles. It had become something of a tradition in Newfoundland to construct a railway prior to a general election. The branch lines were the result. A branch line was a make-work project. A railway would give the unemployed something useful to do and inject some money into the local economy, at least until the votes had been counted. As a legacy of this "enlightened" policy, a traveler going down the main line would encounter long stretches of rusty-looking track that began at no particular point, ended at no particular point, and on which the amount of freight and passengers was not very great. The roadbeds on some of the branches were chiefly used as pathways by flocks of omnivorous goats. Some of the more rambunctious animals were known to leap aboard the slow-moving trains and nip the passengers.

Though chronic money losers and often in a poor state of repair, the branch lines did serve a useful function. Given that the roads in Newfoundland had been described as only "slightly better than [...] secondary roads in the devastated areas of France in the years immediately after the Armistice,"[9] the branch lines were a lifeline to the people lucky enough to live near them. They tapped bays and coves that would otherwise be virtually cut off from the capital.

The train was the only regular connection many small communities had with the outside world. It was quite an event whenever a train pulled into a little station. Virtually everyone in the village would be on hand to greet it. It was as if a VIP had arrived, instead of a broken-down locomotive pulling a few wooden passenger coaches and a boxcar or two. The inhabitants would be thrilled by the sight of the train as it came wheezing into the station. As soon as it stopped, people would clamber all over it, looking at the massive iron wheels, examining the cabin, talking to the engineer, and wandering up and down the cars. There was a good chance that the train was many hours

Locomotive hauling wood across a dam (Canada Science and Technology Museum).

late. But no one minded too much. It was here and it was theirs and that was what counted. The railway company went to the trouble of printing timetables for the branches but they were largely ignored. The Cross-Country Express was on time more often than not, but the branch line trains seldom were. If you were to ask a local what time the train was due to arrive, your informant would probably give you a blank stare and after a moment's reflection reply, "Sometime tomorrow." Seasoned travelers fully expected to spend the better part of a day at the station, otherwise they would run the risk of missing the train when it finally showed up. There were few places that had any telegraph communication with the dispatching office, so as a rule, the stationmaster was as pleasantly surprised as anyone when a train came into view.

Even when the train arrived it was unwise for a traveler to be in much of a hurry. The train was sure to remain stationary for some considerable time at least, loading freight and waiting for stragglers, while the crew talked with their friends, brewed some tea and played cards in the station house. When the big whistle blew and the train slowly pulled out of the station, the townspeople would be on hand to provide a rousing send-off. It was just as well that no one was in much of a hurry because the average speed of the branch lines seldom exceeded ten miles per hour. It often took nine or ten hours to travel the eighty miles of the Placentia Branch and fifteen hours for the eighty-eight miles of the Bonavista Branch. Wags christened the Bonavista Branch "The Newfie Slug." A traveler could not help but develop the virtue of patience after blazing along the rails for fifteen hours and an average speed of six miles per hour.

There were constant delays. Sometimes, on the curves and gradients, the old engines had considerable trouble keeping up a sufficient head of steam and would come hissing to a halt. People would hitchhike a few miles at a time and the train would obligingly stop to pick them up or let them off anywhere they wanted. Trappers flagged the train down in the bush and hopped aboard the baggage car. If it was summer, the first-class coach might be occupied by a party of sportsmen from Europe or the mainland of Canada or the United States. Conversation with them was likely to be interrupted at any moment by a report that a few moose were crossing the track up ahead. At every whistle stop there were packages and mail bags to be picked up and dropped off, berries to be gathered and trout to be hooked.

In winter the wind would begin to blow a gale and before long the track up ahead, the train, the track behind and, seemingly, the whole world, would be engulfed in swirling snow. At such times the engine might freeze, making it impossible to percolate heat to the passenger cars. Starting fires in the emergency stoves, the passengers piled on extra sweaters and shivered in their blankets and coats until a relief team arrived. So strong could the wind get that snow flakes could be driven through the frames of double windows. A passenger might wake up under eleven inches of snow!

A train trip might be an inconvenience, but no matter what happened it was seldom looked upon as a hardship. There would always be friends to talk to and gossip to exchange. The crews were approachable and usually ready to bend regulations if a passenger had a special request. A story is told of an old lady by the name of Aunt

Sophie who boarded the train at Carbonear and asked the conductor to be sure and tell her when the train reached Brigus Crossroads. Unfortunately, the conductor became engrossed in a card game and forgot all about Aunt Sophie until the train had gone two miles past Brigus Crossroads. The conductor informed the engineer what had happened, and the engineer, being a kindly soul, immediately agreed to bring the train to a stop and back it up the two miles to Brigus Crossroads. When they reached the crossroads, the conductor informed Aunt Sophie. "Thank you sir, thank you very much," said Aunt Sophie, "this is where the doctor told me to take my pill."[10]

Then there was the newly-hired conductor making his inaugural run. As the train puffed into the first station on the line, the conductor realized with a fright that he had completely forgotten the name of the community. Rather than risk looking like a fool, he bellowed out in his most confident voice: "Here ye are for where you're goin'! All in there for here come out!"[11]

The passengers generally looked upon a train trip as one big party. In the early days there were no sleeping cars or dining cars on the branch lines, so the passengers, as we have seen, were left to fend for themselves. Generally, those who knew what to expect did not fare too badly. Each family brought a wicker basket well stocked with sandwiches, molasses cookies, cakes, raspberry syrup and whatever else was available. Before long, generous quantities of food were passed around and consumed by everyone in the car. The conductor, who was generally on a first-name basis with most of the passengers, was usually invited to the feast. As his contribution, the conductor would brew up a huge pot of tea on the heating-stove at the rear of the car. As the train crept down the track the festivities grew. Gradually the distinction between first-and second-class broke down as people wandered all over the train. At each stop another old friend and neighbor climbed aboard. Inevitably, someone would have a mouth organ or button accordion. Before long, people were singing songs, dancing jigs in the aisles and clapping time to the music.

The Governor Has a Close Call, 1913

On one of our many train journeys we met with a serious mishap which might have ended in even greater disaster. Travelling on evening in our train at about thirty miles an hour, we were sitting at dinner when, about nine o'clock, we suddenly became aware of smoke in the coach in which we sat, and in a moment we discovered that the sleeping coach next ahead of us was on fire. We made a rush for it to rescue my despatch box and cyphers, but were beaten back. My aide-de-camp then tied a wet towel around his mouth, but that too failed, and in an instant the flames shot up through the roof. Luckily we had a powerful brake on the coach in which we were, and jammed it down, attracting the attention of the engine-driver, and the train was stopped as quickly as possible. The conductor ran back and uncoupled, drawing the rest of the train forward, and not a moment too soon, as a minute later it could not have been done, and the loss would have been infinitely greater. Fortunately there was a water-chute some three hundred yards farther on to supply passing engines, and to that the forward part of the train was taken; but the flames were too violent, and all that could be saved of the burning coach was the floor and under carriage. On the next morning we surveyed our losses, and estimated them, all alas! Uninsured, at about £650 between the five of us. The bedrooms of the ladies were in the after coach in which we were dining, and so their actual personal belongings were saved, with the exception of their furs which, by bad luck, had been removed from their cabins just before dinner; but all our portmanteaus and their contents were burnt to ashes, and everything belonging to my staff and myself went out of existence. Even the silver of our dressing bags was fused into molten lumps. The water which played upon the floor of the coach caused enough of my cypher to be saved to serve for identification, and curiously enough a little silver and ebony crucifix lay at the bottom of the coach blackened but absolutely unharmed, although the triptych in which it hung was burnt. Not one single other thing was saved. The coaches were all lighted which many very powerful oil lamps, and the mass of oil from them caused the terribly overwhelming smoke which so completely defeated our efforts for salvage. We had reason to be thankful that our brake worked as quickly as it did, or there would have been a vacancy in the office of Governor of Newfoundland. We were about twenty hours from St. John's, and of course started back at once, arriving a soiled and bedraggled party, very unlike the usual arrival of His Excellency the Governor at his seat of Government.[12]

Twelve

The New Century

The Reid Newfoundland Company lost $6,000,000 operating the railway in Newfoundland between the years 1901 and 1921. It was not that the company was badly managed. Rather, it was that the company was faced with the impossible task of making a profit in the conditions that existed in Newfoundland. There were simply too many miles of track to maintain and not enough traffic. The population of Newfoundland was too small and too spread out, and the economy too small to support a railway of the size it had.

As the Reid family's advisors had been telling them all along, a railway in Newfoundland could not possibly be a profitable concern. R. G. Reid and his sons after him were all too aware of this counsel. Unfortunately, the profits they expected to make from their six thousand square miles of real estate — the profits they expected to offset the expense of operating the railway — had never materialized. The railway had proven to be a greater white elephant than anyone could have imagined.

The railway was bleeding the Reid empire dry. In a desperate attempt to remain solvent, operating expenses were slashed drastically. The frequency of trans-island expresses was cut back, winter operations on the branch lines were curtailed, and maintenance reduced to a mere fraction of what was recommended. The Newfoundland Railway was beginning its steady decline into decrepitude, a decline that would last until World War II.

With the coming of World War I Newfoundland enjoyed a brief period of prosperity. The sudden flood of men, munitions and material shunted across the island by train helped pay the bills for a while, but just about pounded the old railway to dust in the process. The Great War brought business. It also brought galloping inflation, large wage increases and staggering losses to the balance sheet. The railway lost $340,000 in 1918 and twice that amount in 1919. In 1920, expenses exceeded revenue by the frightening figure of $1,320,000. In 1912, 400,000 wooden ties had been replaced. Six years later, after the punishment meted out by the war effort, only 140,000 ties were replaced. The railway was falling apart. The locomotives were older, the rolling stock rickety, the ties wormy and dry, the track rusty and the roadbed sadly in need of ballasting.

CNR Engine No. 593 (formerly Newfoundland Railway 193) was in service from 1919 to 1957 and has been on display in Corner Brook since 1959 (The Rooms Provincial Archives, VA 29-13 / H. Clayton).

By 1920 the Reids were ready to call it quits. They informed the government that they could no longer afford to operate a railway in Newfoundland. Due to war costs and the world recession that came after, the government was not eager to take responsibility for a proven money-loser like the railway. The Newfoundland government was already saddled with a national debt of such proportions that seventy percent of revenue went towards meeting the interest charges. Nevertheless, they had to come to the railway's rescue. Losing money or not, the railway had become an essential service. A commission was formed consisting of three members appointed by the government and three by the Reid Newfoundland Company to run the railway system for one year from July 1, 1920. Some ballasting and much needed capital improvements were made but, by the end of the year, another $1,650,000 had been lost. During the next two years the Reids reluctantly continued to operate the railway as best they could. They hired a Canadian railway expert named R. C. Morgan to manage the line, while the government agreed to cover operating expenses to the tune of $1,500,000 a year. Capital expenditure was cut to the absolute minimum and maintenance to almost nothing. Employees had to accept pay cuts, the schedules were further reduced, and during the winter of 1922, operations over the Gaff Topsails Plateau ceased altogether. Losses for the period still averaged $1,300,00 per year. But at least that was less than expected. Morgan was a good manager and did the best he could. With careful attention the railway could limp along for a little while, but it could not hope to continue forever. In his year-end report for 1921 Morgan gave a gloomy summary.

> The expectation of the parties to the original contract, as to the amount of traffic has not been realized; and the Reid Newfoundland Railway has always been, and for a long time will be, a line of extremely light traffic requiring the maintaining of large mileage of track for the handling of small tonnage of freight and a limited number of passengers.[1]

Morgan recommended that the Reids continue to operate the railroad with the Newfoundland government subsidizing maintenance and capital improvements.

This was not acceptable to the Reids. It cost the Newfoundland Railway seven and one-half cents to move one ton of freight a distance of one mile compared to the Canadian Pacific Railway's 0.78 cents! In 1919 the Newfoundland Railway was earning $1,542.70 per mile compared to the C. P. R.'s $15,917.61 per mile! Understandably the Reids wanted out. In April 1922 they offered to surrender the entire system to the government. Employees of the railway were notified that there would be no funds available to pay wages after May 15. From May 16 to May 23 the railway was closed down completely. Emergency funds were granted by the government to meet the payrolls and operating expenses until June 30, 1923. In July 1923, the Railway (Settlement) Act was passed. Two million dollars were paid to the Reid Newfoundland Company for the improvements it had made and the government took over the railway, changing the name to the Newfoundland Government Railway. The Reids still owned vast land tracts and would continue to be an economic force in Newfoundland for years to come but their railroading days were over. Thirty-three years of railroad pioneering had come to an end.

What had the government of Newfoundland received for its $2,000,000? A ramshackle transportation system that had already cost the Newfoundland taxpayers $30,000,000 and the Reids millions more; a thousand-odd miles of track, docks, ships, dry dock, telegraph lines, miscellaneous repair sheds, warehouses and stations; all of it was old and much of it run down.

In its first year of operating the trains, the government's railway commission actually broke even. This unaccustomed state of affairs resulted from the fact that the commission spent virtually no money. Though the railway was left to disintegrate for an additional year, it certainly made for an encouraging year-end report. Actually, it was too encouraging. The employees were so bold as to ask for more money! No more year-end reports were published after that.

Seventy-pound rail was ordered early in 1925, along with much-needed rolling stock. Between 1925 and 1929 an average of 400,000 ties were replaced, the main line

2-8-2 Mikado, Locomotive No. 327, 1940s. Twenty-four Mikados were built for Newfoundland (Public Domain).

completely re-railed and the dry dock rebuilt in concrete. A large new coastal ship was ordered, diversions and branch lines constructed (for the same old reason, they were popular at election time) and a steam shovel was purchased to aid in the work of ballasting.

By 1929 the railway, which three years before had reverted to its original name, Newfoundland Railway, seemed on its way to recovery. Wages for its two thousand employees averaged a princely $2.50 per day. Prosperity seemed tantalizingly close. Then disaster struck in the form of the Depression.

Newfoundland was probably hit harder by the Depression than any other country in the western world. The economy of Newfoundland was all but wiped out. Trusted railway employees lost their jobs and wages for the rest were cut back as much as twenty percent. Train schedules were reduced, recently constructed branch lines were closed and the track ripped up for use on the main line. Fifty-seven stations were unable to earn their upkeep, maintenance lapsed, and once again the railway began to visibly fall apart. With the appearance of dirt and gravel roads, anyone who could get a truck went into the transportation business. Between the years 1930 and 1932 road transportation cut into the railway's total volume of freight by a crippling 50 percent. In 1932 400,000 tons of freight were carried by road compared to 320,000 by the railroad.[2]

It was estimated that to afford a bottle of ink for the company's accountant, two thousand pounds of freight would have to be hauled a distance of five miles, or a gallon of oil twenty-five miles. Unfortunately it was politically impossible to raise the rates, as the railway's customers were also voters.

Conditions went from bad to worse, until in 1933 the colony touched bottom. With a quarter of the total population on the dole, Newfoundland was declared bankrupt. About one-third of the public debt could be traced to the cost of running the railway. In an unprecedented step, responsible government was suspended indefinitely in favor of a six-man commission of government appointed by the British crown. The railway was placed under the responsibility of the commissioner of public utilities. By 1936 there was a little capital available, but the railway remained neglected. Equipment and rolling stock were in short supply and revenue was so low that the rails were taken up from the Trepassey, Bay de Verde and Heart's Content branch lines. It would take the catalyst of a second global conflict to lift the railway out of its doldrums.

Until the beginning of World War II, Newfoundland was humbled to such an extent that it had to rely on handouts from Great Britain to keep its head above water.

Carload of bundled wood being hauled to a paper mill in Corner Brook, 1950s (The Rooms Provincial Archives, B4-114 / CNR).

Historic plaque at Ship Harbour commemorating the signing of the Atlantic Charter in 1941 by Franklin D. Roosevelt and Winston S. Churchill. Under this agreement much-needed American equipment was transferred to the Newfoundland Railway (Dianne Taylor-Harding).

But the war brought astonishing changes. Suddenly, Newfoundland was no longer poor — it was experiencing undreamed-of prosperity. Overnight, Newfoundland was transformed from a remote backwater to the bastion of the North Atlantic. American and Canadian troops poured into the island, bringing with them more money than the islanders had seen in a lifetime. For the first time in its history all the island's resources were in heavy demand. Unemployment vanished overnight and the government was faced with the pleasant embarrassment of an annual financial surplus.

The railway was flooded with business and almost overwhelmed by it. In a matter of months the railway went from a state of abject penury to an abundance of wealth. The amount of freight shot up to 700,000 tons a year in 1945, almost double what had been carried in 1940. Employees worked an average of seventy hours per week. Wages climbed from $2,000,000 in 1930 to $5,000,000 in 1940 and $7,000,000 in 1945. The railway, which found itself in the usual position of showing a profit in 1944, was supplied with whatever it needed, much of it courtesy of the United States government.

Under the lend-lease program, Britain, in return for the use of one hundred and forty badly-needed destroyers, granted the still officially neutral United States permission to build military bases in Newfoundland, Bermuda and the West Indies. Before long, the United States Army Corps of Engineers was hard at work in St. John's, Corner Brook and Argentia. Efficient communications between these bases were essential. As roads in Newfoundland were treacherous at best, the railway was the only alternative — but certainly not in its existing state. The twenty-mile branch from the American naval base at Argentia was re-ballasted and re-railed with seventy-pound rail and

Engine No. 1003 (built by North British Locomotive Works) at the turntable, St. John's, 1940s. It was in service from 1935 to 1957 (Public Domain).

Whitbourne train station. Built in 1945, it now houses the Whitbourne Town Council (Hollis Harding).

a new terminal erected. The United States War Department had little alternative but to supply the Newfoundland Railway with new locomotives and rolling stock, seventy-pound rail and modern construction equipment to the tune of $2,100,000.

The Americans built a communications cable network and the railway was assigned a couple of circuits. Prior to the war the railway had relied on a single galvanized wire strung between wooden poles crossing the island. Every winter, under the weight of ice and snow, breaks would occur.

The Canadians were not far behind. The year 1940 saw a number of high ranking Royal Canadian Air Force officers examine the Newfoundland Railway. The train carried them to a place in the center of the island called Gander Lake, and there they decided to have a base and airport constructed. The whole area was soon a hive of activity, as workmen with heavy equipment began clearing the forest and constructing hangers and runways. The Canadians depended completely on the railway and it did not let them down. The Newfoundland Railway did a magnificent job transporting men and supplies, including millions of gallons of high-octane fuel as well as iron ore and newsprint in quantities many times larger than it had been designed to handle. In the process the rolling stock was subjected to a severe pounding. Passenger coaches were in such demand that they were almost constantly in use. Troops were packed on open platforms, in lavatories and on tops of stoves (in summer). Freight cars were routinely loaded twenty to fifty percent over the stated capacity. Before the war gasoline was shipped at the rate of sixty barrels per car. During the war this jumped to one hundred and twenty barrels per car.

A major problem during the war years was keeping the railway supplied with ties for the roadbed. Made locally from untreated fir or spruce, the entire line needed about two million ties. With a lifespan of six or seven years, about 300,000 replacements were required annually. In 1939 280,000 ties were replaced but only 120,000 in 1942. There was an abundance of trees in Newfoundland of course, but it was labor that had become scarce. There were plenty of good jobs available at the bases and on construction projects. When peace came in 1945 the Newfoundland Railway was in need of 750,000 wooden ties.[3]

Surprisingly, serious accidents were few. In February 1943 there were three derailments between Arnold's Cove and Come By Chance. A trainload of Canadian troops leaving Gander, thinking the line was clear, soon found themselves in the same predicament. At midnight, yet another train, the incoming express, made it as far as Arnold's Cove before being blocked by drifts of snow. Within a distance of less than ten miles there were five locomotives stuck in the snow, all of them running out of food and fuel. Headquarters sent a message to "Burn everything in sight," and received the reply, "Everything burnt; expect church next to go."[4]

To keep the trains rolling, improvisation was the name of the game. Many stories were told of keeping a coupling together with a track bolt and a spool of wire. There were no better improvisers than the engineers. One engineer's seventy-five-ton

Auxiliary tool car, Whitbourne (Hollis Harding).

Signal, Whitbourne (Hollis Harding).

locomotive developed mechanical trouble in the front end. He knew that, far from the yards as he was there were no cranes or jacks available to take such a weight. He had to think of something on his own. When he came across a section crew, he had his solution. The engineer instructed the men to dig the ends of two steel rails into the earth in such a way that the other two ends would be placed securely under the front of his locomotive. When this was done to his satisfaction the engineer drove slowly forward. The front of the locomotive was raised off the track, the engineer crawled underneath, fixed the trouble and continued on his way.[5] On another occasion a forty-ton artillery piece fell off a flatcar near Ocean Pond. There was no crane available, but by clever use of jacks and wedges the gun was slowly inched up.

It was about this time that the Newfoundland Railway's passenger train was facetiously called "The Slowest Crack Train in Civilization" and "The Newfie Bullet." For people used to the sleek modern rail systems of Canada and the United States, the Bullet — old, slow, cranky and always overcrowded — was a constant source of amusement. It was said that yesterday's train, or the one from the day before, was the one most likely to arrive today.

Mixed train at Holyrood (Canada Science and Technology Museum).

Newfoundland Railway passenger trains No. 1 and No. 2 meeting at Steady Brook, c. 1949 (Canada Science and Technology Museum).

Despite little idiosyncrasies like the soot which bellowed into the windows of the wooden coaches, hills that gave a distinct roller-coaster effect, the ships' anchors which prevented the train from being blown over and the curves which enabled the traveler to take in engine and caboose in one look, the troops grew rather fond of the old Bullet. It was so friendly and informal they could not help but like it. The soldiers also grew rather fond of the national drink of Newfoundland, a rather fiery version of rum known as Screech. Sometimes they combined these two affections quite cleverly, especially when headed homeward or on leave.

On October 9, 1942, Joan Blondell, the American movie actress, visited St. John's as part of a USO tour. Miss Blondell became so enamored of the funny old train that upon her return to the United States she added a humorous little song about the Bullet to her repertoire and sang the song on national radio.

> A pretty lady passenger was sitting there close by,
> She spied an American soldier with a twinkle in his eye.
> He walked up beside her and asked her for a kiss,
> Up with her hand and knocked him cold on the Newfoundland Express.[6]

Passenger train No. 2, *Caribou*, eastbound at Bear Cove Bridge, 1950s (Canada Science and Technology Museum).

Trainmen with the newspaper announcing the close referendum vote by which Newfoundland joined Canada, 1949 (Canada Science and Technology Museum).

Another verse advised would-be suicides to avoid the Newfoundland train, as they would freeze to death before they could be run over. Expatriate Newfoundlanders, however, taking the song as a racial slur, deluged her with hate mail.

In 1945 the war ended, and the amount of freight and passenger traffic declined almost to the starvation levels of prewar years. For six short years Newfoundland had been thrust into the center of the modern world. It was understandable that Newfoundlanders should wish to become a permanent part of it. After a heated campaign, referenda were held to decide the island's future. The result was that, on April 1, 1949, by a narrow margin of votes, Newfoundland became Canada's tenth province.

On the same day, the Newfoundland Railway became the newest element of the Canadian National Railways. April Fool's Day was held by some to be a suitable day for the takeover. Despite the many improvements made during World War II the Newfoundland Railway was still essentially a nineteenth-century operation. In 1947 it carried only one-seventh the amount of freight it carried during the war years. It lost money at an alarming rate of $1.12 a running mile and its deficit for the year was a whopping $1,355,351.

As of April 1, 1949, the Canadian National Railways took possession of seven hundred and five miles of three-foot-six-inch gauge track, largely unserviced and in need of massive rehabilitation. Rolling stock consisted of forty-six aging steam locomotives, three diesel locomotives, ninety-eight wooden passenger cars, one thousand and four freight cars and one hundred and fifty-four units of work equipment. Also included were the dry dock in St. John's harbour and a fleet of fourteen ships, most of them leftovers from the Reid days.

Passenger train No. 1, westbound over Joy's Crossing, Holyrood, 1940s (Canada Science and Technology Museum).

Curious sheep at Stephenville Crossing station, 1950s (Canada Science and Technology Museum).

After studying its new property the C.N.R. began a series of changes designed to completely integrate the Newfoundland Railway into the modern rail system of Canada. The first change was to immediately raise the starvation wage of the Newfoundland Railway's four thousand one hundred employees by 30 percent to meet national standards.

Mile for mile more money was spent on the railways in Newfoundland than in any other part of Canada. Mile for mile more money was needed! In the first fifteen years of Confederation, Canadian National pumped $80,000,000 into Newfoundland. Traffic increased from 900,000 tons of freight in 1949 to 1,500,000 tons in 1960 and 2,000,000 tons in 1967.

Mindful of the days when the Cross-Country Express was buried in snow for days at a stretch, Canadian National began a three-year program to raise the level of the track bed an average of four feet. From now on the track across the Gaff Topsails would be above the level of most of the winter snow drifts. Bulldozers, snowplows and work crews were at the ready and the tracks were usually cleared in a few hours.

Between 1953 and 1956 the old steam locomotives were replaced by forty-one diesel locomotives specially constructed for narrow-gauge use. A further twelve diesels were delivered between 1958 and 1960. Altogether, 1,400 pieces of rolling stock were added to the system including livestock, gondola and refrigeration cars. Canadian National was the first railway in the world to use standard-size forty-foot steel boxcars mounted on narrow-gauge boggies. About one hundred standard size freight cars

Tilted railway symbol on a boxcar (Canada Science and Technology Museum).

Passenger train en route to St. John's from Port aux Basques, c. 1945 (Canada Science and Technology Museum).

were so converted. The advantage of using them was that they could carry one-third more cargo than narrow-gauge cars.

To enable the railway to handle heavier and faster trains, a program was started to replace the seventy-pound rail on the main line with more durable track weighing eighty-five pounds a linear yard. To handle the increased demands placed upon the system, new marshaling yards were established in Corner Brook, Bishop's Falls and Port aux Basques; existing facilities were expanded by the addition of diesel shops, repair depots, storage sheds, stations, steel bridges and culverts. Untreated softwood ties with a lifespan of five years were replaced by 2,480,000 new ties treated to last twenty-five years. Crushed stone ballast in the amount of 1,600,000 cubic yards was used to replace the previous inferior mixture of clay and gravel. The fleet of coastal boats was augmented by seven new ships, including container carriers and railway ferries.

Prior to this time there were no railway ferries operating to Newfoundland. A cargo outward bound from St. John's might be loaded on the railway at St. John's, transported to Port aux Basques, unloaded, loaded aboard a vessel, transshipped at the North Sydney terminal, and then loaded on to a Mainland train. This was obviously inefficient and costly. In 1967 Canadian National introduced a railway ferry. Cargoes could then be loaded in Newfoundland and not unloaded until they reached their destination anywhere in North America. Associated with the railcar ferry was the only standard-gauge operation in Newfoundland, a single switching engine on a short stretch of track in the Port aux Basques terminal.

In order to handle the increasing flow of automobiles, Canadian National brought into service the world's only narrow-gauge bi-level automobile carriers. Twenty of these cars, each equipped to carry six automobiles, were manufactured in the railway shops in St. John's.

In the first years after the takeover, the C. N. R.'s planners debated the feasibility of flattening the grades, straightening the curves and widening the track to match the four-foot, eight and one-half-inch gauge on the Mainland. It must not be forgotten that the Newfoundland Railway still had grades as steep as two and a half percent and curves as sharp as fourteen degrees; these were steeper and sharper than anything found in the Rocky Mountains and unsafe for a standard-gauge operation. To iron out all the kinks would be prohibitively expensive, between $750 million and $800 million,

The Newfoundland Express crossing the Gaff Topsails, 1960s (Canada Science and Technology Museum).

and would involve the relocation of virtually the entire track. It was decided instead to keep the narrow gauge but improve it as much as possible. The worst curves and grades were eliminated, but the railway in Newfoundland remained steep and twisty. In such a situation there was little advantage in converting to standard-gauge. A locomotive operating on a narrow-gauge track can pull as many cars up a grade or around a sharp turn as can a locomotive on a standard-gauge line.

For the first time passenger service in Newfoundland approached the quality of service long taken for granted on the Mainland. Enough peculiarities remained to give the Bullet its special character. The track remained narrow but at least it was well ballasted and no longer rusty. The engines, coaches and freight cars were as small as before, the difference being that they were now well-maintained and freshly painted. It was ironic that the long overdue improvements to passenger service occurred as paved highways were making passenger trains obsolete.

Most people liked the Bullet. A few travelers rubbing their battered craniums might complain about the limited headroom in the sleeping cars, but the berths were comfortable, even if they were narrower than those found on the Mainland. The only serious inconvenience was the narrowness of the center aisles which made it difficult for two people to pass. When the lights were turned out at night, confrontations were

Coach No. 5019, Avondale. Now used as a diner (Hollis Harding).

liable to occur to the amusement of the whole car. When two people bumped into each other in the dark, a few apologies were muttered and

> the contestants backed away each to the end of the car and politely waited for the other to come through. It was one of those stage-waits which hold an audience spellbound. The second exchange of apologies seemed to lack something of the spontaneity and sincerity of the first, and on the third attempt there were no apologies at all, rather the reverse, if you known what I mean. Then came that sustained silence marking the apex of drama, and after that a rugged male voice, "Look ye, m'am, I'm waitin' here till ye come through, and dammit, I'd be obliged if you'd hurry."[7]

The seats in the new steel passenger coaches were all of the reclining type but closer together, with less leg room than was standard. In place of air conditioning, fresh air was funneled through vents placed in the ceiling. Winter heating was supplied courtesy of a steam generator car. Just in case, each car was equipped, front and back, with old-fashioned oil stoves.

An average passenger train in the 1960s consisted of two diesel locomotives and about a dozen cars; a few more on summer weekends. Each sleeping car was marked

Locomotive No. 940 and baggage car, Whitbourne. The monument in the foreground is the Railroader's Memorial. "In memory of those railroaders who lost their lives in the line of duty during the years of the railway era in Newfoundland." Sixty names are listed (Hollis Harding).

with the name of a Newfoundland community: Fogo, Gander, Humber, Lewisporte, etc. The coaches were numbered. Despite all of Canadian National's costly improvements, passengers were rocked and pummeled mercilessly, much as they always had been for the last seventy-odd years. On every curve the train would sway like a drunken sailor. More than one passenger complained of seasickness.

None of the coaches were equipped with the latest brakes or lock couplings. Every time a train navigated a curve or gradient, the slack played in and out with a force violent enough to shake the entire length of the train.

The run from Port aux Basques was scheduled to take twenty-one and one-half hours, about the same as in 1898. The crew members paid much closer attention to the timetables than in days gone by, but the Bullet was still the Bullet. Delays and unexpected events still occurred, there being little that the C. N. R. could do about the weather. Few places on earth have a wind problem to match that of an area near Cape Ray on the west coast. The railroad track, which was perilously close to the shore, bore the full brunt of the ocean elements, not the least of which are one hundred and fifty mile per hour winds. Trains had to be chained in place with ships' anchors. At a place called Wreckhouse, fully loaded freight cars were tossed off the track like match boxes.

Snow plow No. 3459, Whitbourne (Hollis Harding).

For many years the railway had in its employ the world's only human wind gauge, an old-timer by the name of Lauchie McDougall. Lauchie had lived at Wreckhouse all his life and claimed to know more about the winds than anyone. For twenty dollars a month Lauchie would walk along the track twice a day sniffing the wind. If his sensitive nose detected a big blow coming on, he would immediately telephone the dispatcher at Port aux Basques and all train traffic would be halted.

> Legend has it that Lauchie would gauge the strength of the wind by pushing on his front door. Depending on how hard the wind pushed back, Lauchie knew whether or not Wreckhouse was safe for trains. Lauchie is dead now, his family scattered, and all that remains of their small house is the wind-blasted foundation.[8]

On one occasion an eastbound freight train with two steam locomotives had its twenty-three cars blown off the track. The locomotives stayed on the rails only because of their great weight. At the railway station in St. Andrew's anemometers were mounted on a pole to measure wind speeds. The last recorded measurement was one hundred twenty-seven miles per hour before the instruments were torn from their perch. The gusts of wind were so fierce that they sometimes blew back the flames from a locomotive's firebox into the cab housing the crew. Sometimes the fires were completely blown out.[9]

Even in its last years the Bullet stubbornly resisted becoming too efficient. To the never-ending frustration of C. N. R. planners, the Bullet survived with some of its devil-may-care personality intact. The Bullet was in no particular hurry to arrive at its destination and its passengers were tolerant. Now and then the Bullet put on a burst of speed to show off, but usually it was content to meander along at about twenty miles per hour, not exactly burning up the rails. The surprising thing was that despite all the Bullet's quirks it was seldom more than a few hours late and, more often than not, it arrived approximately on time.

Thirteen

July 2, 1969, The Last Run

In 1967 Canadian National Railways announced a plan to phase out the train it insisted on calling the Caribou #102 but everyone else called "The Newfie Bullet." The "Bullet," or the Caribou if you prefer, was losing money. Operation of this passenger train had cost the C. N. R. and the Canadian taxpayer $900,000 in 1966. The Canadian Transport Commission received C. N. R's application but would permit the railway to abandon the "Bullet" only if it could prove the bus service proposed to replace it with was an adequate alternative.

Locomotive No. 940 and snow plow. The locomotive was built in February 1960 by General Motors Diesel Division, London, Ontario (Hollis Harding).

Top: Canadian National Railway's *Caribou* passenger train leaving Port aux Basques for St. John's, c. 1960 (Canada Science and Technology Museum). *Bottom*: Detail showing the tilted Newfoundland Railway symbol (Hollis Harding).

Top: Caboose No. 6053, Whitbourne. Built in 1961 by National Steel Car, Hamilton, Ontario (Hollis Harding). *Bottom*: Snow plow No. 3465, Avondale (Hollis Harding).

Top: Snow plow No. 3465 and Locomotive No. 925, Avondale (Hollis Harding). *Bottom*: Passenger car on display in St. John's (Hollis Harding).

End view of the same passenger car (Hollis Harding).

For six months "Bullet" and bus battled it out in a contest the former could never hope to win. The buses were gleaming new, air conditioned, and despite an initial tendency to get lost on the highway, completed the St. John's to Port aux Basques run a full ten hours faster than the old passenger train. The buses were widely promoted by an intensive advertising campaign, the "Bullet" all but ignored. One potential traveler in Toronto was even told by a C. N. R. ticket agent that passenger trains were no longer running in Newfoundland.

Not to anyone's surprise, the buses won the contest hands down. The C. T. C. was satisfied that Roadcruiser bus service was more popular and more efficient. From a strict dollars and cents point of view there could be no doubt they were justified in their decision. The passenger train was slow, usually half empty, uncomfortable and creaky. But the Bullet was much more than a mere train — it was an institution, a living piece of folklore. If there was but one train in the world which should not have been judged on purely economic terms, that train was the "Newfie Bullet." Any train that stopped to let its passengers pick blueberries deserved a new lease on life.

Hand car, Avondale (Hollis Harding).

Engine No. 900, St. John's. This was Newfoundland's first diesel locomotive. It is equipped with a steam locomotive–style headlight (Hollis Harding).

Top: Another view of Engine No. 900 with freight cars (Hollis Harding). *Bottom*: Boxcar used as a storage shed, Quidi Vidi (Hollis Harding).

Thirteen. July 2, 1969, The Last Run

Hand car, Avondale (Hollis Harding).

It was July 2, 1969, ten o'clock and a bright sunny morning as the two diesel engines struggled to pull sixteen cars out of the Port aux Basques station for the last time. Aboard were two hundred and six passengers, mostly reporters and American railway buffs. Watching was a small hushed crowd of about one hundred people. Nearby, a more boisterous crowd was jostling to get aboard Roadcruiser buses. The Bullet received little in the way of fanfare and nothing in the way of ceremony to mark its passing. Moments before, the loudspeaker had announced — as it had hundreds of times before: "Train number 102, the Caribou, now boarding for St. John's. All aboard."

As the train pulled out of the terminal, workmen in the marshaling yard put down their tools to stand in a silent tribute as the train passed them by.

There was plenty of rum aboard the train and sporadic guitar-playing but nobody much felt like having a good time. A few passengers tried to liven up the occasion by telling shopworn Bullet jokes. The most popular one concerned an unhappy young man, spurned in love, who tried to commit suicide by lying down across the tracks just before the Bullet was scheduled to pass. A few weeks later a search party found the hapless youth covered with cobwebs and dead from the effects of starvation. His grieving parents sued the company for the unpunctuality of their trains. But the jokes fell flat; it was not a time for laughing.

Top: Locomotive No. 925, Avondale (Hollis Harding). *Bottom*: Passenger car at the Railway Coastal Museum, St. John's (Hollis Harding).

Longest surviving section of narrow gauge track in Newfoundland, Avondale (Hollis Harding).

All along the route little knots of people, some with tears in their eyes, silently waved goodbye to the old train one last time. People stood on the roofs of their homes and waved with both arms; housewives doing their washing in the back garden waved aprons; farmers and grizzled fishermen doffed their caps and remembered the old days. Several small children displayed a homemade sign with the words "Bye Bye Bullet" written on it. Whenever the train stopped, people crowded around asking for menus, place mats, or anything else for a souvenir. Automobiles at every road that crossed the track sounded their horns as the Bullet passed by. Many old-timers were there that day. A few climbed aboard to ride a few miles, while senior engineers and firemen were given turns at the throttle. Among the old-timers was George Tipple, eighty-four years old. George still remembered how it was seventy-one years before, when the first train traveled over that very same route. George was thirteen years old at that time and recalled how he and his school friends stood expectantly beside the track as two small steam locomotives, belching black smoke, came huffing and puffing along the track, pulling passenger cars on the very first trans-island express. George still remembered how the passing train blew off his new straw hat.

At eight A.M. the next day, the final trans-Newfoundland passenger train creaked into the station at St. John's twenty-five minutes early. A small quiet crowd had gathered. The passengers collected their baggage and left without ceremony. The "Bullet" was history.[1]

Epilogue

In 1969 the Newfoundland operations of Canadian National were constituted as an autonomous division known as Terra Transport. Canadian National spent millions of dollars on narrow-gauge cars and improved facilities but the writing was on the wall. In competition with highway trucks, the railway's share of the freight market steadily declined. There was an annual deficit of $35 to 40 million. Ominously, the cross-island trains began to be designated as "Extras." First to go were the branch lines. The last train on the Bonavista Branch ran on November 23, 1983. The Argentia and Carbonear Lines ceased to operate on September 19 and September 20, 1984, and most stations were boarded up. The Lewisporte Line heard its final train whistle in 1987. In December 1987, an agreement was reached between the Canadian federal government and the Newfoundland provincial government. In return for $800 million for highway improvements, all rail service in Newfoundland would cease on September 1, 1988. The last train, in fact, left Bishop's Falls at 10:00 A.M. on September 30, 1988, for the 138-mile run to Corner Brook. With indecent haste, the first track joint was broken at 2:10 P.M. on October 12, 1988 at mile 340.1, seven miles west of Gaff Topsail. At 2:45 P.M. on

November 23, 1990, a few spectators were on hand to witness the lifting of the last spike at the Bishop's Falls railway bridge. The rolling stock — 900-class diesel locomotives, narrow-gauge container cars, ballast dump cars and track equipment — was sold to railways in Bolivia, Chile, Nicaragua and Nigeria. The 547-mile railbed from St. John's to Port aux Basques has been turned into a hiking trail called the T'Railway. The Newfoundland government has declared it to be a linear park.[2]

Fourteen

Railway Mail Service, Dispatching Office, Locomotive Shop, Coastal Boats and More

Railway Mail Service

Among its many activities, the Reid Newfoundland Company and the Newfoundland Railway which succeeded it were responsible for moving the mail by train. The railway's coastal steamers, in addition to moving passengers, livestock, and general cargo, carried thousands of mail bags. On October 18, 1897, a notification of the new service was published.

> On and after Monday, October 25th Regular Trains will run between St. John's and Harbor Grace as follows, daily (Sundays excepted):—
> Leave St. John's at 9:30 A.M., and arrive at Hr. Grace 3 P.M.
> Leave Hr. Grace at 9.15 A.M., and arrive at St. John's 2.15 P.M.
> Special trains will run between St. John's and Placentia, connecting with the mail steamer "Bruce" at the latter place, on Monday, Wednesday, Thursday and Saturday in each week.[1]

The first train carrying mail destined for foreign parts was advertised as follows:

Newfoundland
N. & W. Railway
ROYAL MAIL ...
"SHORTEST SEA VOYAGE."
QUICKEST & SAFEST ROUTE

Sydney, Halifax, St. John, N.B.; Montreal, Toronto, Boston, New York, and all other parts of Canada and the United States, as well as all parts of Europe. Special Mail Train (with sleeping cars attached) will leave Newfoundland Railway Station, St. John's, at 5 A.M. Monday and Thursday of each week, connecting with SS "Bruce" at Placentia and Intercolonial Railway at Sydney.

Fourteen. Railway Mail Service, Dispatching Office, Locomotive Shop, Coastal Boats

Railway steamer *Bruce*. "All Rail, Save Six Hours' Sail per S.S. Bruce" (Harvey, 1900).

> Returning SS "Bruce" will leave Sydney on arrival of Intercolonial Train at Sydney, every Tuesday and Friday Evenings for Placentia, connecting with Special Mail Train for St. John's, and all other points in Newfoundland.
>
> For Tickets, Passenger and Freight Rates apply to
>
> > R. C. [sic] Reid,
> > St. John's[2]

The Newfoundland Post Office also published important information about the collection of mail for the trains.

> Mails for United Kingdom, Dominion of Canada and United States, by train to Placentia and per steamer "Bruce," thence to Sydney, C.B., close at this office every Wednesday and Saturday night at 9 o'clock. Pillar boxes and Branch Offices will be cleared at 7 o'clock. Late letters may be posted at the General Post Office until 4 o'clock on Monday and Thursday mornigs [sic].[3]

Further notices about late fees, receiving boxes and mail trains operating between St. John's and Placentia soon appeared.

> Persons desirous of Posting Late Letters to go by Special Train, connecting with the SS "Bruce" will please take notice that a Special Receiving Box is provided for that purpose at the Railway Station, left-hand side of the main entrance, and beneath the window of the Freight Office. Letters intended for this mail should not be posted in the iron pillar box at the gate after 7 P.M. on Wednesdays and Saturdays. Every such late

letter must be prepaid by stamps, with Five Cents Late Fee in addition to the regular postage.[4]

Late Letters for despatch per steamer "Bruce," will be received at the Railway Depot up to 4.45 A.M. on Mondays and Thursdays, and forwarded by the Special Train. A Late Fee of Five Cents for each letter, in addition to the regular postage must, in all cases, be prepaid by stamp. Letters posted without this late fee, will not be forwarded in that day's mail.[5]

When the first trans-island train ran on June 29–30, 1898, from St. John's to Port aux Basques, it met the railway steamer *Bruce*, which carried passengers and mail bags across the Cabot Strait to Sydney, Nova Scotia. A clerk was on board the ship to sort the mail. The trains had a traveling post office (T.P.O.), with as many as three clerks providing round-the-clock sorting of letters and parcels. The local trains dropped off mail bags at their numerous stops, while the cross-island train carried the mail bound for Canada and the United States. In 1895 it was observed that the train had drastically changed the way mail was carried.

The railway now carries nearly all the northern mails, which in winter used to be conveyed by couriers on foot, or with the aid of dogs over the ice and snow. Small steamers ply from Shoal Harbor, Exploits and Clode Sound around the bays, carrying mail and passengers to and from the various settlements; and thus both social and material progress has been initiated by the iron horse and his satellites, the common roads.[6]

Fifty years later, small aircraft met the trains and loaded bags of mail for remote communities in the Northern Peninsula and Labrador. As early as 1905 the volume of mail bound for the mainland was too much for the clerk on the *Bruce* to handle alone. A mail sorting office had to be established in Sydney, Nova Scotia.

During the 1940s a postal clerk would make four rail trips to Port aux Basques from St. John's each month. The mail car was staffed by four postal clerks. Even though they regularly rode the rails, the mail clerks were not railway employees. Until 1949 they worked for the Newfoundland Post Office and after that date for Canada Post. In the 1930s there were twenty-four railway mail clerks, rising to fifty-four by the 1960s. The mail cars were equipped with two-burner propane stoves and one of the clerks would take on the job of cook. On one occasion the clerks had taken on some juicy steaks but discovered that they had left the frying pan behind. Ever resourceful, they cleaned a broad shovel used for feeding the locomotive with coal, and cooked their dinner on that.

Unless becalmed by winter storms in the Gaff Topsails, the mail train would deliver its cargo the day after posting. Clerks would simply toss mail bags off the train at places where the train was not scheduled to stop. One Christmas at a place called

Left: Newfoundland postage stamp: "S.S. 'Caribou' 9 Hours to Sydney, N.S." 17 Right: Newfoundland postage stamp: "Express Crossing Newfoundland."

Fourteen. Railway Mail Service, Dispatching Office, Locomotive Shop, Coastal Boats   135

Mail coach No. 5015, Avondale (Hollis Harding).

Ocean Pond the mail clerk's aim was faulty. The bag of letters he tossed off the speeding train lodged in the branches of a tree. Upon the return journey, the clerk saw that the mail bag was still in the tree. He sent a note out on the next train. "Please look in the tree near the railway tracks, your mail is in it, Merry Christmas."[7]

When the train could not get through people had to resort to the old methods to get their mail:

> Arrival of Dog-Trains With Mail, c. 1904:
>
> It was a lovely afternoon in early March four or five years ago. The sun shone out with the brightness and power as it sometimes will even in early March. The snow, quite recently fallen, lay on the Humber Sound in dazzling white, and all around on either side the land was clothed with the same beautiful spotless mantle. It was a joy to be out that afternoon, I remember it well, walking up on the [railway] track (the track is largely the public highway in winter at Bay of Islands), walking up the track, just for pure enjoyment of the day, not minding how far I went, nor in what direction, so long as I was out in the glorious brightness and warmth of the sun. For it had been a terrible winter,—weeks on weeks—nay, month after month of intense frost and heavy snowstorms. The railway had been doing some big snow fighting, and nearly for a month or two not a train had arrived and consequently there had been no mail. Not a letter or a newspaper for all these weeks. Day after day we could only go to the telegraph office

and read the latest dispatch about the Russo-Japanese war, but no other intelligence from the outside world had we. And now as I walked along the track, reveling in the delightful day after such a lengthened siege, I espy way off, at the head of the Humber Arm, about four or five miles distant, a dark streak — for a little I descry two, they are in a line, only separated a little, the first longer than the second. It is moving, coming nearer! What is it? Can it be? Yes, it must be, it is the mail on dog sleds, the mail at last, that we have been looking for so long, that we had given up looking for it. On they come. What a long line it is. Now I make out one dog a good bit ahead of the first, and another ahead of the second streak. These are the leaders. I stand watching. Rapidly they draw nearer, for the dogs and drivers are now doing their best, seeing the journey's end in sight. I can make out three men in charge of the first team and two in charge of the second. How well the dogs all pull together, following the leaders and urged on by the drivers. Now they are directly opposite the village at Birchy Cove. By this others have seen them and people are flocking from all directions to the postmaster's wharf where they will most likely land. We had scarcely arrived there when madly they came, tearing, straining, yelping, hot with excitement; fifteen of them as well as I can remember, certainly not less, in the first team, and nine of them in the second. They are soon released. How they jump and scamper and run yelping about. For a time it looks pretty exciting. The crowd think it safest to keep back a bit. By degrees they are quieted and placed in a store to rest before appeasing their ravenous hunger, for they are ravenously hungry — so hungry that it would be death to feed them before they

Avondale train station. Originally used as a telegraphic repeater station, it is now a museum (Hollis Harding).

have had a good rest. They have had a long journey from Millertown Junction, a hundred miles by the railway line, and the last stretch from Deer Lake was both the longest and the hardest, the going being very heavy over new fallen snow.

We couldn't help remarking these dogs, what noble animals for hauling they are; every one with his own name which he knows well and to which he responds at the call of the guide. The leading dogs were very handsome animals and seemed to be proud of their position way off by themselves, without any tackling, and acting simply as leaders.

The following day, after a good night's rest and a good meal, in which hard tack largely predominated, they were on their way back again, making a sight of striking interest as they left the wharf and started off full of life and eager for the journey. This is not a usual scene. It has not occurred since. It may not be seen again, for the Reid-Newfoundland Company seem now, with rotary plow and the experience of the past, as if they had got the upper hand and were determined to keep it.[8]

Dispatching Office

The dispatching office was the nerve center of the Newfoundland Railway. The eastern division was controlled from St. John's and the western division from Bishop's Falls. During World War II the St. John's dispatching office controlled traffic on the Bonavista, Lewisporte, Argentia and Carbonear Branch Lines and the movement of the majority of the railway's coastal steamers. Also coordinated was movement into and out of the American army and navy bases in St. John's and Argentia as well as the Royal Canadian Air Force base at Gander.

Movements on the railway were controlled by what were known as "Written Train Orders." These would be flashed along the telegraph lines to the relatively few stations which could handle trains traveling in opposite directions. For example: The engineer and conductor of an eastbound freight train would receive notification that they were to meet the westbound passenger express at a certain station. If the westbound was not there, the eastbound would pause at the siding, known as the passing track, and wait for the westbound passenger train to tumble past.[9]

Stations were equipped with a standard quadrant signal board. When the signal arm was pointed upward it meant that there were orders for the train and it must stop to receive them. Telegraphs were installed at stations and staffed with telegraphers who were trained to copy train orders sent by the dispatchers from St. John's and Bishop's Falls. The telegraphers would repeat the orders for accuracy and deliver them to the trains in question.[10]

Newfoundland Railway Steamship Service

The Newfoundland Railway was responsible for a marine division. The railway operated a fleet of steamships which made scheduled connections with the mainland via North Sydney, Nova Scotia, plied the great bays of the island, and sailed the remote coast of Labrador. For ease of freight handling, wharves with railway track were built in Port Blandford, Humbermouth, Placentia, and Lewisporte.

In 1897, R. G. Reid purchased the *Bruce* to link Port aux Basques with Nova Scotia.

> Today is a red letter day in our annals, the arrival of the *Bruce* marks an epoch in Newfoundland history. We are no longer isolated. This magnificent ship ... is the link that will bind us to the continent, bring us into closer connection with the civilization and superior advancement of America. Up to the present we have lain outside the strong currents of progress, remote, unbefriended and practically unknown, the helpless victim.[11]

The *Bruce*, equipped with sails and a steam engine, was waiting in Port aux Basques with a head of steam to meet the first cross-island express train on June 30, 1897. The train arrived at 10:45 P.M. and the *Bruce* cast off for Sydney, Nova Scotia exactly sixty-five minutes later. For the next fourteen years the *Bruce* connected the railhead at Port aux Basques with the Intercolonial in North Sydney, transporting nearly one million passengers.[12]

On March 4, 1911, in heavy ice conditions, the *Bruce* was wrecked on the rocks near Louisbourg, Cape Breton Island. Her bottom was torn open and the engine room

The *Bruce* meeting the Express at Port aux Basques (Harvey, 1900).

The *Bruce* meeting the train at the terminus of the Placentia Branch Line (Harvey, 1900).

quickly flooded. On board were one hundred and twenty-three passengers, including many women and children and forty Newfoundland fishermen heading for British Colombia to join the Pacific seal hunt. Two lives were lost. The survivors made it to shore in six large lifeboats. Local people came out with horses and sleighs and the Sydney and Louisbourg Railway ran a special train to get the people to safety.[13]

Almost immediately the *Bruce II* was built in Scotland for the Newfoundland Railway. More than 50 percent larger than the earlier vessel, the *Bruce II* was built to navigate through ice. She did the mainland crossing until 1916 when she was sold to Russia. Upon her first arrival in Newfoundland, the proud captain of the *Bruce II* had said, "As a seaboat I never saw her equal. I tried her in every way coming out, but not a drop of water came over her for'd."[14]

Under the terms of the Reid contract of 1898 the contractor agreed to provide seven additional steamers for passengers, freight and mail. The Newfoundland government agreed to pay $100 for each of one hundred and four trips a year in Placentia Bay; $130 for each of sixty trips in Notre Dame, Trinity and Bonavista Bays; $800 for each of fifty-two trip trips of a steamer along the south coast; $1,500 for each of ten trips per year from St. John's to Labrador; and $195 a trip between Placentia and North Sydney, Nova Scotia. The steamer sailing between Port aux Basques and North Sydney was subsidized to the tune of $130 for each of its one hundred and fifty-six crossings.[15]

Reid ordered steamers from the A. & J. Inglis shipyard of Glasgow, Scotland. Known as the "Alphabet Fleet," they were named *Argyle, Bruce, Clyde, Dundee, Ethie, Fife, Glencoe*, and *Home*. The fleet was augmented by the *Inverness, Kyle, Lintrose*, and *Meigle*. The Reid interests were bought out by the government in 1923 and these and other vessels were operated by the Newfoundland Railway. Between 1924 and confederation in 1949 the railway steamship service ran the *Portia, Prospero, Caribou, Malakoff, Northern Ranger, Baccalieu, Burgeo, Moyra, Random, Northton, Brigus, Springdale, Bar Haven,* and *Cabot Strait*. The Canadian National Railway took over the fleet in 1949 and operated it until 1985. Since that date modern car ferries linking Newfoundland with the mainland have been operated by Marine Atlantic.[16]

SS *FIFE*

The *Fife* was the railway's first marine mishap. She was lost at 11:30 A.M. on November 17, 1900 in the Strait of Belle Island. It was her maiden voyage. An inquiry found that the second mate, who was not a qualified navigator, was guilty of negligence. He had remained in the wheelhouse even though the windows were frosted over. The weather was clear and fine but the second mate could not see where the ship was heading.[17]

SS *CARIBOU*

The *Caribou*, two hundred and sixty-five feet long, forty-one feet wide and 2,222 gross tons, was built in a Dutch shipyard for the Newfoundland Railway in 1925. The ship, which could carry four hundred passengers and fifty boxcars of freight, was put into regular tri-weekly service crossing the Cabot Strait between Port aux Basques and North Sydney. On August 18, 1930 the *Caribou* ran onto some rocks near Port aux Basques, tearing a hole in her bottom. After extensive repairs in the St. John's dry dock, another division of the railway, the *Caribou* was returned to scheduled service.

Tragedy struck in the early morning hours of October 14, 1942. While crossing the Cabot Strait the *Caribou* was struck in her starboard side by at least one high explosive torpedo fired from a German U-boat. The *Caribou* went to the bottom in a matter of minutes. Of the 238 passengers and crew aboard, 135 perished in the icy water. Two others succumbed after rescue. Survivors were picked up by a ship of the Royal Canadian Navy. The Caribou also carried fifty head of cattle, 910 mail bags and ten railcars of general freight.[18]

The enemy submarine which had sighted the *Caribou* forty miles southwest of Channel Head at 2:40 A.M. was the *U-69*. Only four months later, on February 17, 1943, *U-69* was sunk with all hands by a British cruiser, HMS *Viscount*.[19]

SS *DUNDEE* AND *ETHIE*

December 1919 is remembered as the unluckiest month in the history of the Reid Newfoundland Railway. Two steamships were lost. The *Dundee* had been carrying mail and passengers across Bonavista Bay since 1900. On Christmas Day 1919 the *Dundee* ran aground on Noggin Island. The crew and passengers were completely cut off for two days. Heavy seas and ice made rescue perilous. On the second day the *Dundee* began to take on water. Before she sank, another railway steamer, the *Clyde*, managed to get through the ice in the nick of time and got everyone off.[20]

On December 11, 1919 the Dundee's sister ship, *Ethie*, with ninety passengers on board, sank near Bonne Bay on Newfoundland's west coast. The ship had run into an unexpectedly violent hurricane which had driven her onto a reef that ripped open her bottom. There was also a real danger that the boiler would explode. A "boatswain's chair" was rigged up by fixing ropes to a buoy which was floated ashore. Local people retrieved the ropes and a pulley system was set up. Miraculously, all the passengers, including a newborn baby, and the crew were rescued by means of the chair.

A controversy arose over the role of a Newfoundland dog in the rescue. This breed, a large, thick coated, black dog unique to Newfoundland, is renowned for its swimming ability, loyalty and courage. The dog, so the story goes, either retrieved the buoy or swam ashore with the ropes in its mouth. Most likely, neither thing happened. An American reporter from a Philadelphia newspaper happened to be in the area and noticed a mongrel on the beach tugging on the ropes. The reporter probably exaggerated the dog's role to make a better story.[21] The story has grown over the years and is partly responsible for the Newfoundland dog's reputation. Newfoundland poet E. J. Pratt was moved by the rescue of the railway steamer *Ethie* to write "*Carlo*" in 1920. He prefaced the poem by writing, "The dog that saved the lives of over ninety persons in that recent wreck, by swimming with a line from the sinking vessel to the shore, well understood the importance as well as the risk of his mission."

Carlo

I see no use in not confessing—
To trace your breed would keep me guessing.
It would indeed an expert puzzle
To match such legs with jet-black muzzle;
To make a mongrel, as you know,
It takes some fifty types or so.
And nothing in your height or length,
In stand or colour, speed or strength,
Could make me see how any strain
Could come from mastiff, bull or Dane.
But, were I given to speculating
On pedigrees in canine rating,
I'd wager this—not from your size.
Not merely from your human eyes.
But from the way you held that cable
Within those gleaming jaws of sable,
Leaped from the taffrail of the wreck
With ninety souls upon its deck.
And with your cunning dog-stroke tore

Your path unerring to the shore —
Yes, stake my life, the way you swam,
That somewhere in your line a dam,
Shaped to this hour by God's own hand,
Had mated with a Newfoundland.

They tell me, Carlo, that your kind
Has neither conscience, soul, nor mind:
That reason is a thing unknown
To such as dogs: to man alone
The spark divine — he may aspire
To climb to heaven or even higher.
But God has tied around the dog
The symbol of his fate, the clog.
Thus I have heard some preachers say —
Wise me and good, in a sort o' way —
Proclaiming from the sacred box
(Quoting from Butler and John Knox)
How freedom and the moral law
God gave to man, because he saw
A way to draw a line at root
Between the human and the brute.
And you were classed with things like bats,
Parrots and sand-flies and dock-rats,
Serpents and toads that dwell in mud,
And other creatures with cold blood
That sightless crawl in slime, and sink
Gadsooks! It makes me sick to think
That man must so exalt his race
By giving dogs a servile place,
Prate of his transcendentalism,
While you save men by mechanism:
And when And when I told them how you fought
The demons of the storm, and brought
That life-line from the wreck to shore
And save those ninety souls or more.
They argued with confidence.—
'Twas instinct, nature, or blind sense.
A man could know when he would do it.
You did it and never knew it.
And so, old chap, by what they say,
You live and die and have your day,
Like any cat or mouse or weevil
That have no sense of good and evil,
(Though sheep and goats, when they have died,
The Good Book says are classified)
But you, being neuter, go to — well,
Neither to heaven nor to hell.

I'll not believe it, Carlo, I

Will fetch you with me when I die,
And standing up at Peter's wicket,
Will urge sound reasons for your ticket:
I'll show him your life saving label,
And tell him all about the cable.
The storm along the shore, the wreck.
The ninety souls upon the deck.
How one by one they came along
The young and old, the weak and strong,
Pale women sick and tempest-tossed,
With children given up for lost,
I'd tell him more, if he would ask it —
How they tied a baby in a basket,
While a young sailor picked and able
Moved out to steady it on the cable:
And if he needed more recital
To admit it a mongrel without title,
I'd get down upon my knees
And swear before the Holy Keys.
That judging by the way you swam,
Somewhere within your line a dam
formed the job by God's own hand,
Had littered for a Newfoundland.

I feel quite sure that if I made him
Give ear to that, I could persuade him
To open up the Golden Gate
And let you in: but should he state
That from your legs and height and speed
He still had doubts about your breed,
And called my story of the cable,
"A cunningly devised fable,"
Like other rumours that you've seen
In Second Peter, one, sixteen.
I'd tell him, (saving his high station)
I scorned his small adjudication
And, where life, love, and death atone,
I'd move your case up to the Throne.[22]

SS *Kyle*

The *Kyle*, built in Newcastle, England, in 1913, was described as a "splendid specimen in marine architecture." It was 220 feet long and weighed 1,055 gross tons. It could comfortably accommodate one hundred and twenty male and forty female passengers. The ship was strongly constructed to withstand ice pressure, had five watertight bulkheads and reciprocating three-cylinder 1,580 engines. She was also equipped with a recent technological advance, a wireless set with a range of one hundred and fifty miles. The *Kyle* did duty on the Labrador coast and the crossing to Nova Scotia. In 1927 the *Kyle* found the wreckage of the *Old Glory*, an American airplane which had hoped to be one of the first to cross the Atlantic Ocean but crashed off the Newfoundland coast. The *Kyle* was sold to private interests in 1959 who used her for sealing and trading on the Labrador coast. In 1967 the *Kyle* ran aground in her home port of Riverhead, Harbour Grace, where she can still be seen, the last survivor of the railway's steamship fleet.[23]

SS *MEIGLE*

Purchased by the Reid Newfoundland Company in 1913, the *Meigle* (named after a place near R. G. Reid's birthplace in Scotland) was twenty-two feet long, thirty feet wide and fifteen feet deep, with a gross tonnage of 1,060. The ship was put into the coastal service carrying cargo and passengers until 1932 when she was converted into a prison ship and moored in St. John's harbor. The Depression was in full swing and the penitentiary could not accommodate rioters detained for protesting insufficient government relief. The *Meigle* later served as a salt bulk storage hull, then was sold and put into general cargo work. In World War II the ship narrowly survived an attack by a German U-boat. On July 27, 1947, the *Meigle*, with a load of livestock, was wrecked near St. Shotts, Newfoundland.[24]

SS *CLYDE*

When war was declared between the United Kingdom and Germany on September 3, 1939, Newfoundland, as part of the British Empire, was automatically part of the conflict. The Newfoundland Railway played a part on the very first day of the war. A German freighter, the *Christof V. Doornum*, was in the port of Botwood loading lead and zinc. Hearing the news from Europe, the crew slipped the ship's lines and headed out to sea. But the railway steamer *Clyde* was on the spot and immediately intercepted the much larger German ship and towed her back to the wharf. The German crew were placed under armed guard, loaded aboard rail cars and shipped to St. John's where they were interned. The prisoners of war were eventually transferred to a prison camp in Canada. The *Christof V. Doorman* was renamed the *Empire Commerce* and became a freighter in the service of the Allied cause. She was sunk by a U-boat only nine months later.[25]

Locomotive Shop

The Reid Newfoundland Company and the Newfoundland Railway operated a locomotive shop in St. John's which overhauled and rebuilt locomotives. What is not so well known is that the shop built locomotives as well. Between 1911 and 1916 the shop built a dozen steam locomotives. A mixture of locally crafted parts and components supplied by the Baldwin Locomotive Works in Philadelphia were used in the construction. Ten of the locomotives, numbered 111 through 120, were of the 100 class 4-6-0 type and weighed seventy-five tons each. They were deployed on the branch lines, where some of them remained in service until the 1950s. The remaining locally built locomotives, numbers 152 and 153, were manufactured in 1916. They were of the heavier 150 class with eight driving wheels and weighed 113 tons. These trains were comparatively slow and were assigned freight hauling duties. In 1922 the locomotive shop built a seventy-five-ton rotary steam plow.[26]

As early as 1897 the Reid machine shop in Whitbourne built three Pullman passenger cars named after the Newfoundland towns of Placentia, Twillingate and Trinity. A contemporary description reported:

> There are three Pullman cars being built at Whitbourne; they are to be named "*Twillingate*," "*Trinity*," and "*Placentia*." They measure 46½ feet long and will contain smoking room, lavatory, private stateroom, and ordinary day-coach apartments with reclining seats. The sets are to be upholstered in olive green plush, save the smoking room, which will be done in olive corduroy. The draperies will be very elaborate. The fittings, handrails, etc. will be of brass, except in the lavatories where they will be of nickel. The outsides of the cars are to be finished in cherry decorated with gold, outlined by black. The windows will have mosquito shades. The air brakes and couplings are of the very latest improvements. The machine shops are today hives of industry, and a new dynamo has been placed to give extra lighting.[27]

Between 1920 and 1940 the Newfoundland Railway acquired its most powerful units of motive power, thirty 100-class 2-8-2 Mikado-type locomotives, each weighing 130 tons. These and the older locomotives were sent to the locomotive shop in St. John's an average of once per year for an overhaul. Minor repairs were carried out by divisional repair depots located at Port aux Basques, Humbermouth, Bishop's Falls and Clarenville. The most common problems were wheels which developed sharp flanges, leaky pipes and valves, loose and missing bolts, and leaky boiler tubes.

In the St. John's shop a locomotive would undergo a complete inspection. Usually reports from the divisional repair depots were on hand. The first stop would be the coal oil pit where these two commodities, as well as ash and water, would be removed from the tender. The locomotive was then cleaned of dirt and grease by sandblasting and given a coat of prime paint. In the machine shop, the erecting crew used two overhead cranes to lift the cab and boiler from the wheels. All parts and machinery, boiler, tubes, flues and firebox would then be cleaned, removed, repaired or replaced as required. After the work on the boiler had been completed and a hydrostatic test done, the locomotive was carefully reassembled and given a second coat of paint. After a test run the locomotive would be returned to duty. The locomotive shop continued in operation after Canadian National took over. Fifty-six diesel locomotives were acquired and the shop was equipped to service them.[28]

Newfoundland Railway Dry Dock

In 1898, R. G. Reid, as part of the railway contract, purchased the dry dock in St. John's for $325,000. Built of pine, the dry dock was 625 feet long, 132 feet wide and drew twenty-six feet of water. The Reid Newfoundland Company advertised that it ran "one of the best equipped Dry Docks in America. Steamships docked and repaired at the lowest rates. Well equipped and thoroughly fitted with all modern appliances."[29] Transferred to the Newfoundland government in 1924, the dry dock was modernized and reconstructed in concrete. The St. John's dry dock continued to be operated by the Newfoundland Railway until 1949 and afterwards by Canadian National Railways and Terra Transport. The railway dock yard became an essential service in World War II. Hundreds of merchant and naval ships received minor and major repairs and refits.[30] The figures for the war years from September 1939 until May 1945 are as follows:

Year	Ships	Gross Tonnage
1940	160	334,500
1941	172	569,000
1942	287	917,000
1943	310	1,235,000
1944	214	848,000
1945	137	632,000[31]

Telegraph Service

Along with running the railway, R. G. Reid was contractually bound to install a telegraph line beside the track. In 1898 Reid purchased the existing telegraph line for $125,000 and agreed to operate the system for an annual subsidy of $10,000. For $1,500,000 Reid sold the telegraph service to Newfoundland Postal Telegraphs in 1905. Rotary snow plows operating in the storm-ridden Gaff Topsails would frequently break the line with the weight of the ice and snow they threw off.[32]

St. John's Street Railway

Along with his many other responsibilities R. G. Reid was contracted to build and run a street railway in St. John's with electric streetcars. As part of this agreement, Reid had to establish an electric power plant to supply the streetcars and the general public with electricity. Reid's railway company advertised, "All the Electric power supplied in St. John's is generated on this system. City Lighting and Power for Factories, etc., supplied at moderate rates."[33] The hydro plant was built in the nearby community of Petty Harbour and started producing electricity on April 19, 1900.

As a side agreement, Reid was required to pave Water Street, the city's principal commercial artery, with cobblestones. Reid used 770,000 granite blocks, each one foot long by three and one-half inches wide and seven inches thick. Reid was paid $140,000 for the paving work. Reid's cobblestones remained until 1949 when Water Street was resurfaced with asphalt.

The St. John's Street Railway commenced operation on May 1, 1900. The streetcars were manufactured in Montréal, carried fifty passengers, had a top speed of eight miles per hour and required a conductor and a motorman. The cars had a wooden body painted yellow, a cowcatcher, and ran on fixed iron rails. The trolley cars were powered by electricity from overhead wires transferred by conducting rods. In 1924 the streetcars passed out of the railway's control, being taken over by the Newfoundland Light and Power Company. Busses replaced the streetcars in 1948.[34]

Roadcruiser Bus Service

When railway passenger service ceased in Newfoundland, the Canadian National Railway was still obliged to provide transportation for passengers. The result was probably the only bus service operated by a railway. C. N. R. buses crossed Newfoundland on regular schedules from December 2, 1968, until 1995 when the operation was sold to private interests. The railway bus service operated as many as twenty-six Roadcruiser busses and carried 200,000 passengers annually. The busses made the run between St. John's and Port aux Basques in fourteen hours.[35]

Schools on Wheels

Along the main line of the track were more than a dozen tiny, isolated settlements for the families of railway sectionmen. Between 1936 and 1942 the Newfoundland Railway, the Department of Education and the Anglo-Newfoundland Development Company cooperated to run a mobile school for children living in these remote places. The Anglo-Newfoundland Development Company became involved because it had employees in a similar situation to those of the railway. A.N.D. employees and their families were living along the private spurs connecting pulp and paper mills to the main line. The A.N.D. Company donated the school car, the Department of Education provided the teachers and the instructional materials and the railway assumed responsibility for maintenance and moving the school from place to place.

The private passenger coach *Shawnawdithit*, named after the last known member of Newfoundland's Beothuck Indians, who died in 1829, was converted into the school. The car had been for the use of Lord Northcliffe, owner of a British newspaper empire and the A.N.D. Company, whenever he or other VIPs were visiting Newfoundland. The car was fifty-two feet long and nine feet wide, with windows along the sides and open platforms on each end. It was painted dark green and was stenciled on the side in gold leaf letters:

Anglo Nfld. Development Co. Ltd.
Newfoundland Railway
School Car

The traveling school was equipped with a desk for the teacher, a blackboard and removable tables to accommodate different-sized children. A gasoline-powered motor, vented outside, was used to provide power for a radio and interior lighting. A coal furnace was installed for heating and comfortable living quarters provided for the teacher. The car had a regulation school bell but it was seldom necessary to ring it. The school on wheels was so popular the children would usually be outside waiting for the door to open.

The school car traveled the rails from September to June, stopping at each remote settlement for a few weeks at a time. About two hundred children were served by the school. Lessons would be conducted and assignments given which were to be completed under the watchful supervision of the parents. At a typical stop there would be six to fifteen children of all ages and grades. The teacher would also distribute library books and provide literacy training in the evening for any interested adults.

The schools on wheels program ended in 1942. By then roads had begun to end the isolation of the settlements and regular schools were being built.[36]

Railway Fire Patrol

The railway was the cause of numerous forest fires. During the summer months, red-hot cinders from the locomotives would shower the tracks and ignite the wooden rail ties and dry grass. One train started seven fires in only six miles. In 1904 train fires devastated thousands of acres of valuable timber stands. The next year the Newfoundland government passed the Forest Fires Act which stipulated the railway's responsibility for fire prevention. At first patrolmen simply walked behind the trains. Beginning in 1919 the fire patrol traveled the track on light three-wheeled vehicles called velocipedes. While seated, the operator pumped a hand bar back and forth for propulsion. The equipment was primitive: shovel, water bucket and hand pump. A patrolman would be assigned a section of track between four and nine miles long. His job was to follow the trains, extinguishing small fires before they had time to grow into blazes. There were nine velocipedes in service in 1922, twenty by 1930 and thirty-one by 1946. Seventeen speeders — that ran on the tracks — were also put into service. In the last decades of the railway, trucks patrolled roads and watchtowers were erected. The fire patrol was effective. One four-man crew extinguished ninety-one fires in a single day. In 1944 the name was changed to the Newfoundland Forest Protection Association. The cost of operation was shared by the government, the railway, and pulp and paper companies. Even after the introduction of diesels, fires could still be caused by frequent braking which caused hot scale to fall near the track.[37]

There is a great company of pine, birch, juniper, spruce and ash. Alas, near the track havoc has been wrought by the sparks from the trains, and it might be possible to trace many miles of the track from an airplane by means of the black line that has been scarred across the land.[38]

Fourteen. Railway Mail Service, Dispatching Office, Locomotive Shop, Coastal Boats

While winter brings its dangers to the railway, summer makes the railway itself a source of danger. Throughout the greater part of its length the line runs through spruce forests and when these are dried by the sun the sparks from the engine are very liable to start a fire. To remedy this a system of patrols has been instituted. When a train passes a given point a watcher follows it until it reaches the point from which the next watcher is due to start, and so on throughout the danger zone. Frequent notice boards remind one how serious the question of forest fires is.[39]

Fifteen

Wrecks, Collisions and Close Calls

Derailments were a constant danger to railwaymen in Newfoundland. They could be caused by heavy snow, faulty communication, spread rails (rails that expanded because of the heat of the sun), moose or other large animals on the track and curves out of alignment because of slipped ballast. Numerous level-crossing accidents involving pedestrians and vehicles occurred as well. Collisions with other trains were the most serious accidents. There were an extraordinary number of accidents during World War II, with increased train traffic, inadequate equipment, and such improvisations pushing the crews to the limits of their endurance.

July 18, 1882

The first railway fatality occurred near Upper Gullies when a woman asked if she could hitch a ride on a flatcar with laborers returning to St. John's. Her request was denied but she refused to take no for an answer and attempted to board the moving train anyway. Unfortunately the woman lost her footing, slipped and fell between two cars and was killed.[1]

November 18, 1882

At Indian Pond the train collided with a cow on the tracks. A group of laborers on a flatcar were thrown off by the impact. Three of them fell under the wheels and were killed.

August 1897

"A man named Morrissey belonging to Holyrood fell off the N. N. & W. train on Friday last about 1 mile south of Alexander Bay. The train was speeding along at the rate of 30 miles an hour, and those who witnessed the accident became seriously alarmed for his safety. Conductor White and Brakesman Byrne started back on a trolly [sic], one of a number which were being conveyed to the front, expecting to find him a corpse, but they were more than surprised on observing the man pursuing the train at breakneck speed in hopes of catching up with it. How he escaped injury was explained by himself, 'that he fell on his feet like the cats.'"[2]

A Railway Fatality, 1898

"The news of a terrible accident was flashed over the wires last night and was to the effect that Conductor John Day, of this city, had been killed by the train of which he was in charge. The accident occurred at the watering place, Cape Ray crossing, which is near Port aux Basques, at 5.15 o'clock last evening. It appears that when the train stopped Conductor Day jumped off the flat car, but the train started suddenly he had no time to get out of the way. One truck passed over him, breaking one arm and fracturing his skull. He expired after a very brief period. John Day had been constantly employed by Mr. R. G. Reid since the Northern and Western Railroad has been started. He was a man of about 38 years and has never been known to take a glass of intoxicating liquor."[3]

Wreck of a Train Approaching Bay of Islands, May 1899

"It is eight o'clock in the evening, and scarcely dark, although it is cloudy. We are in the depths of the best forest of the West Coast, and are moving slowly up a considerable grade. On the heavy sleeper on which we are now travelling we experience a jerking sensation for an instant or two, and then our car stops completely. We know something quite unusual has happened, but no particular alarm is given, and everything being so quiet we look forward with little foreboding of a serious disaster. But what is our amazement, on looking out, to see the greater part of the train ahead of us lying on its side, and partly off the track; the track torn up, and a number of the train hands and passengers by the "Colonist" car bundling out of the several compartments in their remaining ways.

"A little search, and it is found that no one is seriously injured. The engine did not leave the rail. The baggage-master, and the mail-clerk of the disabled cars were not at their posts, and consequently escaped, luckily for them. Only three were in the colonist car, the rest havin gone to the dining-car for supper.

"A gang is very soon at work building a track around our wreck so that our cars can be passed on. The passengers gather here and there to discuss their various experiences but soon we are comfortably settled for the night, which passes quickly enough.

"The morning is again with us, and we hurry out to see for ourselves the progress toward a start. In the distance we hear the sound of the axes and hammers of the track layers, and now and again the whistle of an engine is heard. The horses that were in the overturned car have been conveyed to another car. The track around the wreck is nearly laid, and in a few hours we will be off again. It is a bright day, and some very good snap-shots are taken, embracing all the notable characters of our company. Last, but not least by any means, we get a picture of our trunk (the same one that fell back in the steamer) just as it is being handed out of the wreck. We felt very much for it when we saw it through a hole in the baggage-car, with a seven or eight hundred weight piece of iron machinery lying on it. At eleven o'clock we were on our way again."

"At a turn the camera is levelled at the 'Royal mail,' with our luggage upon two flat cars at the rear. We feel quite as if they possessed sensibilities, faithful followers of ours as they are. We wonder how they like travelling in this 'come by chance' way. But they are silent."

"The St. John's papers are procured here, and are read with much interest for an account of the railroad wreck. To the amazement of all only a casual mention is made of it in the morning issue following the disaster. All felt certain that their friends in St. John's would be much concerned, but now the probability is that not one word will reach a friend upon the mainland. Had all been killed or seriously injured there is no knowing when correct information would have reached them.

"These questions arise because of a remark heard to the effect that this event is not likely to be known away from the scene of the disaster, for the Reids own the telegraph line and control all channels of information and would suppress all news not favorable to the railway. This may be incorrect, but the fact remains that this presents a fair illustration of what the possibilities are of a monopoly or union of monopolies controlling not alone the railroads, and suppressing all news by which the people may know of impositions practised upon them, but, from indications of the times, it will not be long before the press will also fall into the hands of monopolies and trusts, and even the free distribution of books be governed by ruling bodies preventing all freedom of thought."[4]

1901

A cow on the track caused the derailment of Engine #60 close to the terminal in St. John's.

1901

A passenger train derailed about one mile from Cape Ray. In those days the cars were lit with kerosene lamps. When the car went over on its side, a newlywed couple was trapped in their upper sleeping berth and burned to death when the kerosene caught fire.

JANUARY 1917

A head-on collision between a westbound engine and an eastbound freight train occurred between Gallents and Harry's Brook. A locomotive was badly damaged and its fireman seriously hurt. The engineer of the westbound engine had misread his orders.

FEBRUARY 6, 1917

West of Glenwood a westbound passenger train derailed. Eight passengers were trapped in their sleeping berths and died when kerosene lamps burst into flame.

1930

Ice buildup caused Engine #108 to jump the tracks near Port Blandford.

1930

At Gleneagles a westbound freight was involved in a rear-end collision with a parked train. The caboose and several cars of the parked train were completely destroyed by the impact. The locomotive which did the ramming was badly damaged and some of its cars had their undercarriages bent so severely they had to be written off.

February 9, 1930

A derailment at Lethbridge on the Bonavista Branch Line. At 1 A.M. an extra train consisting of Engine #123, a plow, two boxcars, a combination mail and baggage car, and two passenger cars left Bonavista to clear the track of snow and slush as far as Clarenville. An unexpected block of ice derailed the plow and the locomotive, which tipped over an embankment. Serious injuries resulted from this mishap. Despite a wait of four hours for medical help there were no fatalities. The nearest doctor was in Clarenville, twenty miles distant. The doctor arrived by means of a dog team. No cranes were available. Using blocks and tackles it took two weeks of hard work to get the locomotive back on the rails.

Winter 1940

At Northern Bight Station a westbound freight train pushing a wedge snowplow rear-ended a parked train. A passenger died in the impact. Fortunately, everyone else had jumped to safety with seconds to spare.

1942

On the Bonavista Branch Line an old locomotive found itself unable to haul a heavy load of firewood. It was decided to leave half the flatcars behind and come back for them. On the return, the coupler would not lock and close, and the cars rolled away, quickly picking up excessive speed. The trainman had no choice but to jump for his life. Reaching a curve, the cars derailed and toppled over an embankment.

March 1942

The mixed train operating between Bonavista and Clarenville was derailed by snow buildup in a remote spot. The force of the accident catapulted a traveler the entire length of the passenger car. The crew and thirty passengers were advised that it would be at least two or three days before they could be rescued. Without any food the people, including women with small children, trudged eighteen miles along the rails to safety.

Summer 1942

Due to the heavy demands placed on the rolling stock during World War II there were many serious accidents. One of the worst occurred at Goose Cove. The regular

Bonavista mixed train derailed, killing one trainman. The roadbed had grown soft, sending the cars into an uncontrolled rocking motion which tipped them over. There were no cranes available to lift the cars back on the rails, so jacks, blocking and heavy tackles had to be used in their place.

1942

After doing twenty continuous hours of duty at Argentia, switching war cargoes for the United States Navy, a trainman simply fell asleep on his feet. When the train rounded a sharp curve the exhausted crewman tumbled off. It was some time before his absence was noticed. When it was, his concerned colleagues went back for him in a speeder. Fortunately, the missing man was only bruised and shaken up.

About the same time a passenger fell from a train and had his arm severed. In the 1950s a passenger jumped from a train and was crushed to death.

August 5, 1944

An engineer and a fireman were injured when locomotive #195, an extra work train returning for a load of ballast, tipped on its side while on the Bonavista Line. It rolled down an embankment and landed in four feet of water. A short stretch of track had to be put down to get the locomotive back on the line. The locomotive was repaired and continued in service until 1957. The engineer and fireman were injured to the extent that they needed months in the hospital.

1950

A rear-end collision occurred at Cook's Brook Siding. Steam locomotive #328, pulling fourteen flatcars of pulpwood and a caboose, slammed into diesel #908 parked on the track. The 328 was traveling at about 40–50 miles per hour at the time and several passengers were injured. The parked #908 was on a downgrade on a sharp curve and lacked the proper signal flags. The 328 was derailed and #908's caboose was burned and three cars were wrecked beyond repair.

May 1951

A wreck occurred at Gambo Side Hill when a freight train hauling pulpwood derailed. An axle on her leading engine broke while she attempted to climb the hill. An engineer died and a fireman was severely injured.

July 29, 1954

A head-on collision occurred at mileage 236.1. An eastbound passenger train, #16, had orders to meet the westbound locomotive, #908, with a load of wood at a place called Lake O'Brien. The weather deteriorated and visibility dropped. The passenger train met another wood train on the siding, headed by locomotive #903. In the murkiness the "3" was mistaken for an "8" and the passenger train proceeded on its way. A short time later #16 was on a steep downgrade when it collided with the 908, also on a downgrade. Neither train was able to stop in time. The damage was extensive but miraculously none of the crew or any of the one hundred and fifty passengers were killed, although several were injured.

May 1959

Twelve of eighteen cars jacknifed on the descent into Codroy Pond.

October 3, 1960

At night, a diesel locomotive was backing up fourteen empty flatcars and a caboose near St. Fintan's when the train collided with a cow lying between the rails. The caboose derailed and the cars pressing from behind sliced off its side, killing a conductor and a brakeman inside.

September 13, 1966

A serious accident occurred at Crow Gultch when two trains had a head-on collision at forty-five miles per hour. Three trainmen lost their lives and a number of other crew were injured. The two locomotives were destroyed.[5]

Plaque in Lewisporte commemorating the Salmon River Bridge Wreck, November 15, 1942:

Salmon River Bridge Wreck

During World War II, trains had to bear the added cargo of soldiers, airplane fuel and war equipment. Lewisporte was a strategically important and extremely busy area during this period. Ships entering the harbor supplied much-needed fuel to Gander. To carry the load, extra trains were brought from the U.S. and were often put to work still bearing their American labeling.

At 8:25 on Sunday morning, November 15 1942, steam engine No. 194 was en route from Lewisporte to Gander. It was carrying fuel for the many war planes that passed through the airport. Four Lewisporte men and one Clarenville man were operating the train. Albert Anstey was the conductor, Jim Hobbs and Richard Snow were brakemen; Otto Fudge was the fireman, with William Stone of Clarenville the engineer. About three kilometers east of Lewisporte Junction at Salmon River Bridge, the last few cars of the train derailed, striking the abutment with such force that the train and the bridge collapsed into the river. Jim Hobbs was suspended upside down with his leg trapped in the wreckage for an hour. He fell free and was rushed to the hospital in Gander for treatment of his torn muscles. The other men were uninjured but the train was wrecked and the bridge demolished. Until a new bridge was built, two trains would stop at either side of the bridge, with cargo being unloaded and carried by hand across the river to the other train.

Runaway Trains

Few situations are more dangerous than a train that is out of control. This could happen when a prankster or vandal interfered with the valve controlling a train's air pressure braking system. When the crew, usually navigating a downgrade, realized that the train was picking up excessive speed, they knew what had happened. A trainman would volunteer for the frightening and dangerous duty of walking along the top of the hurtling cars and checking each valve until he found the one which had been turned off. When the trouble spot had been located, the brave trainman would have to climb down the ladder between the bucking cars and, "holding on with both hands, and with one foot on the drawbar, would hook the tow [sic] of his boot on the handle of the valve and turn it by this method."[7] Needless to say, many trainmen were injured or killed.

Appendix One: Travelers, Eye Witnesses and Shameless Boosters

Well Done Ladies, 1895

The excellent series of letters from the pen of Mr. Fretwell are already producing results. Three ladies Mlles. Neville, Cameron and Harvey have crossed country by rail and returned via the S.S. Grand Lake. The tour proved very enjoyable, and was made with ease and comfort. The time from departure to arrival was 8 days, and the arrangements were, we believe, made by Mr. David Fraser, the kindly and popular agent for Mr. Reid. All the walking necessary was seven miles, which doubtless was enjoyed equally with rail and water. We congratulate the ladies on their pluck. Are they the lady pioneers of our great lone land?[1]

The Railway in 1897

But the first railway was got under weigh: and at the close of the working season twenty miles were graded and ten miles metalled.

By this time the fishermen began to look upon the railway in a different light. Caliban was growing tamer. Although he could not for the life of him understand it, he was being paid handsomely to fell trees, to shovel earth, and to load and unload sleepers. Indeed, he was paid so handsomely that the company which had undertaken to build the railway went into liquidation long before the line was even one-half completed. I heard some of the most amusing stories of the fishermen in connection with this first railway experience of the colony; and one can readily believe the process of knocking together a railway to have been highly humorous for all except the contractors.

But the colony was not to be baulked of her line. Little by little the inhabitants began to catch the railway fever — perhaps one of the most virulent of all known infections. From loathing and dreading the railway, they began to admire and embrace it; and soon every legislator in the island was pledged to get a Bill passed for a railway of some sort beginning somewhere and ending somewhere else in his district. Rough-looking citizens began pouring into the capital from the outports, to make inquiries as to why no more railways were being built. At last, the Government, dreading unpopularity, and finding no more contractors ready to build railways, determined to construct a line — a very limited one — on its own account. I may mention on authority, that although anywhere would have answered the purpose, the particular line to Placentia was resolved upon to obtain the political adhesion of the two members for that district, and that it took two years to complete and cost 750,000 dols.

It only remains for me to add that the new railway boasted the inordinate length of 27 miles.

No wonder the fishermen grinned and rubbed their hands! No wonder the more sensible taxpayers of the colony, who had long been advocating railways, began to look aghast at the proceedings. More railway measures were passed; and in 1889 the Government decided to resume the building of the railway to Hall's Bay, which the defunct company had left two-thirds uncompleted. But when ten or fifteen miles had been built, in a most dilettante and rambling manner, a new Government came into power, and a new man came on the scene.

This person, whom I hope I do not libel in referring to as the largest private landowner in the world, was a Montreal railway contractor. In his office in the Canadian metropolis he had been seated one day, with a map of North America hung before him on the wall. He had already amassed a large fortune, and could look back on a long and adventurous career. As a penniless Scotch lad, he had left his home and gone to seek his fortune in Australia, where ability and shrewdness pushed him along, and prosperity came to him wherever he went. He at length migrated to Canada, and in the capacity of contractor, built large portions of the Canadian Pacific Railway. He was now a wealthy man, a thorough master of his business, and, although somewhat enfeebled in health, already looking out for new fields of endeavour. As he contemplated the map, he was immediately struck by the geographical situation of Newfoundland. He remembered the vague reports he had heard of the colony, and he made a X in blue pencil on the map.

"That," he remarked quietly to a friends, "is the coming country."

A short time elapsed and the news reached Mr. Reid that Newfoundland wanted somebody to build the island a railway. The colony was advertising for tenders. In the tender he despatched to the Government he offered to build the road at 15,600 dols. a mile. The offer was accepted. Upon the heels of this acceptance the colony was astonished by the celerity with which the new contractor got to work. Mr. Reid's faith in the colony was greater that the Government's. The latter had only considered a railway to Hall's Bay, the former was ready, not only to build it across the island, and take their bonds in exchange at a time when Newfoundland bonds — technically known as "Fogs" — were at a low ebb, but also something more. A railway is a useless concern if it be unoperated. Mr. Reid offered, then to operate the new railway.

The cost of operation was estimated at £20,00 sterling annually.

The Government then agreed to "grant in fee-simple to the contractor 5000 acres of land for each one mile of main line or branch railway throughout the entire length of line to be operated," in respect of its operation for ten years. Also, in addition to pay 60,000 dols. a year by way of a mails subsidy.

When the news of this arrangement became public, not a little indignation prevailed among a large class of respectable persons in the capital. They felt that Mr. Reid had been imposed upon. One gentleman overwhelmed the new contractor with his condolences.

"I'm really very sorry this thing has happened," he said. "Why didn't you come to me? I could have told you all this land wasn't worth a d____d red cent."

The millionaire smiled inscrutably. He is still smiling; his descendants will go on smiling even onto the third and fourth generation. Mr. Reid is not a young man, but he has associated with him three clever stalwart sons, who promise to be among the wealthiest and most powerful men in the world.

From the moment the first sod was cut they became Newfoundlanders. They did not delegate the work to others, but went at it tooth and nail, toiling with the men, sharing their fare and hardships, and even their personal risks. And now the last sod is cut, the last spike driven, and the Newfoundland Railway is finished. I was talking with a man who said to me, I know not by what authority:

"Reid has built a first-class road; but his profits will be at least half a million sterling. In other words, the profits and the subsidy will more than operate the line, and he has got 2,500,000 acres, much of it rich timber, agricultural, and mineral land into the bargain."

Supposing that to be true, and I will not vouch that it is, how many millionaires would have approached such a projects with a pair of tongs? To take its bonds and its lands in payment required more confidence in the colony than any other man has ever shown since it was discovered by Cabot.... I do not think a Scotchman like Mr. Reid ever dreams of the picturesque side of his position. The idea of erecting a baronial castle on his vast domain and inviting over brother princes to a house-warming has probably never entered his head. It has several times entered mine: it is rather a fascinating notion — the largest landowner on earth![2]

Rapid Transit, 1898

A Record Trip
Sydney to St. John's, 24 hours

We can at last realize what rapid transit means. The S.S. Bruce has just completed a record trip. From the hour the mails were placed on board the steamer at Sydney to the time of the arrival of the train in this city, the time occupied was exactly 24 hours. Letters from Halifax written on Tuesday morning were read at 11.10 o'clock last night

(Wednesday) in St. John's in time for an answer to reach Halifax Friday night. Think of the old time system and the present! Mr. Reid has truly revolutionized our mail and passenger service.[3]

On an Iron Horse, 1898

It was the first excursion train — well it was the first passenger train of any sort — that left St. John's station, at 7.20 P.M., on Wednesday, for Port au Basque [sic], and being an excursion about one hundred passengers availed of the comforts of Messrs. Reids' sleeping, dining and Pullman coaches for a run across the country.

There were seven cars and two engines; and since the day the first through train was announced we were turning over in our minds how it was possible for the News to write itself down in history regarding this first through train. It was accomplished in this way: Through the courtesy of Mr. Harry Reid we were permitted to mount from Iron Horse No. 11, which was in charge of driver Byrne and fireman Foran, and from our appreciation of riding the four-footed beast, we concluded that a still greater treat was in store when not having to run the risk of broken bones on a stubborn mule or a thoroughbred. Our pleasure was somewhat disturbed by the snorting beast which we had mounted, and frequently it emitted such guttural sounds from its "throttle" that we were concerned for our own safety as well as that of the panting (Iron) Horse. But it was not until the gong sounded and we tugged everlastingly at the bell cord did the real sensations commence, which at once assured us that a canvas jumper and duck pants were more suitable to ride with that even our own humble tweed. But after the first neigh, (whistle) didn't that horse plunge! Old No. 9 "loco" was in front and the horrid thing kept belching forth soot and smoke until we thought that No. 11 would become blinded and cease to move. But no! On they sped, and the more fuel the faster they would run. Just before reaching Topsail we examined our "railway" watch and discovered that the excellent speed of one mile for every two and a half minutes was being attained by the two engines. Suddenly, when near Kelligrews, there were two unearthly yells from No. 9 followed by equally awful ones from No. 11, caused by four sheep being on the track and about twenty others surrounding it; and for the first time we witnessed the antics of half-crazed animals before the gigantic locomotive. At first the ram thought it was great sport to butt the engine while the more sensible sheep scampered off to the meadows nearby, and it was not until the exhaust pipe of the engine threw forth a volume of steam did the sheep of the masculine gender deem it advisable to depart from his adversary, the engine. Now, we were told as we once again "got up" that record speed, we were approaching "Duff's grade," and soon the slowly moving engines intimated that we were climbing the incline. It was puff! Puff! Sish! Sish!! For about three minutes, after which we had ascended the "up grade," and tugging again at the bell cord we drew towards the siding where the Bruce's express train was to pass us, en route to St. John's, with the mails from all parts of the world (brought to Placentia by the Bruce) on board. One thing one could not help observing was that, no matter where or when the engines sounded their whistles, Mr. H. D. Reid was giving every detail his personal supervision. His practical direction and personal service convinced all that he is a "thorough railway man." While thus admiring Mr. Reid's movements that phrase which makes every passenger hustle to his seat — "all aboard" — was shouted by Conductor Liddy, who, by the way, made his passengers as comfortable as he just knows how to do, either on regular or special occasions. But we haven't explained how we know that Mr. Liddy was attentive to his passengers. When the engines stopped for water we had a consultation with the engineer, the result of which was that our argument that plush-cushioned seats with the absence of smoke and soot was beyond all question more comfortable than an engine room, i.e. for pleasure, prevailed.

When we were leaving the Port au Basque [sic] train great preparations were going on in the dining car; tables were being set up here and there and the spotless damask cloths with all the other beautiful paraphernalia made the scene somewhat like a miniature hotel.

The excursion trail did not stop at any station on the road from St. John's until Whitbourne was reached. It was like approaching a city. The twinkling electric lights, the well-lit shop windows, the active operation at the railway station and machine shops, with engines moving to and fro and freight and baggage piled up all around presented quite a busy scene and exemplified that the railway tends to make the town.

Several horses caused some trouble by running along the track at one point on Wednesday night, but not the slightest damage or accident occurred during the trip.

The excursion train was delayed an hour in reaching the Bruce at Port au Basque, caused by the breaking down of a freight car on the Northern road....From the train windows one can count twelve icebergs in Conception Bay.[4]

A Trip to Clarenville in 1898

A drive by train, through the darkness, from St. John's to Clarenville, although somewhat uneventful is nevertheless interesting and enjoyable. As we glided along so comfortably on Thursday night last we were reminded of the "Puffing Billy," projected in Newcastle-on-Tyne sixty years ago, and the wonderful improvement made in locomotive propulsion since that time. We were agreeably surprised to be informed by a tourist on the train that the cars were gliding along even more smoothly than they do on some of the Canadian-Pacific and other lines. It was an agreeable surprise, at least to a novice, that Newfoundland could, *in one particular*, boast of being in a position to compare favourably with the neighbouring provinces. Out informant also assured us that rates of traffic, passenger rates, accommodation, charges for sleeping compartments and refreshments were equally accommodating and satisfactory with the same provisions outside this colony. From what could be observed in the night a great deal of interest seem to centre at the stopping places along the line. Crowds of juveniles and adults gather at these places to await the approach of the trains and receive visiting friends or bid departing ones "good bye." the juveniles board the train and cram themselves in everywhere, where an *opening* occurs, with small paper dishes of native fruits, and many a face of these shoeless urchins brighten at the sight of a five-cent piece or a few loose coppers. We were agreeably impressed with the decorum of the train officers as they moved about in the discharge of their various functions, seeming to be "all eye and all ear." We thought we could discover a very marked mingling of suavity with unswerving decision in carrying out the rules of the road. An occasional accident to cattle happens along near the harbours, but such accidents are regarded even by the people themselves, as simply unavoidable, and the opinion very largely prevails that the people themselves ought to unite and fence off headlands or other suitable places where their live stock may be secured from danger of being broken up by the locomotive.

―∽∼―

The inhabitants along here already appreciate, very highly, the advantages accruing from the railway. Many a man, in the winter season, can have direct traffic with St. John's, ship their rabbits, venison or other commodity and get his barrel or bag or anything else in return, while under other circumstances he would undoubtedly have to suffer extreme want, and such advantages from railway extension and operation, under the genial contractors, will increase as time rolls on. It is hard to find any place this side of paradise — where the trains don't run — without the tendency of some querulous character, but apart from the possibility of having such a sublunary genius in this quiet and orderly neighbourhood, there is not a word of fault-finding, or disrespect or even a dissentient expression of opinion as to the Messrs. Reid, in their conduct and management of the Newfoundland railway system, whatever may be said by cynical or sinister individuals to the contrary.[5]

The Railway in 1899

The puff of the steam engine is no longer confined to the saw-mill or the ship; for these are already augmented by the equally shrill whistle of the locomotive. Our hitherto locked-up country is partly intersected by lines of railway, and the impenetrable forest is now thrown open, and its fastnesses laid under tribute to the rails of the iron horse. The solitudes of the interior are broken in upon, and where the scream of the lonely night owl, and the yelping of the wolves, were once the most familiar sounds, the voice of man is now heard in superior tones. The stillness is broken by the approach of busy men from the city, and the ancient Indian trail, is superceded by the railroad. Our interior is now accessible, and that which lay so long unknown is no more a mystery. The solitude of ages has been intruded upon by the ruthless (?) hand of advancing civilization, and now in the closing days of the dying century we are having our own doors thrown open to us. How opposite,—A closing century, but an opening country.... Who of us ten years ago would have thought that a railway would so soon tap our bays and cross the country? Who five years ago would have indulged the fancy of sleeping and dining cars for Newfoundland? ... We speak of our railways and dock, our telegraph extension and steam communications; and we rejoice in their conveniences and comfort. It is by these agencies that we are making such rapid advance towards a better era in our history. But we seem to be losing sight of the name which was so prominently identified with the introduction of our railway system, and to forget how bitter was the opposition to his measure. Our country's development lies in the operation of her railways, and whatever success attends these developments, will add lustre to the gentleman who first introduced the railway Bill. Since that date— 1881— he has had many severe attacks in public life ... but he has lived to see the railway completed, and he now enjoys the quiet of life's evening, in the land for which he did so much. To the strenuous efforts of the Right Honorable Sir William Vallance Whiteway, K.C.M.G., the railway of to-day owes its inception.[6]

Hunting Woodland Caribou, 1900

I landed in Newfoundland early on the morning of October 26th, 1900, and started at once for Howley Station, where a telegram had informed me I would find my guide and camp equipment awaiting me. The journey by rail from Port-aux-Basques to Howley occupied nine hours, but the time passed quickly, as the country we travelled through was always wild and interesting. Much of the ground was covered with dense forests of spruce and juniper, but the individual trees in these wooded tracts looked very small and slight in comparison with the giant timber, amongst whose tall and massive stems I had lately been hunting moose in Canada.

I must confess that all I heard and saw concerning caribou sheeting on the evening of my arrival at Howley, impressed me most unfavourably, and all I subsequently saw of shooting these animals from ambushes during their annual migration across the railway line, confirmed my low estimation of the attractions of this form of game killing.

As I stepped from the train I saw that there were several carcases of freshly-killed caribou lying on the platform of the little railway station. These were all does and fawns, which I was subsequently informed had been killed that day whilst crossing the line quite close to the station. In addition to these entire carcases there were several heads, skins, and haunches of stags, but not a good or even moderate pair of horns amongst them. Seeing me examining these trophies of the chase, my guide, who had introduced himself to me as soon as I stepped from the train, remarked jovially: "Ah! You've come to the slaughter-house now." ... Day was just breaking ... after a most uncomfortable night in that wretched "go-as-you-please" or "accommodation" train, already several hours late on schedule time, I reached Terra Nova station.[7]

Along the Railway, 1900

The first through train carrying mails and passengers left St. John's July 24th and Port-aux-Basques July 27, 1898. It is the grand trunk line of Newfoundland and traverses the entire island, opening up the most important farming, lumbering and mining districts. It is the connecting link between Canada and the United States and Newfoundland, and will be the main artery of communication between the island and the North American Continent. It involves a sea passage of but six hours, across Cabot Strait from North Sydney (C.B.) To Port-aux-Basques, distance ninety-three miles, in a swift and well-equipped steamer. By this route the insular disadvantages of the island are reduced to a minimum. In increasing numbers travelers, tourists, health-seekers and sportsmen will find their way to this almost newly-discovered country, attracted by the salubrity of the climate, the beauty of the scenery, the novelty of Nature's aspects and the abundance of game. The line is solidly built; the rails heavy and of the best material; the bridges and culverts of granite and steel. The passenger cars are of the same style as those on the Canadian Pacific Railway, the first-class being dining and sleeping, fitted up with every attention to comfort. The second-class passengers have also sleeping and dining cars. Nothing has been left undone to render the line popular and attractive. In addition to operating the railway the contractor is to run steamers of a superior class on the principal bays to connect with the railway, thus linking together the various centres of population and rendering the fine scenery of those bays accessible to tourists. Hotels will be erected for the accommodation of visitors in the most attractive centres.

The S.S. "Bruce" is a noteworthy steamer, specially built for this service at the cost of $250,000. Her fittings, berths, saloon, etc., are not inferior to those of a Cunarder. Nothing is left undone to ensure the comfort of passengers. Her steam power, in proportion to her size, is very great, so that she makes fifteen knots per hour. She is specially fitted to encounter ice, having a perfectly solid bow and sheathed throughout. In the winter of 1897—98 North Sydney Harbor was covered with ice two feet thick, but she made her way through it without an effort, to the astonishment of those who witnessed the performance of "the ice crusher," as she is called.

On reaching Port-aux-Basques, a small but safe harbor open all the year round, passengers are transferred to the train which moves along the first nine miles to Cape Ray, through a rugged track of rocky barrens. Then passing behind the Auguille hills it enters the fine valley of Codroy ... Codroy — twenty-nine miles — Robinsons and Fischel's stations are passed and St. George's Bay station — eighty-nine miles — is reached.... Bay of Islands is 141 miles from Port-aux-Basques. Here the Humber, the second largest river in the island, discharges its waters into the sound, an arm of the bay.... From the train, as it glides along, charming view are obtained of the Humber.

Travelers by the train will be struck with the fact that scarcely a house is seen after leaving Codroy till Bay St. George is reached. Here the line takes a southeasterly direction, but the paucity of houses continues till within seventy or eighty miles of St. John's.

This admits of easy explanation. The population of the island is settled along the shores, mainly engaged in fishing. Until now the interior has been a *terra incognita*. The railway has been built to promote settlement and open up the country for industrial enterprise. The railway precedes settlement and makes it comparatively easy. The mineral wealth, the timber, the good lands, the marble quarries and coal beds amply justify the construction of the railway and the development of these resources will transform these unpeopled wastes into the smiling homes of men in the not distant future. The enterprise and energy of the colony in constructing this line at a cost of some $17,000,000 will yet be amply rewarded.

At Deer Lake station, 172 miles from Port-aux-Basques, the valley of the Humber widens and spreads out in several directions.... Grand Lake, 183 miles from Port-aux-Basques, is fifty-six miles long and five miles in breadth, with an island twenty-two miles long near its western extremity....

The line now passes along Kitty's Valley — 203 miles — and Gaff Topsail is reached — 213 miles — the watershed between Exploits and Grand Lake, the highest point on the railway, 1,700 feet above the sea — "the roof of the island," as it is called — being its most elevated plateau. Protruding through this roof are three remarkable granite eminences called "The Topsails" — detached masses of granite springing from the plateau to a considerable height. All around are bare granite ridges and huge boulders of granite strew the surface....

The train now enters the great valley of the Exploits, containing much fertile soil and good timber. In summer, wooded hills, with their dark green foliage and wild flowers of various hues on the level places along the track, make a charming scene. The stations along the valley are Caribou, 224 miles; St. Patrick's Brook, 231 miles; Winter, Dawe, 252 miles; McCallum, 268 miles; Bishop's Falls, 280 miles, and Exploits, 292 miles on Norris Arm, Notre Dame Bay is reached. The scenery here is exceedingly fine. The river is crossed by a splendid iron bridge, having a span of 250 feet. The course of the line is now southerly, and at Glenwood — 316 miles — crosses the Gander river, which flows through the finest lumbering region in the island. Here at Benton — 342 miles — and Gambo — 356 miles — are several lumbering establishments. The Gambo is crossed by a steel bridge 240 feet long, resting on piers of solid masonry....

Passing Alexander, Terra Nova, 381 miles; Clode Sound, Thorburn Lake, Shoal Harbor, 412 miles; Clarenville Station is reached, 416 miles. Here again the line touches salt water, the scenery being very fine. Port Blandford is on Clode Sound, an arm of Bonavista Bay....

The stations from Clarenville to Whitbourne are Northern Bight; Whiteway, 443 miles; Arnold, La Manche, Rantem, 458 miles; Tickle Harbor, Placentia Junction, Whitbourne, 449 miles. From Whitbourne, the train runs to St. John's, distance 57½ miles, by Holyrood and the shore of Conception Bay.[8]

Marconi's Train Trip Out of Newfoundland, 1901

[On December 11, 1901 Guglielmo Marconi made history on Signal Hill, St. John's. On that day he received the first transatlantic wireless signal from a transmitter at Poldhu, Cornwall. Shortly after, Marconi traveled across Newfoundland by rail.]

Under instructions from the Reid Newfoundland Company, we desire to call your attention to statements made editorially by the Herald, on the 30th and 31st instant. On the former date you say: "Passengers tell of terrible washouts on the West Coast." The only washout was at Bay of Islands where it occurred in consequence of a very severe gale, and a most unusually high tide. Further in the same article you say: "Passengers outward Tuesday night, Marconi and others, spent a dreadful time Wednesday night, the seas washing up to the car floors. The train was some hours late." On the 31st, referring to the above, you say: "Our information originated with a friend of the Reids, who crossed the country in the storm, dined with Marconi in the private car, and stated that they could not enjoy the meal owing to the water washing up against the car floors." We wish to point out that Tuesday's outward train passed Bay of Islands about midday on Wednesday, several hours before the storm took place, and therefore there can be no truth whatever in the statement with reference to Mr. Marconi and his friends.[9]

Railway "Sport," 1903

There are, it may be mentioned, a certain number of individuals who never attempt to reach the interior, whose ambition is satisfied by what may be called the "railway sport," and who possibly deserve any disappointments that fall to their lot. The term "railway sport" needs elucidation. Twice a year the caribou in Newfoundland migrate; in the spring they move from south to north, and in the autumn travel back from the north to their winter feeding grounds. It happens that the railroad from St. John's to Port-aux-Basques intersects a main route of migration, and immense numbers of deer cross the line, the bulk of them reaching it near a station called Howley. This is the spot hunted during the earlier part of the shooting season by the "railway sports," for it is often possible to shoot the three stags allowed by the law without walking out of sight of the metals. Yearly, as might be expected, a multitude of immature stags are slaughtered in this way, and the ears of the passengers in the passing trains may be filled with the report of guns, as if a small skirmish were taking place!

From this form of shooting all the chief elements of true sport are eliminated....

The railway is now under the control of the enterprising Reid Newfoundland Company. Through forests, over rivers, beside lakes, the line runs with a station every dozen miles or so, a station that often consists of no more than the wooden cabin of a section-man, whose business it is to keep the permanent way.

My destination, Terra Nova, lies one hundred and seventy-one miles distant from

St. John's, and is reached in something over eight hours by the express; thus it was far into the small hours — shortly before three o'clock, in fact — when the train attendant put his head into my sleeping-car and informed me that twenty minutes more would bring me to my station. The train was running with a roar and a creak between deep woods of spruce, that flashed at intervals into star-lit waters. But at that hour, between night and morning, one thinks little of the charms of scenery, the more especially as there was barely time to dress before we began to slacken speed and finally to draw up. My baggage, my "camp" as it is called in Newfoundland, was dropped out and stacked beside the metals, the conductor's voice echoed through the frosty air, and the train swung away out of sight, the louder clang as it disappeared telling of the trestle bridge across the head of Terra Nova Lake.

I found refuge in the single wooden house of Tim Hawco, the section-man. Lonely as was the spot, it knew nothing of the silences of solitude, for in the little room of the railway agent the telegraph machine never seemed to cease its clatter for ten minutes, day or night. Such was Terra Nova in 1903, but since then a lumber mill and the men employed in its working have altered the place a good deal.

I found that my men had not yet arrived from Alexander Bay, but was not much surprised, as they were to come by an "accommodation." The trains run by the Reid Company are of two kinds — the express and the accommodation. How the latter came by its name I do not know, unless it be that it is the duty of the accommodation train to accommodate; but, to judge from the opinions freely offered by its passengers, it does not altogether achieve success in this respect. Its speed rarely averages fifteen miles an hour, with further delays of stoppages to collect or to set down freight, or to allow the express to pass — delays which sometimes run into hours, a hardship not a little accentuated by the fact that nothing in the shape of food is procurable on board. There is, I have heard, a rule on the Reid line that any train twelve hours behind the scheduled time becomes a special — a great many accommodations must become specials! Many people, especially sportsmen, grumble, which is, after all, rather absurd, as they always have the alternative of the express, which, considering the route, is punctual and certainly more comfortable.... But it is the fashion to deride the accommodation; and what has justice to do with a time-honoured joke?[10]

A Little Journey to Northern Wilds, 1908

To reach the heart of the caribou one starting from the United States has some distance to go.

Those of our party who live in the East sail from Boston, whence the ocean liners bound for Liverpool proceed by way of Halifax to St. John's, the capital of Newfoundland. At St. John's the travelers do not tarry, for the railway which crossed the island is not entirely reliable, and since a train is "in," they board it, and ride off into the interior, where the caribou abound.

Those of us who start from the West go first to Montreal and Quebec, and thence by rail, out across New Brunswick and Nova Scotia, till we come to North Sydney, at the easternmost tip of the latter.

From here a miserable steamer conveys us across Cabot Strait to Port-au-Basque [sic], on Newfoundland Island. The passage, though one of only ninety miles, keeps us aboard the steamer all night. A Newfoundland storm all but tosses us from our bunks while we try to sleep, and when we go on deck in the morning we find ourselves enveloped in a heavy fog. A spitting rain is falling and we stand about, feeling very miserable indeed while undergoing a searching customs' examination.

Then we take the island train mentioned above — at its western terminus, however — and in a poorly-heated car, tired and sleepy and shivering, speed on to the caribou country.... we begin to catch snatches of a conversation between some men across the aisle from us, and it does not take us long to perceive that one of the party is a famous caribou hunter of the island. He is giving some newcomers pointers on the hunting of caribou, and we beg to be included in his audience. He receives our advances with true Newfoundland friendliness, and, continuing his recital, turns directly to the chase.

Caribou? Yes, indeed, there are lots of caribou up here. Sometimes in October the animals are so numerous that they cross the tracks of the miserable little island railway in mighty herds, just as buffalo crossed the tracks of our great transcontinental lines in the sixties. At Howley's we may see this, if we have a mind to.... The true sportsman, our hunter states, stalks his caribou, camping out at night and shooting him, then bringing the meat in to the railway.... The line of the railway, in fact, is so thoroughly shot over that a hunter himself is not secure against occasional bullets, among those coming from all directions.[11]

A Trip to Newfoundland, c. 1908

In the spring I had made all preparation for a trip to Newfoundland, and arrived at North Sydney to take the steamer *Bruce* for Port aux Basques. Walking into the office of the company upon the dock to make arrangements for my passage, my attention was attracted to a little group of men. I learned that the Government doctor was vaccinating every passenger before allowing him to enter Newfoundland, because at this time Sydney had an epidemic of smallpox. One of the officers shouted to me: "Here you, going over? Bare your arm." I answered, "Not for me," knowing it would be useless to go into the woods with a punctured arm. Just a little while before the boat cleared I slipped aboard, heard the officer shout "Cast away!" and we were off for Port aux Basques.

The sea was rough and in the morning all the "landlubbers" were "pale behind the gills." On landing, every person called upon the customs officer to have his baggage cleared, and I was required to leave a deposit of fifty dollars for the return of my Auto

Graflex camera. The train was scheduled to start in a few minutes, and all the passengers were aboard waiting for more than an hour, wondering what was delaying the start. Inquiry developed the fact that the trainmen were waiting for the wind to subside before they would venture across the viaduct over a swamp a few miles out. It seems that the train had been blown off the track several times by a strong wind. We finally crossed in safety.

Among the passengers were several fishing parties, and they were bubbling over with good fellowship in anticipation of the excellent sport they were going to have in pursuit of their favorite pastime. I believe every person should have a hobby of some kind to divert his mind from his burdens and petty cares. A chance to do something that we like fills us with pleasant thoughts, both in anticipations and realization. Several of the fishermen returned on the same train with me; they looked much better and were quite talkative about "whipping the stream." their "wonderful casts," and the "big fellows" they didn't get. Their hearty appearance confirmed my theory.

Passing though the country, as far as the eye could reach we looked out over barrens covered with moss. Here and there a small body of blue water, like a jewel, broke the monotony. Perhaps a solitary duck floated peacefully on its glossy surface, waiting for the little brood soon to appear. Away over yonder on the opposite shore of one of the lakes stood a sentinel, the sandhill crane (*Grus mexicana*), knee-deep in the water, sedate and motionless, waiting for an opportunity to catch some unsuspecting fish that might fortunately pass his way. The countless herds of caribou had returned to the north and were scattered all through the woodland hills, attending to their domestic duties. Towards evening the fishing parties began to drop off, one by one, at Middle Brook, Fischel's Brook, and Harry's River, all ideal streams for salmon and trout. They seemed scarcely able to restrain themselves until the morrow, when they could joint their rods, wade the crystal water, and cast the Jock Scott or Silver Doctor into the riffles again and again in anticipation of a strike.

―※―

While at Bay of Islands and old sailor came into port with a young man aboard, penniless and very sick. He lived in the interior and the captain was trying to raise money to send him on the train to his home. The lad knew he was going to die and was anxious to reach home to make amends to his old father and mother for seeking, against their wished, a life on the seas. Passengers contributed the money and sent word to the captain, but before the train arrived the poor boy died.

The train pulled in, not in due time, but several hours late. The conductor shouted "All aboard!" and as it slowly left the bay my thoughts turned homeward. It is then I begin to feel anxious about the folks at home and wonder if all is well.

―※―

The Glencoe turned up at 1 o'clock on the 26th and the next afternoon we reached Placentia, where the train was waiting. We got away about 5:30, but did not reach St.

John's (80 miles) till 2 A.M. the following morning, a very poor performance. The engine could not pull us up the inclines. We made a rush and each time stuck halfway and had to run back a couple of miles to make a fresh try. However, it seemed a usual occurrence, for every one on board took it quite philosophically, many recounting their reminiscences of when they had to stop all night in the train.

In the train was Mr. Job, just returning from a good grouse shoot. He told me he had in his office a sixty-four pointer caribou stag shot by an Indian and brought by his brother. He very kindly allowed me to see it the next day, and a very remarkable head it was; I could make out at least sixty points.

I left St. John's at 6 P.M. on the 29th and as we approached Gaff Topsails, about the highest point of the railway, sleet and light snow were falling and a bitter wind was blowing across the open barrens.[12]

With the Newfoundland Stags, 1908

Before the days of the railroad, hunting parties were limited to the country which they could reach by some water course if they wished to get into the interior. It so happened that the largest river on the island, the beautiful Humber, emptying into the Bay of Islands on the west course through a cliff-walled gorge of wonderful picturesqueness, led to the most excellent hunting grounds. That is the country north of Grand Lake and east of the Humber, of which Howley — three tar-papered, barrel-chimneyed cabins along the track at the time of my visit there — appears as the metropolis on the railroad map, the best one there is, by the way, though it is inaccurate in a good many details.

When the railroad was put through to Howley those who had formerly come into the district from Bay of Islands by the river arrived at their old hunting grounds by the train. They went no further because there was no need of it. They could get all the caribou they wanted there without leaving the tracks. Those to whom the fame of the district had come came to Howley because it was the only place they knew anything definite about. They too went no further because they found there was no need of it, and camped down along the railroad track or went up Sandy Lake stream two miles north of it.[13]

To Newfoundland, 1910

Getting away at eleven o'clock, and after a rather rough passage, for the *Bruce* is only about 800 tons, we arrived at Port aux Basques at 7 A.M. on the 17th [of August].

It was a lovely morning, and the rocky shores of Newfoundland looked particularly wild and attractive in the bright sunshine. Port aux Basques is a small settlement, and so far as I could ascertain does not contain an hotel, but no doubt some form of lodging exists, where, as throughout the island, the visitor would be given a warm welcome and whatever was going, be it little or much.

The train was waiting for the steamer. The line is a narrow-gauge one, but the cars were quite comfortable, and the prospect of seeing a new country is always attractive. But how we did bump over that line ... however, no one seemed to mind, and after all passengers should be grateful for having a line at all.... Getting away at 8:15 we passed all along the west coast, through a most beautiful country, teeming with salmon rivers, most of them I fear much over-fished, for the west coast rivers are the favourite haunts of the American angler, being easily reached from New York and Boston.

Thompson's Hotel, prettily situated on the Little Codroy River, looked particularly attractive, and two American anglers got off there. I was told there was a late run of big fish in August, an exception, for as a rule all the Newfoundland rivers are early ones.

At Crabbes a local guide, on the look-out for a job, deeply deplored the fact that Crabbes should be neglected for the better-known Little and Big Codroy Rivers. He assured me there were two rivers, the one ten minutes, the other about two minutes, from the station, "crawling" of course with fish, and that a thirty-five pound salmon had been caught by a local angler a few days before....

As we slowly bumped our way north, the scenery became more and more beautiful, until it culminated in the views as the train skirted the Humber River, then along Deer Lake, gradually rising towards the barrens of the centre of the island. All along the sides of the railway the ground was carpeted with wild flowers, a perfect blaze of colour. Nightfall found us at the north end of the Grand Lake, where is situated "The Bungalow," a sporting hotel recently established, which from the train looked most comfortable.

The food in the dining car was quite good, but by no means cheap.... On Thursday the 18th I arrived at St. John's at 12:30, having traveled without a stop from the previous Sunday at midnight.[14]

Migration to Canada, 1910

On a Thursday evening at 6 P.M., about the last half of November, 1910, I boarded the Newfoundland cross-country express train, to, first of all, cross the island of Newfoundland to Port-aux-Basques, a distance of almost five hundred and fifty miles.... As that train, which was composed of a couple of sleeping cars, a dining car, two or three ordinary passenger cars, as well as a baggage and mail car, pulled out on time from the railway station, I, together with Mr. Phelan, stood on the tail end of the rear sleeping car and waved goodbye to all the members of my family.... Mr. Phelan and I had dinner or supper on that train. At that time I thought it was a wonderful experience to be able to ride on what I then considered was a most modern and comfortable means of transportation. In my inexperienced mind, I really thought that the speed of this mode of conveyance was miraculous. In fact it is evident that later, under the supposedly efficient powerful and heavier locomotives, with the better ballasted roadbeds and the rerailing of the entire cross-country system with seventy pound steel, it took longer for an express train to cross the island.... I did learn, however, that this express train, the most modern and luxurious form of transportation ever introduced into Newfoundland, was rolling along like our old coaster, *Mary*, in a calm swell in the middle of Cape Broyle Bay. In fact there were times when one would think that this future *Newfie Express* would overturn ... we ultimately came to the foot of the Gaff Topsails. The weather was cold. There was no snow yet to be seen on this most rugged part of the Island of Newfoundland. Slowly we climbed the steep grade, and I was able to see for myself the loneliness and isolation of the people employed by the Reid Company to keep this so-called modern railway in actual operation. When this train ultimately arrived at the peak of the Gaff Topsails, it was then I was able to see the majestic grandeur in the ruggedness of the surrounding mountains.... We had breakfast between Grand Falls and Humbermouth and the dinner hour was approaching when I would have my last meal of Newfoundland codfish for several years. We pulled out from Humbermouth on time. There was nothing at Corner Brook at that time.... We stopped a few minutes at Curling and had a beautiful view of the picturesque Bay of Islands. We approached the beautiful Codroy Valley during the afternoon and one could seen the many small farms and salmon rivers — rivers world famous for their salmon fishing at certain periods of the year. Finally, we arrived at Port-aux-Basques, the terminal of this wonderful railway — wonderful in my mind at any rate, because I had never been on a railway before.[15]

Boosterism, 1911 Style

The railway is very substantially constructed and very efficiently operated: the road-bed is splendidly built; the rails are the best procurable; the bridges are of steel with granite abutments, and the rolling stock is the finest that is made. Express trains cross the island every alternate day in either direction, and the present summer will see a daily express service inaugurated. These trains are made up of ordinary baggage and mail cars, coaches for second class and first class passengers; dining car and sleeping cars, all of the style used on the Canadian Pacific Line. Through freights trains are run every day, and morning and evening trains ply between St. John's and Carbonear, along the shore of Conception Bay, and likewise to Placentia, the chief town in the Bay of that name. A splendid granite station in St. John's; machine shops of the most approved type are established in the vicinity and available both for the repair and construction of railway equipment and for steamers and vessels effecting changes in the Dry Dock near by. At all the principal points along the main line and the branches, substantial and commodious stations have been erected, and at the terminals point, where several bay steamers connect with the trains, substantial wharves and adequate freight ships are provided....The growth of the traffic of the Reid system the past six years is attested by the following figures:

	1903–4	1909–10
No. of passengers carried	136,010	194,844
Tons of freight carried	122,935	173,343
Miles run, Passenger Trains	150,425	297,573
Miles run, Freight Trains	51,296	78,366
Miles Run, Mixed Trains	200,821	287,529
Passenger Traffic Earnings	$206,940	$274,490
Freight Traffic Earnings	$159,941	$231,266
Mail Traffic Earnings	$41,812	$42,000
Other Earnings	$22,724	$43,834

The railroad starts from the Dry Dock in St. John's, which is the deep water terminal and runs through the Waterford Valley, a delightfully picturesque suburb of the city, for about four miles, when it traverses the section of the peninsula to Topsail, in Conception Bay, a beautiful watering place, much affected by the city's residents during the summer months. Then it skirts the South Shore of Conception Bay, keeping within sight of the ocean and of farming villages the whole way. From Holyrood, at the head of that Bay, it runs inland a few miles. At Brigus Junction a branch line continues along the north shore through several populous centres to Harbor Grace, the second town in the colony; and three miles further, to Carbonear, the present terminus there, though it is proposed next year to extend this branch to Grate's Cove, the tip of that peninsula. From Brigus Junction the main line continues to Whitbourne, where another extends to Broad Cove in Trinity Bay and across the peninsula also to Harbor Grace. The Broad Cove branch is being extended the present year to Heart's Content, the landing place of five submarine cables. Seven miles beyond Whitbourne is Placentia Junction, whence a line of twenty-six miles extends to Placentia and taps that Bay, all of this country being more or less settled and given over to agricultural pursuits. Thence the road traverses the Isthmus of Avalon, where, from the car windows can be seen the waters of both Trinity and Placentia Bays. Still going north, the railway crosses the Terranova, Gambo and Gander Valleys, through tracts extensively wooded and which it is hoped with pulp and paper enterprises in the future.

Two important points passed in this section are Clarenville, the terminal for the Trinity Bay Steamer, and Port Blandford, the terminal for the Bonavista Bay ship. About 240 miles from St. John's, Notre Dame Junction is reached, whence a spur, nine miles long, connects with Lewisport, the terminal for the steamer on Notre Dame Bay, while seven miles further Norris Arm is reached, where the valley of the Exploits is centered and beautiful panoramas of fiord scenery are disclosed. The Exploits is crossed at Bishop Falls, twelve miles from its mouth.... At Badger Brook the road leaves that valley, takes a north-west route across the White Hill plains, climbing these to the Topsails country, the great central plateau being crossed at an elevation of 1,737 feet above sea level. The line then follows the course of Kitty's Brook to the north-east of Grand Lake, continuing along the south side of Deer Lake and down the delightful Humber Valley to Bay of Islands, which it traverses completely, circling around towering bluffs, and then through the Harry's Brook valley to Bay St. George. From this point it passes back of the Anguille mountains along the valley of the Codroy Rivers to Cape Ray and skirts the seaboard to Port-aux-Basques, which is its western terminal.

Last year the Reid Company took further contracts to construct branch lines of railroad; from Clarenville through the Bonavista peninsula in Bonavista town, the work of which was about four-fifths completed last year and will be finished early this summer; from Broad Cove to Heart's Content; from Carbonear to Grate's Cove; from St. John's along the eastern front of the Avalon Peninsula to Trepassey, near Cape Race; from the Avalon Peninsula south-west to Fortune Bay; and from Deer Lake to Bonne Bay. The total mileage is about 300 and the construction figure is $15,000 a mile, payable in cash, as against $15,600 a mile, payable in bonds in the past; with 4,000 acres of land per mile for operating for forty years, as against 5,000 acres for the fifty-year operation of the main line, ten years of which have practically expired.[16]

Beginning the Ferryland Branch Line, 1911

Tuesday, May 9th, was an eventful day in the section of the peninsula of Avalon which is known as the District of Ferryland, because that day witnessed the cutting of the first sod for the new Railroad, which is to traverse that District, and end, for the time being, at Ferryland. The function was performed by the energetic and able Executive member for that district and its senior representative for the past twenty years, Hon. M. P. Cashin, Minister of Finance and Customs, and was witnessed by a goodly gathering of citizens, including the Acting Premier, Hon. D. Morison, D.C., Minister of Justice...

The Minister of Finance showed the important part Ferryland had played in the ancient history of our island, its progress in recent years, the possibilities of developing agricultural, fishing, and other operations there, and the special interest which this line of railroad would serve in running to Trepassey, which could be made a Winter port for the Island, enabling Steamers, to transfer mails, passengers and freight at times when St. John's might be blocked with ice, and possibly in the future becoming a port where big Atlantic Liners could call the whole year round, and thus avoid the divergence from the regular route which a call at St. John's would imply. He also emphasized what benefits had accrued to the country generally through the Railway policy, how the critics of its earlier days had been converted into its present-day advocates, and how all had come to see that bound up was the prosperity of the Island with the development of its resources through the agency of the Railroad.

Mr. Morison reminded the gathering that the Railway extension was a chief feature in the present Government's policy, and that the Premier, though absent in person, was present in spirit on the occasion, having for long years advocated the providing of Railway facilities for the Colony as fast as such could be granted.... Mr. P. F. Moore, junior member for Ferryland district ... expressed his satisfaction that the district was at last to receive the benefits of railway extension for which it had waited so long and patiently...

The line will be about one hundred miles long, stretching from St. John's to Trepassey, and will run through or within immediate touch of every important settlement along the Coast, so that the people of these thriving fishing and farming settlements will be able to derive the very best advantages from this construction.

Exceptional progress has already been made with the construction of the line, the grading of the road-bed having been completed by Coronation Day to Witless Bay, twenty miles from the city, while gangs have partly graded sections further along so that the Company entertains the hope of having the whole of the road-bed constructed right to Trepassey before the snow comes and the rails at last as far as Renews, sixty miles from town, which section will probably be operated the coming winter. This will make a record unique in the local annals and will give the people of the greater part of the Ferryland district an opportunity of enjoying the advantages of daily intercourse, by train, with the capital, which they have been waiting the past thirty years to avail of.[17] [Despite the evident boosterism the line to Ferryland and Trepassey operated only from 1914 until 1934.]

Opening of the Bonavista Railway, 1911

The opening of the Bonavista Branch Railway by His Excellency Sir Ralph Williams is a memorable event in the History of the Colony. The arrangements made by the Messrs. Reids for the comfort of their large number of guests were simply perfect, and were admirably carried out by W.D. Reid and R.G. Reid, and their valuable assistants.... From first to last everything went merry as a marriage bell. In the party were Sir Edward and Lady Morris, and his Ministers and their wives.

We left St. John's in the evening of Tuesday, 7th November, 1911, about 7 P.M. the party numbered over eighty persons, not including the Newfoundland Highlanders' Pipers. The train consisted of engine, baggage car, two dining cars, day coach, four sleepers and two private cars. We woke up in the morning at Shoal Harbour so as to go down the new line in day-light. We rounded into the beautiful land-locked arms of Trinity early in the day. The country here is exceedingly picturesque and beautiful. All the inhabitants who greeted our party with enthusiasm were dressed in their best clothes, and everywhere all along the line the whole country was *en fete*.

Both His Excellency the Governor and the Hon. Premier made excellent speeches which were received with great applause. Whatever other opponents of the Government might say about the Branch Railways, there could be no doubt that the people of Trinity and Bonavista most heartily appreciated the great boon thus conferred on them by the Morris Government. Everywhere when we stopped there was the same warm welcome from the people, and the same overflowing popular enthusiasm. We had so many speeches and addresses that it was quite late when we reached our terminus at Bonavista — famous not only for its fine fertile lands and extensive business, but also memorable in History as the undoubted landfall of John Cabot in 1497 on his famous voyage of discovery.[18]

Ned Brewster's Caribou Hunt, 1914

The minute our eyes rested upon the great rocky shores about Port aux Basque [sic], we felt that we were not to be disappointed in our venture. The whole country was unlike anything we had ever seen. The great, flat-topped mountains lying off in the purple haze, suggested strange caverns out of which primitive monsters might crawl, while the whole land gave the suggestion that some mighty creature had suddenly lifted the bottom of the sea until the waters had receded, leaving the country strewn with rocks and boulders.

Even the people who gathered about the dock as the ship slipped into her place were like fairy people. Most of them were undersized, and their brown, sea-beaten faces seemed to put them in a race by themselves.

When we stepped into the Pullman car of the little, narrow-gauge railroad, we felt indeed that we were in a fairy world. The little thing went puffing up the grades, whizzing around the curves where one could look into deep gorges, racing down the steep mountainsides, just like the play railroads at Coney Island.

The whole country was new and fresh. We had left Boston the first of July, when everything was hot and dusty, and all vegetation had lost the freshness of spring. But here the ferns were just beginning to push through the ground, the leaves had only attained their growth, and the birds were still singing their love songs.

"We have made no mistake," said dad, as we flew across the island in the narrow gauge, darting through ever varying scenery, until we stepped from the train at Glenwood.

The little narrow gauge pulled into Glenwood a few minutes past midnight. The porter announced that we were at our station, took our luggage, stepped from the car, and left our bags somewhere in the darkness.

"You don't mean to say there is a station here, porter?" asked dad, as he stood looking into the night.

"Dis is where your ticket says you git off."

The train moved along and left us standing in a night as black as ink. The dim light from the rear of the train disappeared, and we could not hear the voice of a human being nor discern even the outline of a building. The heavy clouds shut out every ray of light, threatening to drench us any minute, while we sank in wet moss, and water slushed beneath our feet every move we made.

"Cheerful, to say the least," dad exclaimed.

"Case of sleeping on the railroad, it seems to me. No train comes along until morning, so it will be safe." ... The light soon revealed the fact that close by stood an old shack with a rickety platform in front where it was unwise to walk unless one carried a heavy accident policy. Just across the railroad was a long row of shanties, all built in the same way and mostly deserted.... When we stepped out into the room that led to the front door, we found a policeman sleeping on a couch. He sprang to his feet when he heard our steps and sat looking us over, but did not say a word.

"Disturbing you, neighbor?" asked dad, by way of salutation.

"Just waiting for the early train," was his reply." "Can't tell when she will come so I slept here that I might hear her coming and not miss her." ... Just then the whistle of the train was heard a mile down the track, and the puffing of the tiny engine over the steep grade was distinctly audible. The policeman buckled on his belt, put his handcuffs in his pocket, and started for the station...

"De train, he leave at midnight," said Billy [the guide]. "Dare little station up de railroad from Glenwood. You go dare, get on de car, and no one know we come from de woods." ... The whistle blew far away and in a few minutes the little narrow gauge engine came puffing along. We stepped into the car and waved a final good-bye to Billy, until he disappeared in the darkness.

"The greatest trip we have ever had in the woods!" exclaimed dad, as he sat down in the car.

"And hardships only added to the interest."[19]

A Hunting Trip, 1922

On the morning of September 1st the steamer "Kyle" drove into Port aux Basques at full speed in spite of the narrow, torturous channel that in places leads close to the rocks. It was hard-a-starboard, then hard-a-port until a hundred yards from the dock the anchor rattled out to swing us around and we backed into our berth at the railroad wharf. The overnight run from North Sydney had been smooth as a pond, so Laura and I left the ship with healthy appetites at 6 A.M. However, we were destined to undergo a lengthy customs examination and purchase our shooting licenses before we could obtain breakfast on board the narrow-gauge train that stood waiting.

We heard mostly pessimistic reports about this railroad but our inspection disclosed a train or two sleeping cars, spotlessly clean, an excellent diner where the food was ridiculously cheap in comparison with New York prices, two day coaches and two baggage cars — quite a long train for the diminutive locomotive. Our speed during the next ten hours averaged less than eighteen miles per hour and there was considerable jolting and rocking but the ever-changing view from the car window fully compensated for the rough roadbed. Altogether we were agreeably disappointed as not once did we leave the rails as we had been led to believe was this train's invariable habit at least once each trip.

The country around Port aux Basques is a bleak, barren waste with not a tree in sight. It is "the country God gave Cain." The houses of the villagers cling to the rocky walls and cod drying frames are perched on every semi-level spot. It is fortunately true that exposed coastlines the world over are not to be taken as indicative of the true character of the country behind them. And so here it proved, for before many miles the aspect changed. First scrubby trees and alder brush added a touch of green to the brown marshes, then a dense growth of spruce, "var" and birch covered the gently rolling hills.

At Curling, on the Bay of Islands, the [rail] road skirts a bluff that falls precipitously to the ocean. Below us the narrow arm of the sea lay shimmering in glorious sunlight. To make the picture complete and to add a thrill, a whale spouted. Here and there dories "jigging" for cod dotted the water and offshore a short distance lay at anchor a fleet of "bankers," as the fishing schooners that go out to the Banks of Newfoundland are called. There was a coldness in color of the water; a hardness in the grey lichen-covered rocks; the air had lost its languor. Here the North begins.

At Humbermouth the railroad leaves the coast and winds up the narrow gorge of the Humber River. This is one of Newfoundland's best salmon streams and its dark pools at the foot of white rapids held out a tempting invitation.

We were only two hours late in reaching Grand Lake where Mr. J. H. Whitaker took us to his house, the Bungalow, and whetted our appetites for the hunt by giving us our first dinner of caribou meat....

We left the Bungalow on the afternoon of September 3rd by rail. The [rail] road reaches its highest elevation (about 1,500 feet), at the Topsails. This must be a stormy place in winter for on both sides of the track for many miles were snow fences eighteen to twenty feet high. In spite of this protection, every year there are periods of several weeks when the train cannot get through because of the snow drifts.[20]

The Reids Bow Out, 1923

REID NEWFOUNDLAND COMPANY, LTD.
OFFICE OF THE PRESIDENT

August 30th, 1923

To all Employees in the Railway, Steamship, Dock and Express Services.

On the occasion of the retirement of REID NEWFOUNDLAND COMPANY, LIMITED from the transportation and docking business in Newfoundland I desire on behalf of the Directors and Shareholders of the Company to convey to you our best thanks for the loyal service rendered to us in the past and our sincere hope and belief that the like service will be given by you to your country, which, through its Government, is now operating these services.

During the thirty-three years which have elapsed since the Reids first became connected with the railway system of this Dominion the most satisfactory feature of their operations has been the sterling loyalty which has been displayed towards them by the staff and employees generally. Without that spirit of loyalty and co operation the difficulties which we have had to face would have been insurmountable. The hardships and dangers of snow-fighting, for instance, are imperfectly realized by the general public.

I should like here to make a special mention of the period of the Great War, throughout which those of "the outfit" who were not actually in the fighting line with the Regiment or in the Royal Naval Reserve did equally valuable service to their country by keeping our transportation services going while Newfoundland was otherwise practically cut off from the rest of the world by the submarine campaign.

In taking leave of you I wish you to believe that you have our best wishes for your future happiness, advancement and prosperity, and for the greatest possible success of the new management.

Faithfully yours,
R. D. Reid,
President.[21]

A Railroad That Cultivates Adjectives, 1925

You may have ridden over the rocky road to Dublin; you may have loitered with the trains on a little branch railway that trails off to some little known town; but you have not enjoyed the fun of railroading on the funniest road until you have crossed Newfoundland on the Daily Express, which doesn't run every day, despite its name.

Let no one think that the Reid-Newfoundland Company Railroad is carelessly run and that it is a dangerous trip. You can take it safely. I believe it is a safer road to travel on than many of the standard gauge roads of Canada and the United States. I presume had we the statistics the records would be entirely in favor of this road. They are careful of their passengers and the station agents are instructed to drive the cows off the tracks before the trains stop at the stations. When one takes eight hours to make an eighty-two mile trip, as we did going to Placentia, the chances of a serious accident are minimized.

Further, I do not wish to in any way criticize the railway officials, for they are evidently working under handicaps of several kinds, some of them indigenous to the land itself. The officials were kind to me and, perhaps realizing what delays might hinder my work, gave me permission to ride on freight trains and hand-cars and the train crews were so instructed.

The trains in summer run across the island once in two days and are usually late, even with a very liberal time allowance. In summer they may be from a half to a day late and in winter the days have been known to run into weeks.

In February, 1912, the Methodist minister at Lewisporte tried to go to St. John's, two hundred and fifty-five miles away, with an ailing wife and children. It was only a few hundred yards from the parsonage to the station and, flogging through the drifts, they reached it on an ox sled. At a house by the station they waited two weeks for a train, finally a train started, moved by five engines, two rotary plows and a hundred shovelers. But it was two weeks more before the train made the two hundred and fifty-five miles and reached St. John's. A carload of beef which the railway company furnished kept the passengers from starving.

The storekeeper at Petrie's Crossing told me that in February, 1920, he went down to St. John's to get goods and was thirteen days in reaching home. He said, "I got home two days before the train by walking the last ten miles." One winter it took the Daily Express twenty-six days to cross the island; the distance is five hundred and forty-six miles.

The great foe in winter is ice, which freezes to a depth of several feet upon the tracks in the centre of the island. The bright sun shining upon these ice sheets has caused the natives to call it "the glitter."

The Daily Express carries sleepers, and it is fortunate that this is a narrow-gauge road, for sometimes the upper berth passengers are joggled out and land across the aisle.... One has a chance to take the vibratory treatment most of the way and to get thoroughly used to bumps....

The natives find fault with it, as do the tourists who come here in quest of salmon and caribou; but the natives usually conclude their criticism by saying, " It is all the railroad we have, and we don't want to lose it." The tourists use adjectives frequently, for the road somehow seems to make it easy to use adjectives.

The railroad will take you to many a place that maybe you have wished to reach. There's a branch line out of Whitbourne that runs to Heart's Delight, Heart's Desire and Heart's Content, the last named town is at the end of the line. The Bona Vista [sic] Branch will take you to Brickyard, Goose Arm and Brooklyn. Trepassey Branch stops its trains at Petty Harbor, Hell Hill, Aquaforte, Renews and Chance Cove. The Daily Express stops at Come-by-Chance, Topsail, Black Duck, Upper Gullies, and may another place that makes the traveler wonder.

The steamboat lines under the control of the same Reid System stop at equally interesting points,— Fox Cove, Paradise, Ireland's Eye, Cat Harbor, Three Arms, Comfort Cove, St. Jones Without, Leading Tickles and Spanish Room. All of which may suggest that the early settlers had imaginations and let their fertile minds attach convenient names. The sea's way accounts for a good many of them, if you examine and trace them carefully.[22]

A Winter Journey, 1926

The wisdom of annexing a freight-train for cross-country travel in winter was vindicated. I had meant to spend twenty-four hours in Corner Brook, but my actual time was more than double as much. The passenger-train, for which I might have waited at Grand Falls, was reported two hours late. On this I was to continue the journey toward home. Then word came that the two hours had grown to four. That meant mid-afternoon. At three o'clock all news of the train ceased. No one knew anything. I went to bed secure in a promise of being called. Morning came with no news. Then there were rumors that she was past the Topsails and only a few hours away. Next we learned that she was stalled on the Topsails with vague promises of being relieved. I had begun my watchful waiting on Friday morning. Sunday at noon the train came along with a tale of adventure. It had begun to blow when she was approaching the Topsails and the prudent engineer advised pulling into a handy train-shed to await events in safety. The confident young conductor overruled him and she went on — but not far. Soon she was engulfed in snow and overborne by a furious wind. Though steam was kept up in the boiler, the engine froze and could not be made to stir. Steam refused to percolate through the cars. The passengers in the sleepers kept on their clothes and snuggled up in their berths. So strong was the wind-pressure that it drove snow through the frames of double windows. The good priest of Corner Brook was found under a foot of flakes; he was quite comfortable. His bishop was almost as well covered, but was blanketed in his sealskin coat.

Fire was started in the end of the sleeper where a precautionary stove existed. Then coal gave out. Some one braved the elements for half a mile and brought a bagful. The second-class car stayed warm and the diner kitchen had plenty of food. By and by the wind slowed down, and a rotary snow-plow rescued the beleaguered passengers. They were fifty hours late in getting to Corner Brook.[23]

Caribou and the Railway, 1928

So it is with the caribou of Newfoundland. For centuries the herds of the North have annually migrated to the South and those of the South have migrated to the North with equal regularity. During all these ages the caribou suffered little at the hands of man in this uninhabited forest country. But when the railway came, cutting across the island from East to West, it cut across the route taken by the migratory caribou. Then, before the game laws came into force, the destruction of the caribou by man was great. Men posted themselves along the railway line during the migration and slew deer by the hundreds as they passed. Still the migration went on each year, as it does to this day, always crossing the railway line between the same two places, Howley and Gaff Topsails.[24]

The Dining Car, 1931

The food in the dining-car was quite good but by no means cheap. Why one should pay 40 cents ... for a slice of fried cod in the very home of cod, when a whole fish can be purchased for half the money, I could not understand, and although Newfoundland abounds in fish neither trout nor salmon were once served in the restaurant.[25]

Hitching a Ride on the Newfoundland Railway, 1932

Hearing the train approaching, I walked down the track, carrying a large, lighted lantern and stood waving it vigorously around my head. The signal was seen; I heard the brakes applied and the long train came to a sudden stop. Four or five men, the engineer, the conductor, the fireman and one or two train hands leaped out and came running toward me. "What's the matter, is the track washed away?" I answered, "No, we wish to get on board." The conductor appeared to be angry and said, "Did you stop the train just to get on?" I replied, "Certainly, we have to get on." He said, "I'll take you along to St. John's and leave you in the jail"; to which I answered, "That's all right, conductor; here are five dollars for you and five for the engineer, and if the train hands have been put to any inconvenience, I'll give them a little too." this had a good effect and he said, "Thank you kindly, sir, that's plenty, I'll have the berth made up for you, but do hurry, please, or you'll get us into trouble." In two or three minutes all my property was bestowed in the baggage car, except my canoe which, as it was too long to go in, the engineer very obligingly secured to the tender of his locomotive, and we proceeded.[26]

A Rail Journey, 1935

From the platform, certainly, we found it impossible to tell when the train was starting. Some sort of telepathic communication seemed to exist between driver and guard. Aboard the train, on the other hand, there could be no doubt: it gave an epileptic jerk and flurry which might stretch you lengthways along the corridor if you were unused to it.

Throughout the night the bell continued to clang and the train stopped often. Since it was unfenced, cows and other domestic animals stayed on to the line, and the guard, as part of his duties had to dismount from the rear of the train, walk to the front and shoo them off. If he saw that a spark had ignited the grass or undergrowth he had again to dismount to put out the fire by means of a long watering can which he carried for the purpose. As the snorts, jerks and clangs woke me spasmodically during the night I would try to guess in my mahogany bunk whether it was a cow or a fire. One noise of the night which was never explained was the spasmodic occurrence of a gigantic, almost superhuman laughter from beside the line whenever the train stopped for one or other reason. It sounded as though the inhabitants amused themselves at night by coming down the line in parties just to rid themselves of a healthy accumulation of laughter.[27]

Cross Country Service, 1939

The cross-country service is thrice weekly, from June 1st to December 31st, trains leaving St. John's on Sundays, Tuesdays and Thursdays, and arriving at Port aux Basques on Mondays, Wednesdays and Fridays respectively. Returning trains leave Port aux Basques on Sundays, Tuesdays and Fridays respectively, arriving in St. John's on the following day. The running time for the one way trip in approximately twenty-five hours. At Port aux Basques, immediate connection is made with the Newfoundland Government steamer "Caribou," running across the Cabot Strait to North Sydney in Nova Scotia, and the passage occupies eight hours.

During the winter months, from January 1st to May 31st, the cross-country rail and connecting steamer services are reduced to two connections weekly, viz, leaving St. John's on Mondays and Thursdays and arriving at Port aux Basques on Tuesdays and Fridays respectively. The S.S. Caribou also conforms to this schedule, leaving Port aux Basques on Tuesdays and Fridays, arriving at North Sydney on Wednesdays and Saturdays.... The cost of the combined steamer and rail trip between North Sydney and St. John's is $20.00 one way and $35.00 for the round trip. The cost of meals en route is extra. The sleeper rate between St. John's and Port aux Basques is $5.00 for a lower berth and $4.00 for an upper berth. The cost of the drawing room is $15.00. Stateroom accommodation on the S.S. Caribou is included in the through ticket.... The wider scope for the use of a car in Newfoundland is confined to the east coast, in the St. John's area, and there are many who ship their cars through from North Sydney to St. John's via the railroad in order to enjoy the motoring attraction of Avalon Peninsula. The railway has special freight cars to handle automobiles, and a rate of $50.00 is quoted for transportation of a car, when accompanied by a passenger holding a return ticket, from North Sydney to any rail point on the Newfoundland Railway system and back to North Sydney. Transportation arrangements can be made through the Newfoundland Railway Agent at North Sydney.

The original railroad was laid out on the narrow gauge plan and it has not been altered. Considerable improvements and additions to rolling stock, equipment and road bed have been made in recent years, particularly since the system has come under control of the Government, and up to date dining cars, sleepers and coaches of the same pattern, but on a smaller scale, as those used in Canada and the United States, make travel on the Newfoundland railway comfortable and agreeable.

The main line is operated all the year through, though for a few weeks during the winter months the service on some of the branch lines is discontinued. The railway is the sole method of overland transportation across the island from east to west, for as yet no highways enable passage by vehicle from coast to coast.[28]

Fishing Days in Newfoundland, 1942

It would need the pen of a Thoreau properly to describe the delights of our camp life on the Humber. So far were we from the anxious haunts of men! For days and days no message from the outer world did or could reach us. Only the section man on the railway so many miles from us was in touch with the world and he only when one of the infrequent trains of the Reid Company came toiling its great engine bell through the forest or the tingling telegraph wires brought him a message. Whatever our sport during the day there was always at night the talk round the camp fire as its sparks flew upwards and its incense pervaded all the woodlands around.[29]

A Trainman's Memories, c. 1942

I remember the first trip (or run) that I made as a trainman, was from St. John's to Gander and return.... We were ordered for duty at seven o'clock at night, but did not depart until midnight, owing to having to wait for a locomotive on an incoming train.

We departed St. John's and ended up in Gander and after switching in the rail yard for several hours, returned to St. John's half starved and dead tired. We had been on duty continuously for approximately forty hours. After a rest period of ten hours, I was again called for duty.

Oh the lonely whistle of the train, how they stirred one, and it seemed that being a trainman on those trains would be far better than being in the highest office in the country.

More curves and reverse curves, which made you feel face to face with eternity, for it seemed impossible for the locomotive and cars to hold the rails, and you felt every hair on your head tingle at the roots, as your train screeched and jerked itself around those hair pin curves, straightened out, and readied itself for the next ones.

In the hot summer weather, the steel rails on the railroad expand, and if there is not enough space at the end of each rail, the expansion will cause the rails to form themselves into what is known as a "sunkink." I have witnessed several of those during my years on the railroad, and they were very dangerous to say the least.

For those who stretched the rules and were caught, they were disciplined or were dismissed by management for doing so. Prior to 1949, Newfoundland railway passenger trains developed a tradition of comfortable accommodations, efficient service and very dedicated employees....

Our little railway operated those trains for around 107 years, so we knew a little about it. Our passenger trains were killed by two things that hit us back in the 1950s, the jet liners and the Trans Canada Highway. It is now sad indeed and very touching to see the abandoned roadbed, which just a few short years ago had rung to youthful shouts and sounds of toil.[30]

Impressions of Railway Travel in Newfoundland, 1954

The railway is the only one of my acquaintance on which travel is so precarious that the safe arrival of a train is reported in the local paper just as in other lands the coming of a ship is recorded. The normal arrangement was that on three days in the week a train left St. John's for Cornerbrook [sic](the other terminus), and that three days in the week a train left Cornerbrook for St. John's. In the summertime this service operated with considerable regularity, but in the winter it was a very different matter and in bad weather a train might be as much as some days late.

The carriages were arranged on the American principle — a sort of tramcar with two tiers of bunks screened by curtains, behind which the sixteen occupants of each carriage undressed at night as best they could. Each coach, however, had a small separate compartment, known as a "drawing room," for four passengers, and we managed to reserve one of these for ourselves as the train was not full.[31]

A Journey in 1965

The train trip to St. John's from Grand Falls took fourteen hours, all night. It was a long night. I didn't sleep much. The bed was comfortable but how that train rocked, rolled and pummeled me! I was up. I was down. I was in and out of bed. I tried to read. I tried to sleep ... why in the world can't somebody do something about this? It all seemed so stupid. How could Newfoundland ever get tourists to ride such a rocky old thing ... but in spite of my irritation, I never got mad at The Train. Although it was violent and at times a little unreasonable, and always extremely noisy, it had a personality all its own. Even though I couldn't seem to cooperate with this creature, I found it interesting and challenging. Even in the dead of night.

The night on the train passed. Passengers at breakfast next morning were a bit groggy. Among the groggiest were those who had not stopped off en route, but had come straight through Port aux Basques. After breakfast everyone was happier. CNR couldn't afford new tracks. It could afford excellent meals at very low cost and fares had been reduced since Confederation in 1949.

We arrived in St. John's at 10:45 A.M. only ¾ hr. late. I was glad to get off the train.[32]

Memories of the Age of Steam

The most vivid of my early memories is of standing at Princeton station, where my father was station master, watching the Bonavista mixed disembark. When the engineer opened the throttle the locomotive spun its wheels in short bursts until it finally got the impossible mass of freight and passengers rolling. Since that time I have not experienced anything to match the magnificence of a steam locomotive, nothing that could convey that same feeling of sheer power. Man's technology has produced many wonders, but nothing can capture the imagination like the trains of my youth.

It was during my own career as a railwayman that the steam era came to an end. The Newfoundland Railway began to experiment with diesels in the 1940s. By the late 1950s the changeover to Diesel power was in full swing. Any railwayman could see the advantages: better mileage without requiring the frequent overhauls typical of the age of steam and coal. Yet, those of us who experienced the changeover were all touched by sadness, seeing one classic engine after another broken up for scrap.[33]

Appendix Two: To the Old Capitals by the New Way: Crossing the Ancient Colony by Rail, 1899–1900

On an evening in the early part of September we step on board the S.S. "Bruce," at North Sydney, Cape Breton, to take passage to Port aux Basques; a port at the southwest extremity of Newfoundland, close in beside Cape Ray.

We are apt to consider, by what we have believed good authority, that between Cape Breton and Port aux Basques lies the highway of the seas, over which only the daring and adventurous would care to journey. But here we are tonight confidently looking forward to a speedy and comfortable passage over the Cabot Straits; full of anticipation of what is to be learned of the land discovered four hundred years ago by him whose name these Straits bear.

We are now out upon this water, with the Gulf of St. Lawrence at our left, and the limitless expanse of the Atlantic, and the starry unknown, to our right. At eleven o'clock we seek our state-rooms, and find bright electric lights to show us that our rooms have all the appointments of the present century. And musing on what Cabot would think of all this were he journeying about these coasts again, we repose ourselves to rest.

The sea is smooth, and all the circumstances reconcile us to await in peace for whatever the fates have in store; and we are soon fast asleep.

At four in the morning — the very peep of day — we are awake, and immediately seek the deck, for we are nearing the coast, and do not want to miss the first sight of it.

A little more than two years ago we passed this way up the Straits, on a voyage from Liverpool to Montreal. We remember that on that day the fog was so dense that nothing was seen of the coast. How different this is! This glorious daybreak! The myriads of stars are still twinkling brightly overhead. In the east a radiant streak of red is extending landward and seaward, from a point to increased brilliancy. Soon we are able to trace the irregular rocky coast; following it around to the left, a view is obtained of the end of the mountain range which forms Cape Ray. Far out upon the end of its rocky point is the beacon-light, still faithfully at its good work of guiding the mariner.

The welcome harbinger of day is coming apace, and the streak in the east grows wider and more beautiful in colour. Gradually it is shaded delightfully from the dark yellow to the brilliant orange, while the rocky mountains by the coast assume all the shades of the lead colour by the water side, to the richest purple at their summits; blending all this glory with the splendour of the yellow sky above, and making it all a gorgeous picture. "The great beacon fire of the sun" burns out, the mountain tops are gilded, and the orchestra of the wilds begin to hum their welcome. The little homes by the sea — the village of Channel and the more scattered hamlets — sparkle in these first rays of the rising sun, as if they too were on fire, but that other beacon upon the rocks at the Cape has given up its effort.

It is indeed true that no atmosphere is so conducive as this for those marvelous gradations of colour which are dependant upon the peculiarly rare air of these latitudes. Mariners have told us before of the Gulf of St. Lawrence, and its brilliant sky effects, but the half could not be told. Would not a Ruskin exult in this!

The fleet, staunch ship bears us rapidly in by the coast; and now we are passing that beacon which marks the way to the entrance of Port aux Basques. In this beacon we find an interesting object, not only pleasing to the eye, but because it represents a structure from which issues at regular intervals, in stormy weather, a danger signal to anxious mariners by the coast; an automatic gun, which ever does its duty, whether the keeper be awake or sleeping. We are informed that this one, and the one on Cape Spear, near the entrance to St. John's harbour, are the only structures of the kind on this side of the Atlantic.

We glide smoothly and rapidly to our moorings, and thus ends a very pleasant and comfortable trip across the Cabot Straits.

Having passed through the formality of a customs entry, we find ourselves located on the "Cross Country Train." The only incident to disturb our serenity of mind during this usually trying ordeal is an attempt on the part of the "Bruce" luggage department to hoist our heavy trunk about thirty feet out of the hold of the ship to the wharf by the trunk strap, although we had simply placed it around the trunk as a safety, should the lock give way. They, it seemed, chose to consider it put there for their convenience. Fortunately, however, the strap broke before the trunk left its resting place. Nevertheless this is but a trifle, so must not disturb us thus early in our Cross Country experiences. We expect to enjoy them very much.

Our train (the "Bruce Train," or "Cross Country Train") is one that performs a large number of important functions, and in its own way is equipped for the various needs of a long journey, where little for comfort or convenience is supposed to be found at the stoppings. Its arrangements are peculiar. We note this fact in a general way during the few moments of our change from the boat to the train, and when starting off. For our attention is soon directed to the glimpses which we catch, as we move out upon our journey, of the great works of nature displayed here upon every side.

It is a unique country, — not to be forgotten, — although we have, to our regret, but a few instants to look at any particular picture. The rock and water scenes vary so constantly upon this irregular coast, and the road-way winds about in such a circuitous manner, that we find ourselves entertained by a veritable, ever-changing panorama.

A few miles to our left stretches out that extreme end of Cape Ray, where its light stands — that light so often eagerly looked for by the mariner who comes this way in his coursing up and down the gulf. Near us to the right is the lofty range of Ray Mountains, which extend far away into the interior of the island. Their towering rock peaks are landmarks, and give them in so many different aspects, and with such differing combinations between — one moment on the sands at the sea-side, then climbing the rock hill, and then a stretch of heath rolls between us. Now on our left are the broad waters of the gulf rolling their tidal way far beyond our vision.

Both on the 7th of last September, and on the 17th of January, we passed this way. Those were totally different seasons of the year, and now on our May trip something new will undoubtedly be afforded. About two miles out from Port aux Basques we passed that winter night in our sleeper, fast in a snow-drift — four months ago. We came to a stop about eight o'clock in the evening, and at nine o'clock in the morning we were still in the drift. The engine had gone on to Port aux Basques for help, and water, and coal. Close by us were the Ray Mountains; and quite near, the coast, where, before this snow blockade, the drifting sands had been blown upon the rail track, and had delayed the trains. Now squalls of snow were sweeping down from the mountains; but although it was a dark day, the kodak did its best, and thus a picture of a portion of the pinioned wreck is preserved.

Not far from here was the scene of the recent disaster, when a train was blown twenty feet from the track by one of the fiercest blasts known, which came down the Ray Mountain gorges.

These glimpses remind us that we are still by the coast. It is but a few instants only that we can have such assurances at any time, for the rocky points and massive barren islands are constantly cutting off the more extended vision.

What rocks! What sharp, unrelenting points pierce the sea! And then what perfect havens behind! It is indeed a wonderful piece of God's creation.

An hour has sped rapidly since our departure from Port aux Basques, and so far we have only seen rock and water scenery. But we are now making a plunge inland, to a wooded country. The birch, the spruce, and the larch are becoming stronger and more lofty, indicating that the soil must be deep and good, and not too rocky. And there are splendid — almost tropical — feathery ferns behind the deep evergreens. And what beautiful wild flowers in the open spaces! And what rich colouring! The wild weeds are almost gross in their immense, broad, dark leaves. Here Nature seems to be making a special effort to display the rich and the strong in vegetation. In the midst of these bounties and this luxuriant growth, this beautiful day, it is hard for one to believe the assertions made, that this is a country where, for a considerable portion of each year, existence for man is intolerable.

As we want to fix these particular spots upon our memory, and have something which will recall all this beauty to us again (so far we have found no railway literature to supply any clue to our whereabouts), we venture to ask the conductor, who is polite, and apparently very obliging, if he has anything in this line. With a beaming countenance of friendliness the good fellow produces a very long sheet of legal cap, with a typewritten time-table, giving the names of all the various stations upon the 548 miles of road over which we are to travel to reach St. John's. It is perused with much interest, for the names of the stations are quite new and strange, suggesting many conjectures as to their origin, and what circumstances made them a mark in the history of the country. And we devoutly hope that this history may be perpetuated through these very names.

This is a fine, elaborate time-table, which describes the chances of travel by the Newfoundland Railway. We are not pleased, however, with the liberty that someone has taken in altering so many of the names of the stations. It makes us wonder why people persist in changing the historic names of places, which commemorate events in the history of the country, to others of little or no importance, with apparently the one object of pleasing a fancy. Government might take a hand to advantage as regards this.

It is all copied in our diary, the while our conductor never makes the first intimation of a protest. No doubt he has already done much to entertain the weary traveller. We wish that we might make the whole trip with him. While we ruminate thus, we come to our first station,—there are forty-two of them by the route,—a twenty-nine hours' ride.

The first station is Codroy, twenty-nine miles out on our journey. It is properly named in one respect. This, we are told, is one of the spots where those who are looking for the future of the Colony expect the farmer to thrive. It is the most fertile vale on the whole Island.

The station of Codroy is a combination of station, residence, church, and school, and how much more we do not venture to assess. Upon the top is mounted a cross—so much the better for the station it is presumed. Horses and waggons are evidently owned here; for a little distance away, fastened to a tree, is a veritable horse with his waggon; the first out-fit of this kind which we have seen since landing.

Quite a number take the train at Codroy, about fifty labourers, and of particular note, a Roman Catholic priest, and a doctor. And now we begin again to become interested, and to enquire of those whom we have for travelling companions. This becomes an important matter where the passengers are quite limited in number, and may be one's familiar neighbour for several days. The conductor very complaisantly informs us that one of the owners and managers of the road is with us in another compartment; and also a distinguished gentleman and his wife — the gentleman a successful merchant, or merchant's confidential agent. There is also among us a gentleman bound for a point up the coast, who is in charge of a gang of men with appliances for conducting an oil enterprise. We are told that the railway magnate of the Island is a partner is this worthy adventure. The oil operator is communicative, and tells much about his experiences in former undertakings of this kind. He will soon leave us and take sail for further up the coast. We question how long it will be before his enterprise has passed the pioneer stage to become a subject for the clutches of a greedy Rockerfeller or his agent, out of which a fat margin may be made to bribe legislators, and hypnotise Divines.

We find the doctor an agreeable companion, and we are soon engaged in conversation with him. He came down the coast from Bay of Islands to Codroy in order to extend his professional services to a young man who had just been seriously injured by a railway accident. It seems a long distance, but doctors are as rare, or nearly so, as horses in this country.

First of importance among our travelling companions on one of these trips, which have gradually assumed the nature of holiday excursions, is the inspector and superintendent of the Church of England schools of the Colony. He appears a very intelligent gentleman, an agreeable companion, and an authority on Colonial affairs, of which information is given in the most opportune time. Another gentleman is from the eastern part of Nova Scotia, and bound for Bell Isle on business in connection with the iron mines of that mineral Isle. And another is, with his family, from Michigan, and the Lake Superior mineral region prospecting on the Whitney areas in this country lying near the Harbor Grace district. Another is from British Columbia, where he has been prospecting the Seal Fishery of the Pacific. Besides these, there are two Newfoundlanders just returning from a journey to Europe. Then in another car is a Newfoundlander who served in the American army at Cuba in the late war. We saw him only a few days ago marching with his regiment — the eighth — on its arrival home. So our conversation is of necessity quite varied, as the hours of the trip are passed. This is another illustration of how this island of the fishery banks — in the midst of the icebergs of the north — men of such wide experiences and varied pursuits journey.

At forty-seven miles from Port aux Basques the clergyman of the Church of England parts from us. He has six miles to walk in order to reach the next scene of his priestly labours.

It is now ten o'clock, and we are stopping to take water for the engine in the depths of a fine hardwood forest. This would be a choice spot for the settler to make his start; building his cabin exactly where the train must stop for water. Here are stumps of trees lately felled which measure three feet in diameter. We leave our car while the train stands to pluck a leaf from a huge weed. The trefoil spreads out eighteen inches by eighteen inches.

A start is made. It is gently up grade. We have learned that our train travels up and down hill a great deal; all around the hills, too, so that it appears sometimes as though our engine must be turned about and returning. We have not gone very far before the train is brought to a standstill, but not by the will of the train officials. We cannot proceed, so back the whole goes for a good start from the hill we left behind. Off again, and up to the opposite hill-top at full speed, and soon we are whiling through most delightful scenery. At the right, now and again, are distant, but fine views of the lofty Ray Mountains, mostly immense bare rocks, naked as when first thrown into these great winnows; sometimes with deep gulches or ravines indenting their massive sides, where a stunted soft wood, and bush life are seen. Now and then a lake is passed, resting by the base of these towering rocks. All the lakes are called ponds here.

As the run is made beside Robinson's Brook — or River — and then upon a high elevation farther on, there is a fine view of the vale of the Robinson District, of the sweep of land lying beyond, and of the range of rocky hillocks far out by the sea. By our track the soil appears deep and fertile, and not too stony for strength, the huge boulders scattered through this section of the country being the only apparently useless element.

We are now told that all must now take a look at the "Horseshoe," for we are at Fischel's. The "Horseshoe" is the name for a very decided turn in the road, and we twist and turn in a horseshoe shape by a bridge suspended above the tree tops around and over a deep gulch, at the bottom of which is Fischel's Brook. As we sweep down by the side of one nearly perpendicular mountain, we look across the deep, beautifully timbered gully, and see the picturesque bridge over which we are to pass, and swung around, parallel to us, is the road by which we are to climb the side of another mountain. As we rise up again, we look back at the bridge we have crossed, and gaze upon the white gypsum face of the mountain upon the opposite side of the veritable abyss — as grand a bit of scenery as we have ever looked upon.

Nearing Bay St. George the land about the road is not so good as that which we have been passing, and the rock hills are good as that which we have been passing, and the rock hills are not far away, lying like piles of huge boulders one upon the other.

Sandy Point village is seen in the distance. It is situated upon a long, sandy peninsula — quite an island, in fact, as it appears today. It was expected that our train would transact a large business here. On enquiry it is found that the people of this section use little merchandise; it is said that what one dollar per week will purchase is quite enough of the outsider's goods for the requirements of the average citizen. The miserable looking creatures trying to handle the freight just landed demonstrates the fact that the inhabitants of this vicinity lack the necessaries let alone the luxuries of life.

There is no station at Sandy Point, not even a platform, and everything is most primitive. The oil venturer's goods are pitched off into a deep ditch; some of the heavy pipes are almost lost to view in the soft soil, and one looks as though broken in two. It will be no small matter to convey these heavy iron pipes over miles of country where horses cannot travel.

"Bay of Islands next," so the brakeman cries. As the physician has arranged for us to be let off at the first siding upon the Bay, we gather up our parcels and stand waiting our chance to alight, for we are running at break-neck speed down an awful hill — but what scenery!

Approaching our landing place at Bay of Islands the scenery becomes grand. Blomidon rising over two thousand feet, stands conspicuous above everything; but as one sweeps around Mount Moriah, and catches a view of the Bay lying almost beneath them, a distance of five or six hundred feet, the high mountains by the opposite shore but two or three miles away, the pretty villages, and churches, and the shipping at the base of the almost perpendicular formation close by the water, one has indeed a delightful picture.

The passage down Mount Moriah is as pretty as ever. A stop is made for a moment just where we first landed that delightful day last September.

Again we are off, and this time a passenger is left behind. What a lovely place to be lost in! We almost envy him. To his utter amazement, the train has started without the customary half-hour to hour's notice. He is completely bewildered, but finally runs and grasps the forward part of the cattle car at our rear. It being a down grade, the speed is high and although he protests against it, he is forced to let go and is left behind.

Either the man's faith in his own ability to match the "Cross Country" train is great, or he hopes more from the accommodating character of this train than its name implies — express, for he is seen for more than a mile giving us chase.

A dog drawing a boy upon a "slide," followed us for a long time last winter out from Sandy Point station. Evidently these people know something of how they, with their powers of locomotion, compare with us.

It was here at Carter's we stopped for four hours when on our cross-country trip last winter to change cars, to take water, and to take coal. The very necessary preparations for another run were then all attended to in the most deliberate and methodical manner, and one thing at a time, just as we were told to do things by those of experience when we were children.

On that winter's day we had plenty of time for snap-shots of this delightful scenery. The skating upon the Bay was then very good; our parlour-car occupants availed themselves of this excellent opportunity for having a turn. We pictured them in the very act. How will it be this time?

Our unfortunate traveller has caught up to us — it was only four and a half miles. He expresses great indignation at the conductor and threatens to expose the whole circumstance to "Mr. Reid."

All breaks are pressing to their utmost; are we to go plunging into the sea off a huge rock? We have whirled past our intended "stop off." But at last we do slacken speed and in quick time are by the roadside, with our half-dozen pieces of luggage scattered up and down the track for about fifty yards. There is no station, no station master, and the train has gone on; we would have been in a sorry plight had not the doctor helped us in our perplexity.

And with this sudden an precipitous landing we end our first chapter on railroading in Newfoundland. It was three days before we were able to get our luggage together for another ride.

The scenery by the Humber River for several miles from its estuary is indeed grand. The train is skimming along by one of its perpendicular mountainous banks, which reach at times to nearly a thousand feet in height. As we look ahead by a turn, and catch a glimpse of the way we must travel, there seems no escape from an awful plunge down by the rock side into the river immediately below.

It was indeed a clever stroke of ingenuity and enterprise which pushed this railway through these tremendous wildernesses (piled in almost inaccessible heaps of towering rocks, ravines, gorges, and precipices), and across the Colony. It would seem to the stranger an impossible task, so remote is it from all the necessary implements for such a development; yet this is only in keeping with the way the people of Newfoundland have battled with obstacles all through history.

Apparently we are expected to take turns watching the progress of our luggage, as we see it swaying about on the flat car behind. And it proves to be a constant excitement. Now the word goes around that our mail clerk is missing. He is not seen upon his mail bags. Was he left behind at Bay of islands? Has he fallen off his "postal flat car office"? What has become of the registered letters? Who knows?

And now it is reported that bags are lost, and back we go. Whose bags are they? That's the question; and how many more have been left at other times? We must have a look. After a mile's run back they are caught up. Only mail bags, after all.

Imperfect as our train service may be, we vastly enjoy the trip, and will always be glad that we have known this titan Island in all its primitive conditions, and we have witnessed the brave struggles, and supreme efforts of those who strive to bring this isolated colony under the advantages of other lands.

At 2.40 p.m. we are travelling by Deer Lake — a long narrow body of water with a pebbly bottom — eighteen miles in length, and a mile or two wide. The River Humber flows in at one end, and out at the other. The railway runs along by nearly the whole length of this lake; and not a sign of a settlement is to be seen; yet it looks to be a fine district for a community of farmers — the land so rich, and the situation so fine. Both sides of the lake are densely covered with a tall slim growth of spruce, just such a growth as farmers in some countries "up along" would like to find when they went to the woods for poles, in the days of worm fences.

At 3.45 p.m. we are at South Brook, and here we meet the passenger train from St. John's, which is an event. We exchange mails and current news. Our postal clerk gives us every chance to get stamps, and mail our letters. The good fellow runs all the way through the 548 miles, it is said without sleep, and is required to attend to the receipt and delivery of the mails at all the stations. We think he might have half a night's sleep, and possibly do that too? We eagerly grasp the newspapers for "news," and behold, they bear the dates of the last week of August and this is the ninth of September. Our world is truly very much by itself.

At 4.10 p.m. we roll into Grand Lake station, finding only the station, two shanties, and two residents — composing the whole town which has, in fact, turned out to meet us.

The conductor tells us that we may see deer [caribou] today or tonight; this is the region where they are found, and he has often seen them. Indeed, in this season three have been run down and killed by the trains. He himself has seen as large an herd as sixty running from an approaching train. And we are also told of six seen running from a train that came this way but a week ago. All this proving to us the wildness of the country we are now passing through.

This narrow neck of the great straggling island, lying between the head-waters of the Humber and the Lake, and the deep bays at the northeast on the other side, is the route of the deer in the autumn, from their summer feeding ground in he north, to the treeless and mossy rocks of the south — their winter ground. In the spring they go north again. On the first appearance of winter they gather in great herds, from five hundred to a thousand, and away they go.

We are on time at Sandy Pond Stream — "Sandy Bottom." This stream flows into Grand Lake, which in its turn flows into Deer Lake, and that into the Humber, and so on to the sea. We are off again shortly, and have not gone far when we see indications of civilized life, and judge we must be approaching an important station.

We are now at the Junction — this name has been changed to "Howley Station," we believe.

At 4 p.m. we are at Howley, running exactly on schedule time, — except that it is the wrong day by twenty-four hours, — and here we wait another hour for our engine to recuperate, as it is reported to have given out seriously. However, after a time it is patched up, or another one secured, and we are on our way once more.

Shortly after leaving Howley, someone sees Caribou, and now we are told to look toward the woods at our right, which we do, and are rewarded, for about one hundred yards away we see four white caribou trotting from us as we have seen cattle do at the approach of a train, but with heads higher in the air. They stop for a second just as we get opposite to them, to give us the attention our importance deserves, as disturbers of the peace to the denizens of the forest, and then disappear into the woods at a rapid trot. A good shot from our train could easily have felled one of them. In all nine were seen.

The meeting of the trains today is of more than ordinary interest, for now we shall know something more of the condition of the road over which we are to travel to our destination. Deep snow at the Topsails — ninth of May — is the report. The snow seen on the cow-catcher of the approaching train from the east fully confirms this interesting report. But we thoroughly enjoy the novelty.

To our right are the much talked of coal deposits, owned by the Reids. They are worked by Mr. Reid, and the coal is used upon this railway. We secure a lump from a loaded car upon the track near us to examine it. It does not seem very good, but experts say it will be better farther down. There is plenty of this coal within five miles from the main track. If it proves good, it will be of great value to the Island.

At this point we stop to take water, which is led from a stream forming a pretty fall from a perpendicular height of over two hundred feet. The leader is so constructed that the fireman can turn the connection on or off without leaving his engine.

And now we pass through a most miserable country, bogs that cannot be drained, and rocks that cannot be cleared away — miles and miles of it. And after this a grand scene. Far off, to our left, is another long lake — Sandy Point Lake. We appear to be elevated four or five hundred feet above it. Where at one "eye sweep" there seems to be ten miles of lake within our reach, and miles and miles beyond of forest, wilderness and rock. What a grand view it is!

At 5.45 we are working up a very steep grade; it is as much as our engines can manage. We are approaching The Topsails — the highest, wildest, most rugged, and coldest part of the Colony. Far ahead is a great mountain range of solid rock, and farther still, in the distance, seem great plateaus — also of bare rock — surrounded by lumpish hills of the same.

Three conical peaks attract our attention, ten or more miles away. As they are seen now they look like the figures of couchant lions.

And again we travel by lakes, rivers, snow, and ice, upon a vast scale. For we are at the highest elevation on the island, and the view for many miles is unobstructed, except by The Topsails, which this evening appear in shape like huge rounded sugar-loafs. They tower above us many hundred feet, and yet we are told that this is 1800 feet above the sea. Notwithstanding, there are cuttings for our roadway here, and beside us for a good distance we have, at times, snow above the tops of the cars. It is very novel and to be enjoyed, but not for long, as it is decidedly colder.

Our grade is now far down toward the bay coming in from the north. The rapidity with which we rise and descend is shown us by a gentleman traveller, who has an altitude barometer which gauges the height and depth of our descent.

As we wind our way up by the side of one of these mountains of rock, we find that the conical heaps, which verily pierce the clouds, are on either side of our track. We can also see, in the distance to the right, the Fore Topsail, and the Main Topsail; and on the left, towering right above us as we pass them, the Gaff Topsail, and the Mizzen Topsail.

They constantly change form as we watch them, until they are finally lost to view, after having seen them for over two hours. This must indeed be a trying place for winter railroading; this land of never ending rock!

A short time after leaving The Topsails we arrive at Quarry (now Cabot Station). This is quite a settlement, with low log and earth shanties, and canvas tents. Quarry takes its name from the industry of the place — the quarrying of granite, which is indicated by the large piles of granite cubes lying by the track, and which prove to be for "Mr. Reid's" street improvements in the city of St. John's.

As night closes in before we reach West Brook, Joe Glades Pond, Badger's Brook, and Bushy Pond, we do not see all of this section of the country that we wish, but make the best use of our chances.

Notre Dame Bay is the junction with a short road of about twenty miles to Burnt Bay. This is one of the greatest thoroughfares for the steamers plying about the numerous bays at the northeast part of the Colony. In the winter all these bays are frozen over, when the only conveyance is by sleighs over the ice, which mode of travel is often difficult and dangerous. But the summer tour through this part of the country is very delightful, for the scenery is magnificent; by this way one may also reach the rich copper mines of Bett's Cove and Tilt Cove.

At Glenwood, the first important station after leaving Notre Dame Junction, we cross the Gander River. This is another of the large rivers of the Colony. The Gander takes its rise far to the southwest, beside some conical mounts called Partridge Berry Hills, not more than fifty miles from Hermitage Bay on the southern coast. After running its course about one hundred miles, it drops into the long, narrow lake called Gander lake, into which a number of other rivers and brooks flow, while the Gander rushes on, past Glenwood and our track, away to the sea with all the united force of these rivers.

At Benton, twenty-six miles from Glenwood, is Soulis Brook, over which the railway crosses. This is another centre of a lumbering enterprise. Large piles of lumber are passed. On enquiry it is found that they belong to "Mr. Reid." Passing on to Gambo, Alexander Bay, and Terra Nova, some considerable tracts of fairly good land are seen, but much of it is useless for tree or plant life.

At Gull Pond the train comes to a standstill. The engine has given out, and as we apparently must stay here an indefinite time, all make the best of the situation. A large party is put out on the lake trying the skating. We must have passed thousands of acres of the most perfect ice in the last two or three hours — smooth as a mirror. Another party is looking for berries that may have escaped destruction by frost. Finally, however, an engine from St. John's comes to our relief, and we move on our way.

At "Come by Chance Station" is the overland path, or "patie" to the head of Placentia Bay, and the site of a large pulp manufacturing business. Arrived at Tickle Harbour, the interesting discovery is made that we are travelling over a very narrow isthmus, with glimpses of Placentia Bay on the right, and then of Trinity Bay on the left. The track is now elevated upon a high ridge between these waters, and the scenery becomes varied and fine.

Placentia Junction takes its name from the fact that here the Cross Country Road connects with the road which runs between the present capital, St. John's, and Placentia, which was the capital set up by the French, and was thus occupied during a term of dual occupancy of Newfoundland by the French and English.

Ferryland was the English capital long before St. John's was known as such. Government was established in Ferryland by George Calvert, the first Lord Baltimore, who colonized that part of the Colony known as Avalon. He was later founder of Maryland, and the city of Baltimore.

The next station after leaving Placentia Junction is Whitbourne Junction, where a line branches off to Harbor Grace, and Carbonear, the two largest outports of Newfoundland. They are respectively twenty-four and thirty-six miles from Whitbourne, which is the only inland town in the Colony.

Soon after leaving Whitbourne we reach Brigus Junction. From here runs another branch of the railway to the seaport, Brigus. Carbonear, Harbour Grace, and Brigus are all important fishing stations, situated by the small harbours around the larger water — Conception Bay.

At Manuels and at Topsails, the last stations of importance before arriving in St. John's, the scenery is very beautiful. Here are rushing rivers, and pretty brooks; their bold, craggy banks winding among rich sylvan glades, and jutting tree-faced hillocks. Here one sees fine specimens of matted solid blocks of the typical Newfoundland spruce grove — so thick and firm that they might be walked upon, so closely intertwined that no storm could penetrate them. And then there are the pretty opens, where dew and rain and sun can have their way; where the flocks can find food. And there are the dingles and the dells, through which are the glimpses of the sea. It is really enchanting today in its quiet beauty, and makes one long to choose some fair, gentle, summer day to ramble about the beautiful spots without care or thought, except for the joy of it all.

The new approach to St. John's, at the end of the Cross Country journey, brings us to another striking feature of the peculiar Colony. On every side is seen what appears to be a very prosperous section of country. Indeed, from some distance back one is struck with the indications of thrift in agricultural matters.

— Elliott, James Rupert. *To the Old Capitals by the New Way.*
Boston: J. R. Elliott, 1900.

Appendix Three: Poetry and Song

Hall's Bay Line

You rambling boys of pleasure,
Come join me in my song,
With me combine your muses nine,
It won't detain you long.
In vocal strains your voices raise,
Like birds in summer time,
That sing their songs with liberty,
Away by Hall's Bay Line.

One morning as I walked abroad,
Just at the break of day,
The early thrush perched on each bush,
Melodious sung its lay.
The sun sent forth its tinted rays,
With grandeur most sublime,
To sip the dew, where lilies grew,
Away by the Hall's Bay Line.

The verdant leaves bedecked the trees,
Beneath the sunny glade;
And opening buds, their tiny heads,
Submissive homage paid.
While twice ten thousand humming birds,
Their notes so clear define,
In raptures swell, o'er brook and dell,
Away by Hall's Bay Line.

The angler with his hook and line,
Glides through the sunny nooks,
Enamored with those dazzling scenes,
By babbling, purling brooks.
To catch the trout that bask and play,
In Indian Summer time,
In placid streams, there most serene,
Away by Hall's Bay Line.

The sportsman with his dog and gun,
Join in the eager chase,
To hunt the deer that frolic there,
Beneath that moss-clad waste.
Or roving through some lovely copse,
Or down some deep ravine,
They are trapped by wily man,
Away by Hall's Bay Line.

— Nickolaus Peddle, c. 1908[1]

The Newfoundland Railway

I hear, I hear, I hear a lot of noise
'Twixt pressmen, lawyers and political hobbledehoys,
About this railway line that passed through our isle:
Good luck to it, I say, may Heaven on it smile.

Chorus:
Shoo fly don't worry us;
Ho boys we'll get our rights
Ho boys don't flurry us,
For we belong to the Railwayites.

Ding, dong! ding, dong! Here the engine comes along;
Puff, puff! ding, dong! from Harbor Grace into St. John's,
Ding, dong! puff, puff! let the Heaven's shine or lower!
Off we go, hurrah, my boys at forty knots and hour.

'Twill populate our isle, 'twill open up the soil,
'Twill give a fair day's wage unto a fair day's toil,
'Twill work our copper mines, 'twill search for the ore;
In short, 'twill do for us, what was ne'er done before.

All praise upon the man who saw his country's need,
All blessing upon the man who bolsters merchant greed;
A blessing those attend who gained for us the prize,
The other thing attend who voted otherwise.

— Dr. Dearin, c. 1885[2]

Newfoundland Railway Guide

The "Depot" is located where
Fort William long did stand,
And Trains leave here at stated times,
At the Word of command.

The next station is called "St. Ann's,"
About seven miles from town,
At "Irvine" they do sometimes stop
When Mr. Boyd gets down.

"Topsail! Topsail!" next," Liddy says,
And passengers away;
Spence shouts the same at two o'clock
When he comes from "The Bay."

This station, an important one,
Is all the summer long;
Many St. John's folks here reside
And here the weak get strong.

At "Manuel's" in summer time
To spend the day folks stay;
Next "Kelligrews" by the sea side,
Is a place that will pay.

Then "Seal Cove" is a seaside stand
To suit the fishermen
And "Duffs" also by the seaside
For fishermen again.

At "Brien's" they stop if they have freight,
But "Holyrood" is near,
A paying station this will be
As Western folks come here.

Then round the arm to "Woodford's" go,
Where folks from Harbor Main,
Themselves and freight have to unship
And come to meet the Train.

To "Salmon Cove" we spin along,
And here we leave the shore,
"Brigus Junction" and "Hodge Water"
What's for these places lower.

"The Junction" as its name implies
Is where the Branch line joins,
That comes from Harbor Grace, from whence
We hope to see branch lines.

There Mrs. Davenport you'll find,
Who can accommodate
A friend, and also by any one
Who'll pay for bed and "*mate.*"

And from the Junction soon we hope
To see the Line extend
To Hall's Bay, then across the Isle
And at some Gulf port end.

A Branch line is now being made
To Placentia's Old Port,
Where in Terra Nova's young days,
The French held Town and Fort.

At "Broad Cove" and at "New Harbor"
The traffic will increase,
Bay Roberts via Spaniard's Bay,
From "Tilton" soon you'll reach.

At the West end of "Harbor Grace"
The Station you will see,
Where Quinton is the Agent
And as busy as a Bee.

Two Engineers well trained we have,
T. Brine, and Trainor see,
Two Coughlans' with the mails in charge,
For safe delivery.

For brakesmen we have trusty men,
Whitehead and Howlett too,
And others, so that each train has
A full and careful crew.

And then for Track master we have
T. Connors kind but true,
He'll have the line in order kept
By section men all through.

And then for Engineer in Chief
We have a Mr. Stiene,
He has a shop and staff of men
for all work of the Line.

The Station Agents at their posts
Attentive you will find,
And skilled in flashing messages
Of any length and kind.

Then success to the "N" railway,
May it the owners pay;
Three cheers for Evans and all here
Who got it under way.

— W. Swansborough, 1885[3]

Arrah go on!

The Fogo Girl on the Street Car
Oh I met a fair charmer that came up from Fogo,
To look for a place in a Water Street Store,
And being a stranger she struck on yours truly,
Got down on her knees and did humbly implore.
We got on the street car and went for a ramble,
We went up the town and came down again
To the candy-man's store for five cents worth of suckers,
We then went inside to get out of the rain.

Chorus:
Arrah go on, you're only joking,
Let me alone, you're only teasing,
Behave your simple fooling;
Arrah go way, go off, go weddy, go way
Go weddy, go weddy, go on.

I searched everywhere for my sweetheart next morning,
I walked up and down till I nearly was dead,
When I saw her at last giving change at a counter,
Where the railway runs up with the balls overhead.
I blushed with delight and my blood it ran warm,
I then got my nerve and I spoke out quite bold.
When I saw a sly blush from her eye in the corner,
Be off we you now, sure I know you of old.

We promised to go for a walk Sunday evening,
I walked up and down till my feet they were sore,
Sure I knew very well she was only deceiving,
And my eyes they were strained peeping through the door
When at last she appeared and she dressed like a monkey,
She pushed me aside and she walked very fast
Linked on to a fellow I took for a flunky,
A calico clerk with his trousers half mast.

— James Murphy, c. 1910[4]

The Wreck of the Steamship *Ethie*

Come all you true countrymen, come listen to me.
A story I'll tell you of the S. S. *Ethie*,
She being the steamboat employed on our shore,
To carry freight, mail, and passengers down on the Labrador.

On the tenth of December, as you all well may know,
In the year nineteen nineteen, on her last trip did go;
Where she leaved Daniel's Harbour about four P.M.,
With a strong breeze from the south'ard, for Cow Head did steam.

The glass indicated a wild ranging storm,
And about nine o'clock the storm did come on.
With the ship's husband on board, the crew had no fear;
Captain English gave orders straight to Bonne Bay to steer.

At first to the storm the brave ship gave no heed,
Until at length it was found she was fast losing speed,
And the great waves all round her like great mountains did rise,
And the crew all stood staring with fear in their eyes.

The orders went round to preserve for their life,
For the ship she is doomed and it's perish we might;
But still there is hope; there is one brave man on board
Who says he can guide her safely on to the shore.

Walter Young been our purser, as you may understand,
Volunteered for to guide her safely in to the land;
John Gullage, our first mate, bravely stood to the wheel;
Captain English gave orders and all worked with a will.

Up off Marin's Point about one o'clock,

Through bravery and courage, she escaped every rock,
And the people on the shore saw the ship in distress;
All rushed to the spot for to help do their best.
And then we were landed in a rude boatswain's chair,
Taken in by the people and treated with care;
We stayed on the point until the storm it was o'er,
And the brave little *Ethie* lay standing on shore.
O, what of the fright, the exhaustion and the cold,
The depth of my story will never be told!
And all you brave fellows gets shipwrecked on the sea,
You think of the fate of the S. S. *Ethie*.

— Maude Roberts Simmonds, 1920[5]

Appendix Four: Connections Far and Wide in 1900

The Intercolonial Railway of Canada

The Intercolonial Railway enacts an important part in eastern communication. Starting from Montreal it extends to St. John, Halifax and the Sydneys, and embraces in its system more than 1,600 miles. It follows the course of the St. Lawrence River to the ancient city of Quebec, includes the interesting Maritime Provinces of New Brunswick, Prince Edward Island and Nova Scotia, to all of which it affords a good service.

The scenery along its line embraces a wide range of attractions. The picturesque St. Lawrence, the romantic Saguenay and the famous salmon and trout fishing region of the Metapedia Valley. This wild and beautiful country is steadily growing in popularity and as its surpassing charms shall become more generally known as well as the ease with which it can be reached by the Intercolonial, it is sure to attract a large and an increasing tide of tourist travel.

Prince Edward Island, with its fertile meadows, the many beautiful farming sections and pleasant scenes of Nova Scotia are followed by the antique beauties of Cape Breton and the charming Bras d'Or lakes....

The Intercolonial connects at North Sydney with the elegant S.S. "Bruce" for Newfoundland, thus giving excellent communication with that ancient colony, which is becoming, with the completion of the Newfoundland Railway, a popular resort.

The Intercolonial's imperial vesitbule trains, just placed in service represent the most recent and the highest attainments in modern railway travel. The coaches composing these trains are elaborately fitted up, and with the full complement of drawing-room, dining-room and sleeping cars, are practically an elegant hotel in motion. Here one may enjoy every comfort and luxury, and at the same time be pleasantly transported through a lovely country and behold ever-changing views of its charming scenes.[1]

Canadian Pacific Railway: The Great Transcontinental System

The tourist may now leave St. John's, Newfoundland, the extreme eastern point of the continent, and proceed, with but a single short break of ninety-three miles in railway travel, until he reaches the Canadian Pacific Line, which conveys him over its fine road to the extreme western boundary. Here, by boarding one of its magnificent steamships, he may pursue his journey to the Orient.

The Canadian Pacific Railway is the pioneer of a wonderful development, It has carried the standard of civilization, in defiance of great natural barriers, to the remotest confines of the continent, and has transformed the wilderness into the abodes of a prosperous people. It is in this wise that a great public enterprise becomes a most potent force in the progress of mankind in the peaceful arts....[2]

Maine Central Railroad

The Maine Central Railroad embraces points of large manufacturing and commercial importance, as well as some of the most interesting resorts in the country. Bar Harbor and the entire Maine coast, with summer resorts on almost every projecting cape and placid bay ... Portland, the gem city of Casco Bay; Lewiston, the great cotton manufacturing city; Augusta, the beautiful capital city; Bangor, the important lumbering centre ... Its Canadian and maritime relations are of the most comprehensive kind.

In the case of the latter it affords communication with the remote East and its numerous interesting points, which are at the present time attracting increasing attention....

All the places on which we have so briefly touched may be visited en route to Newfoundland, and afford a pleasant diversion on a trip to that far eastern country, from which it is but a day's journey to Labrador, the Land of the Midnight Sun.[3]

Boston & Maine Railroad

The Boston and Maine Railroad is so intimately related to the industrial, commercial and social affairs of New England, that any new opening for business is of great import. At present it traverses Maine, New Hampshire, Vermont and Massachusetts, affording for each and all an admirable service.

The new field of activity and enjoyment to which the Boston and Maine opens the way is the Island of Newfoundland, which has during the past season attained an unwonted popularity by the completion of the trans-insular railway. Leaving Boston by the Boston and Maine, the traveler may enjoy an entire Newfoundland rail journey, broken only by a short trip of seven hours by an elegant steamship. All the coast scenery of Maine, with views of its many thriving towns, the quaint scenery of the Province of

New Brunswick and Nova Scotia, including the Lake Bras d'Or section of Cape Breton, may be enjoyed on the route. At North Sydney, in Cape Breton, the S.S. "Bruce," a fine ship built for the service, conveys passengers to Port-aux-Basques, where a train completely equipped with buffet service and sleeping coaches is waiting to carry the tourist to St. John's, the chief city of the island. The journey affords views of rare scenic beauty, embracing sea views, lakes, forests and mountains. The variety of charming natural aspects lends peculiar interest to the trip, and affords a new and a delightful experience.

When the attractions of this interesting island shall be known, it will become a popular resort for those seeking the rare and the beautiful in nature.[4]

New York, New Haven & Hartford Railroad

An interesting country has just been opened to the outside world by the completion of the Newfoundland Trans-Insular Railway. This great work has, by persistant enterprise and by a large expenditure of capital, been successfully accomplished. Its beneficial effect upon the fortunes of the colony are beyond computation, while its bearing on the world at large is weighty and far-reaching. In connection with existing railway systems if forms a through line to New York, which is of the utmost importance.

The New York, New Haven and Hartford system, with its direct land routes and its fine steamboat lines, is a leading factor in this great chain. This system reaches all the chief points in Connecticut and Massachusetts. It is a model line in respect to its efficiency, and offers the most varied, pleasant and expeditious routes of travel. It embraces a territory which, for the variety and magnitude of its industrial operations, the density, wealth and intelligence of its population, is unsurpassed elsewhere in the country.[5]

Grand Trunk Railway

The Grand Trunk Railway System is known throughout the world as the Great International Tourist Route of America and the leading commercial highway between the Atlantic Ocean and the Great Lakes. The total mileage of this extensive system in 4,186 miles running through the most prosperous and thickly populated parts of Canada, and traversing the States of Maine, New Hampshire, Vermont, Michigan, Indiana and Illinois. Chicago is its western terminus where connection is made for all points in the Western and Northwestern States and the Pacific Coast. Its extreme Eastern terminus is Portland, Maine ... Other points reached on the main line are Montreal. The connecting point for passengers and tourists from Newfoundland and the maritime provinces.... All trains are equipped with the latest appliances for safety and speed. The only double track line in Canada.[6]

Appendix Five: Miscellaneous

The Longest Train Yet, 1895

It was a peculiar looking train that ran between Manuel's and Topsail to-day. A special lumber train from Whitbourne, under the care of Mr. Arthur Noble, preceded the regular by some minutes, but found her engine overtaxed in attempting to ascend the steep grade between the two stations. Meanwhile the regular train gained upon its brother in distress, and uniting with it, attempted to force it up the grade, and at the same time to pull up its own, by no means light load of combined freight and humanity. After one or two ineffectual attempts the sinuous monster breasted the hill, and proud of its victory, steamed triumphantly into Topsail Station where the friend in need parted from its friend in deed, but only for a time. A little further on a repetition of the trouble occurred. This time the engine of the regular was detached and the lumber train backed by it was pushed on to more level grades and less greasy rails. Then Driver Candow came back, and after backing down grade some distance, the regular was pulled up and started once more on the homeward stretch, arriving here about 3.15 P.M.[1]

Sunday Trains, 1898

I notice in to-day's issue of your valuable paper that the Methodist Conference sent a deputation to the C. of E. Synod requesting united action re protesting against the running of Sunday trains as proposed by R. G. Reid's new Time Table. Now I as a humble Churchman protest against this interference of our rights and privileges on the part of these two great religious bodies. The hard-working citizens who have no prospects of enjoying a mouthful of, fresh country air after the week's hard work and close confinement must not be deprived of this small luxury which they can only avail of on this one Day of Rest. I feel satisfied Mr. Editor, that in uttering this protest against any interference in running of Sunday trains I voice the sentiments of hundreds of Churchmen in this city and a good many Methodists as well. In every part of the civilized world there are Sunday excursions by land and water which are gladly availed of by all classes and creeds. I think the Messsrs. Reid ought to be eulogized for granting us this great blessing.[2]

There has been a great deal of angry and, perhaps, unnecessary discussion going on recently in reference to the Reids running railway trains on Sunday and a certain sanctimonious writer, under the nom de plume of "Watchman," one of those creatures who strive to make silly people believe that it is sinful even to kill a fly on Sunday, has been writing a lot of arrant rot and nonsense on the subject that inclines one to believe that he is nothing but a canting hypocrite, a class of men which we already have too many in this community. If it is such a great sacrifice to run trains on Sunday as he would fain make silly mortals believe, I would simply ask him how is it that up to this time such an awful violation of the Sabbath, as he terms it, has escaped the attention of all the great dignitaries of both the United States and Canada. In these great countries trains run incessantly on Sunday; and the people there can compare morally, socially and religiously with us at any time, and on the whole are far more civilized; nor is there any attempt made to impose such foolish and arbitrary restrictions on a people's conscience as 'Watchman' would like to see carried into effect down here. 'Watchman's' ideas are those of a Dedimus Dunderhead, and are too crude for the people of this enlightened 19th century. There is no sincerity about him, to put it mildly he is only a religious fraud and humbug, and silly is the man to be guided by his counsels.[3]

Air Whistle Signals, 1906

In using the air whistle signal, pull directly down on the cord for one full second, and allow two full seconds to elapse between each pull.

In starting a train the air whistle should not be used. The signal to start should always be given by hand or lamp.

Two blasts of the air whistle when the train is running, is the signal to stop at once.

Two blasts of the air whistle when the train is standing, is the signal to call in the flagman.

Three blasts of the air whistle when the train is running, is the signal to stop at the next station, and must be acknowledged by one long and one short sound of the engine whistle.

Three blasts of the air whistle when the train is standing, is the signal to back the train.

Four blasts of the air whistle when the train is running, is the signal to reduce speed.

Four blasts of the air whistle when the train is standing, is the signal to test brakes.

Five blasts of the air whistle is the signal to release brakes, or to release a sticking brake while running.

Six blasts of the air whistle when the train is running, is the signal that more steam is required for heating the cars.

When one blast of the air whistle is heard while the train is running, the engineman must immediately ascertain if the train is parted, and, if so, be governed by Rules 17 and 114.

Note

The engineman of passenger and freight trains leaving a terminal, or at any point where the makeup of the train has been changed, must, after starting and before running 1000 feet, apply the air brake sufficiently to know that the train air brakes are in good working order.

Conductors and enginemen will be held equally responsible to see that the terminal standing test is made on all train air brakes before leaving terminal, or at any point where the makeup has been changed between the air brake cars, and the engineman must be kept advised of the number of air brake cars put in and in working order.[4]

Useful Information, 1929

Ticket Offices—Passengers are requested to procure tickets at ticket offices and in ample time to enable proper checking of baggage. When tickets are procured on train the Conductor will collect ten (10) cents additional to regular fare.

Tickets, Direction Honored—Tickets of all classes are good for passage only in the direction printed.

Children—Children not exceeding five years of age, accompanied by their parents or friends will be carried free. Children over five and under twelve will be carried at half fare.

Stop-Over—Will be allowed in exchange on such tickets as entitle holders to stop-over and when so stamped.

Lost Tickets—Proper care should be taken so as to guard against the loss of a ticket, as Railways are not responsible for lost tickets; also, care should be taken of baggage checks, making a memorandum of check numbers for use in case of loss.

Personal Baggage—Consisting of wearing apparel only, and not exceeding 150 lbs. Weight, will be checked free on each whole fare ticket. And 75 lbs. Free on each half fare ticket. Baggage in excess of free allowance will be charged for, and passengers paying excess charges will receive an excess baggage ticket which must be delivered to Agent with baggage check when baggage is claimed. Storage will be charged on each piece of baggage, either checked or not checked, remaining at stations over twenty-four hours.

Baggage for Flag Stations—Must be claimed at baggage car door immediately on arrival, otherwise it will be carried to next station where agent is on duty and held for further orders.

Caution— It is unlawful to carry dangerous articles, such as gunpowder, matches, etc., in baggage.

Customs— When baggage is examined at Canadian and Newfoundland points, passengers are required to attend to this personally, otherwise baggage will be held by the Customs.

Time of Trains—It is not guaranteed that the starting time or the arriving time of trains shall be as published herein, neither will this Railway be liable for loss or damage arising from delays or detentions, nor will this Railway assume any responsibility beyond its own line.

Reference Marks—

*— Flag Station — Trains stop only when signalled or when there are passengers to set down, and under the conditions named herein.

†— Indicates that trains do not stop.

Disputes— Conductors and Agents are governed by rules which they are not authorized to change, therefore, in the event of any disagreement about tickets required, privileges allowed, etc., passengers should pay Conductor's or Agent's claim, obtain receipt and refer the matter to the Central Passenger Agent for his decision.

Seat Space—A passenger is entitled only to seat space in car sufficient for one person; baggage and parcels that cannot be placed under car seat or in the passenger's portion of the parcel rack must not be taken into the car. Baggage which cannot be stowed away as above mentioned should be delivered at the baggage room. If found in the car it will be removed.

Obstruction of the Car Aisles Will Not Be Permitted.[5]

Confederation Propaganda, 1948

To All Railroaders

You will become employees of the biggest railway in the world, the C.N.R. You will have SECURITY and STABILITY as C.N.R. employees. Your wages and working conditions will be the same as on the C.N.R. Under Responsible or Commission you face sure and certain wage-cuts and lay-offs. You, your wives and sons and daughters and other relatives should flock out on June 3 and vote for Confederation.[6]

Dining Car Luncheon Menu, C. 1950

Luncheon

Prices Immediately Below Include Soup, Vegetables, Dessert,
Bread and Butter, Tea, Coffee or Milk
Cold Tomato Bouillion or Chicken Okra Soup

Fried Mackerel with Lemon Butter.......................... 90¢
Lettuce and Cucumber Salad, French Dressing................. 90¢
Boiled Leg of Mutton, Caper Sauce......................... 1.00
Cold Sliced Chicken with Potato Salad 1.00
Boiled or Mashed Potatoes   Garden Peas
Choice Of: Banana Creme Pie   Fruit Jelly with Whipped Creme
Ice Creme with Wafers
Canadian Cheddar Cheese with Crackers
Bread or Roll
Tea, Coffee or Milk

A La Carte Suggestions

Soup, Tureen, 30¢: Cup, 20¢

Club Steak, $1.00   Lamb Chops, 65¢
Broiled Bacon, 55¢   Grilled Sugar Cured Ham, 65¢
Ham or Bacon with Fried Eggs, 65¢
Eggs, Boiled, Fried or Scrambled, 35¢   Poached on Toast, 40¢
Omelettes: Plain, 45¢   Tomato or Cheese, 30¢   Ham, 60¢
Cold Meats, 75¢; with Potato Salad, 90¢
Chicken Salad, 65¢
Potatoes: French Fried, 25¢   Hashed Browned, 25¢
Vegetables, 20¢
Desserts, 20¢ & 25¢   Preserved Figs, 30¢: with Cream, 40¢
Bread or Rolls with Butter, 15¢
Tea (per pot), 25¢   Coffee (per pot), 25¢   Milk, 15¢

Please write on meal check items selected to ensure prompt service.

No order served for less than 25¢ to each person.[7]

Chronology

1881 Newfoundland Railway Company incorporated.
1884 Railway from St. John's to Harbour Grace completed.
1888 Railway from Whitbourne to Placentia opened.
1893 Railway extended from Placentia to Norris Arm, Hall's Bay
1897 Railway extended from Norris Arm to Port aux Basques.
Name changed to the Newfoundland Northern and Western Railway.
1898 Reid Newfoundland Company takes control of the railway.
June 30. First train crosses Newfoundland from St. John's to Port aux Basques.
Branch lines to Lewisporte and Carbonear opened.
1910 Line from Grand lake to Bonne Bay authorized but not completed.
1911 Branch lines to Bonavista and Port Union opened.
1914 Branch line to Trepassey opened.
1915 Branch lines to Heart's Content and Grate's Cove opened.
Carbonear Branch extended to Bay de Verde.
Branch line to Fortune begun but never completed.
1917 Opening of the Port Union Branch to Port Union Junction.
1921 Branch line to Argentia opened.
May. Railway shuts down due to disagreement between Reid Newfoundland Company and government.
1923 Reid Newfoundland Railway becomes the Newfoundland Government Railway.
1926 Newfoundland Government Railway resumes its earlier name, Newfoundland Railway.
1931 Port Union Branch Line closed.
1934 Abandonment of the branch lines to Trepassey, Bay de Verde and Grate's Cove.
1939 Abandonment of the Heart's Content Branch Line.
1949 The Newfoundland Railway is absorbed by the Canadian National Railways.
1969 July 2. Cross-island passenger service ends.

Glossary

Accommodation train—Mixed train running on a branch line.

Air brake—A brake operated by air pressure.

Anchor—A hand brake. Sometimes in Newfoundland a ship's anchor was used to secure a train to the tack during a heavy wind.

Apron—Steel perch for the engineman to stand on while a tender and steam locomotive were coupled.

Ballast—Broken rock or crushed gravel used to form a stable bed for steel rails and wooden ties.

Ballast car—An open top car with a trap-door at the bottom used for spreading ballast on a roadbed.

Blow around—Injecting water into a locomotive's boiler and building up sufficient steam pressure.

Boiler—A metal tank in a locomotive where water is converted into steam.

Boxcar—An enclosed railcar used to move freight.

Brakeman—Railway employee who operates hand brakes and assisted the conductor adding and uncoupling cars.

Cab—The part of a locomotive housing the operating levers, the engineer and the fireman.

Caboose—Traditionally the last car on a freight train where the crew eat, relax and do paperwork.

Car—A railway carriage or wagon.

Carman—Crewman who repairs and inspects rail cars.

Combination train—A local passenger train and mixed freight.

Conductor—Railway official in charge of passengers and examining tickets.

Cowcatcher—Wrought-iron bars extending from the front of an engine to push animals and other obstacles off the track.

Cut—The narrow passage through a snowbank made by the passage of a rotary plow.

Damper dogs—Pancake-like dough often fried on a shovel. A staple of the navvies who built the railway. Also called damper devils.

Depot—A railway station.

Diesel— A locomotive powered by a diesel engine.
Diner— Dining car attached to a passenger train.
Dispatcher— Person who makes sure that trains are on schedule and meet at the correct time and place.
Dispatching office— Office where he dispatcher controls the movement of trains.
Division— A section of the railway separated by terminals where crews and engines could be changed.
Double header— Two locomotives yoked together for increased motive power.
Doubling— Taking half a train's cars to the nearest station and returning for the remainder.
Engine— A locomotive.
Engineer— Locomotive driver.
Engineman— Fireman or driver on a locomotive.
Firebox— The chamber in a steam locomotive where the fire is established to build up steam.
Fireman— Employee responsible for feeding the fire on a locomotive with coal and keeping the steam pressure up.
Firing— The act of feeding the fire on a locomotive to keep up the steam pressure.
Fish plate— A steel plate used for fastening rails together.
Flag— To signal a train to stop by means of flags or lights.
Flange— Blade-shaped projection used on a locomotive or plow to clear snow close to the rails.
Flatcar— A railway freight car which has no roof, ends or sides.
Giving water— Taking on water into the tender from a water chute.
Gradient— Degree of slope of a railway track.
Hand car— Small four-wheeled vehicle propelled by a two-handed pump.
Head-on— A head-on collision.
Highball— A signal, either by lantern, word or hand, indicating that the way ahead is clear.
Hostler— Employee who services a train when it has completed a run.
Hot box— A wheel bearing that has overheated.
Injector— A device for feeding water into a locomotive's steam boiler.
Iron— A length of railroad track.
Kink— Poorly ballasted track warped by the sun.
Knuckle— Rotating pin which connects railcars together.
Lining bar— Heavy metal bar used to line up steel rails.
Locomotive— Self-propelled vehicle used to push or pull railway cars.
Lost their air— Loss of braking power due to loss of air in pneumatic brakes.
Mail clerk— Postal employee who handles mail on trains and ships.
Making the meet— Passing another train on a siding at least five minutes before it is scheduled to depart.
Mikado— A locomotive produced by the Baldwin Locomotive Works of Philadelphia for the Japanese railway. Also used in Newfoundland.

Mixed extra— An extra train consisting of passenger and freight cars.

Mixed train— A train made up of passenger and freight cars.

Motive power— Locomotives and diesels used to pull and push rail cars.

Narrow gauge— A railroad with rails less than the standard width apart, four feet eight and one-half inches.

Navvy— An unskilled manual laborer.

Operator— The person who gives orders to the conductor to add and drop off cars.

Plow special— Extra train pushing a rotary plow for snow clearing.

Point— The intersection between a siding and the main line, controlled by a switching lever.

Pony wheels— Small wheels at the front of a locomotive.

Pullman— Passenger car which could be converted into sleeping compartments. Named after its inventor, George M. Pullman.

Railbed— The graded right-of-way upon which ballast, ties and rails rest.

Rocking up the grade— Sprinkling pebbles or gravel on a slippery rail or incline to increase traction.

Rolling stock— Wheeled vehicles pulled or pushed by locomotives.

Rotary plow— Steam-powered plow used to clear snow from the tracks.

Roundhouse— A circular building connected to a turntable where locomotives are repaired or stored.

Sectionman— Railway worker responsible for the inspection and maintenance of a section of track.

Semaphore— A signaling device on a mechanical arm using flags or lights.

Short line— To operate trains over a relatively short distance.

Shunt— To move a railcar to a different track or couple it to a different train.

Siding— A short section of track parallel to the main line used for shunting, loading and unloading and parking rolling stock.

Sleeper— Length of treated wood positioned on a ballasted roadbed to hold steel rails in place. Also called a tie.

Snow-fighting— Keeping the rails clear of snow and ice by plowing and shoveling.

Spareboard— Employee kept in reserve to be sent where most needed.

Speeder— Small motorized vehicle used to transport sectionmen and for forest fire prevention.

Spiker— Laborer who drives spikes into wooden ties to secure steel rails.

Standard gauge— Railroad tracks which have a width apart of four feet, eight and one-half inches.

Sun kink— Rails which have expanded due to hot sun.

Switch— A device controlled by a lever on a stand used to send a train from one track to another.

Switchback— A zigzag route up a steep incline.

Switcher— An engine used to move cars around the railway yard.

Tender— A car attached to the rear of a locomotive carrying its fuel and water supply.

Tie— A length of treated wood, usually fir or spruce, positioned on a ballasted roadbed to hold steel rails in place. Also called a sleeper.

Timetable— Published schedule of passenger and freight train arrivals and departures.

Train making up— Placing all the freight and passenger cars on a train in the correct order prior to departure.

Train order— Order given to a train's crew, e.g. departure and arrival times, picking up cars.

Trainman— Conductor's assistant who helps pick up and drop off cars.

Trucks— Pairs of wheels at the front and rear of rail cars.

Turntable— A circular revolving platform used to turn locomotives around.

Water chute— Hinged pipe used to pass water into a steam locomotive's tender.

Water up— Filling a tender with water.

Wiggly-jiggly— Eleven-ton ore car whose short wheelbase caused excessive rocking.

Wye— Tracks forming the letter 'Y' used for turning engines around when no turntable is available.

Notes

Chapter 1
1. Rogers, 1911, p. 159.
2. O'Neill, 1976, p. 385.
3. Journal of the House of Assembly 1880, pp. 125–129.
4. Dearin, J. J. Public Ledger, May 14, 1878.
5. *Evening Telegram*, October 1, 1888.
6. Hillier, 1981, p. 3.
7. Ibid., July 9, 1880.
8. Ibid., July 10, 1880.
9. Winton, F. Public Ledger, April 16, 1881.

Chapter 2
1. Information about the Battle of Foxtrap is taken from several different accounts: Millais, 1907, pp. 79–81. Grant, 1898, pp. 471–472. Willson, 1897, pp. 170–171. Prowse, 1895, pp. 511–513. Fairford, 1912, pp. 9–10. 2. *Evening Telegram*, July 27, 1880.

Chapter 3
1. The story of the All-Red-Route and the Great American and Short Line Railroad can be found in: Fleming, 1876, pp. 243 ff. Harding, 1980, pp. 60–62, 65.

Chapter 4
1. Cormack, 1822, pp. 139 ff.

2. Murray, 1876, p. 4.
3. Prowse, 1895, p. 500.
4. Murray, Op. Cit., p. 11.
5. Ibid., p. 15.
6. Ibid., p.17.
7. Ibid., p.17.
8. Ibid., p. 27.
9. Ibid., p. 21.
10. Ibid., p. 24.
11. Ibid., p. 33.
12. Ibid., p. 34.
13. Penney, 1967, p. 475.

Chapter 5
1. *Evening Telegram*, August 20, 1881.
2. Ibid., "Obituary," June 17, 1908.
3. Ibid., August 8, 1881.
4. *Patriot*, August 19, 1880.
5. *Evening Telegram*, June 15, 1880
6. Ibid., June 30, 1880.
7. Ibid., July 5, 1880.
8. Ibid., July 10, 1880.
9. Ibid., July 9, 1880.
10. Ibid., July 12, 1880.
11. Ibid., July 23, 1880.
12. *Newfoundlander*, August 19, 1881.
13. *Evening Telegram*, August 20, 1881.
14. Prowse, 1895, p. 507.
15. *Evening Telegram*, October 8, 1881
16. Ibid., October 26, 1881.
17. *Newfoundlander*, December 16, 1881.
18. *Evening Telegram*, December 14, 1881.
19. Ibid., July 25, 1882.
20. Ibid., August 16, 1882.
21. *Times*, July 19, 1882.
22. *Evening Telegram*, July 9, 1883.
23. Penney, 1967, p. 478.
24. *Standard and Conception Bay Advertiser*, October 18, 1884.
25. Harvey 1900, pp. 133–135.
26. Baggs, 2003, p. 54.

Chapter 6
1. *Evening Telegram*, March 31, 1886.
2. Ibid., March 31, 1886.
3. O'Neill, 1976, p. 462
4. Thomas 1913, p. 181.
5. Phillips, 1968, pp. 69–72.
6. Mifflen, 1972, pp. 7–9.
7. Harvey 1900, pp. 135–136.
8. Bartlett, 1925, p. 169.

Chapter 7
1. Penney & Kennedy, 2003, pp. 58–64.
Smallwood, 1968, pp. 568–573.

Chapter 8
1. Penney 1967, p. 492.
2. Ibid., p. 492.

3. Hillier, 1981, p. 12.
4. Chafe, 1992, pp. 13–14.
5. Cook, 1996, p. 101.
6. Lingard, 2000, p. 42.

Chapter 9

1. Morine, 1933, p. 9.
2. Hillier, 1981, p. 14.
3. Cook, 1996, pp. 109–110.
4. Coish, 1976, pp. 41–42.
5. Smallwood, 1968, p. 570.
6. *Evening Telegram*, July 18, 1897.

Chapter 10

1. Colonial Office Dispatch, February 23, 1898.
2. Ibid., February 23, 1898.
3. Op. Cit., February 23, 1898.
4. Rogers, 1911, p. 178.
5. *Evening Telegram*, February 28, 1898.
6. Ibid., February 28, 1898.
7. Colonial Office Dispatch, March 23, 1898.
8. *Daily News*, February 26, 1898.
9. *Methodist Monthly Greeting*, March 1898, p. 41.
10. Smith, 1920, p. 148.
11. Debates of the House of Commons of Canada, 1911–1912, p. 6354.
12. Penney, 1967, p. 490.
13. *Times*, October 31, 1901.

Chapter 11

1. Rogers, 1911, pp. 160, 163.
2. Seitz, 1926, pp. 239–240.
3. Millais, 1907, p. 134.
4. Ibid., p. 135.
5. Ibid., pp. 135–136.
6. Ibid., p. 136.
7. Ibid., pp. 136–137.
8. Ibid., p. 261.
9. Lodge, 1939, p. 206.
10. Mifflen, 1972, p. 9.
11. Ibid., p. 9.
12. Williams, 1913.

Chapter 12

1. Brown, 1949, p. 788.
2. Stevens, 1973, p. 412.
3. Penney & Kennedy, 2003, p. 120.
4. Russell, 1965, pp. 38–49.
5. Penney, 1967, p. 499.
6. Ibid., p. 499.
7. Smith, 1952, p. 37.
8. Kearley, 1995, p. 7.
9. Cook 1991, pp. 62–63.

Chapter 13

1. *Evening Telegram*, July 3, 1969.
2. Cook, 1991, pp. 8–9. Lingard 1996, pp. 99–101.

Chapter 14

1. *Evening Herald*, October 18, 1897.
2. *Evening Telegram*, October 19, 1897.
3. *Evening Herald*, October 20, 1897.
4. *Evening Herald*, November 3, 1897.
5. *Evening Herald*, December 22, 1897.
6. Davis 1895, pp. 81–82.
7. Lingard 2000, 99. 91–93.
8. Allan 1909, p. 60.
9. Cook 1996, p. 12.
10. Cook 1991, p. 8.
11. *Evening Telegram*, October 13, 1897.
12. *Encyclopedia of Newfoundland and Labrador*, vol. 1, p. 279.
13. Chirgwin 1962, p. 191.
14. *Encyclopedia of Newfoundland and Labrador*, vol. 1, p. 279.
15. Cook 1996, p. 34.
16. Ibid., p. 34.
17. Penney & Kennedy 2003, p. 200.
18. Cook 1996, p. 38.
19. Cook 1991, pp. 25. 26.
20. *Encyclopedia of Newfoundland and Labrador*, vol. 1, p. 654.
21. Ibid., pp. 782–783.
22. Pratt 1920, p. 55.
23. Cook 1991, pp. 24–25.
24. *Encyclopedia of Newfoundland and Labrador*, vol. III, p. 501.
25. Lingard, 1996, p. 98.
26. Penney & Kennedy 2003, pp. 213–215.
27. Lingard 2000, p. 12.
28. Cook 1996, p. 53.
29. *Encyclopedia of Newfoundland and Labrador*, vol. IV, p. 565.
30. Lingard 1999, pp. 53–54; *Encyclopedia of Newfoundland and Labrador*, vol. I, pp. 646–647.
31. Cook, 1996, p. 31.
32. Lingard 1999, p. 54. *Encyclopedia of Newfoundland and Labrador*, vol. V, pp. 348–349.
33. *Encyclopedia of Newfoundland and Labrador*, vol. 4, p. 565.
34. Lingard 1999, pp. 57–58; *Encyclopedia of Newfoundland and Labrador*, vol. V, pp. 317–318.
35. Lingard 1999, pp. 58–60.
36. Noseworthy, 1997.
37. Lingard, 1996, pp. 86–87; Lingard, 1997, pp. 101–104.
38. Bartlett, 1925, p. 183.
39. Lewis, 1954, p. 135.

Chapter 15

1. Penney & Kennedy 2003, p. 13.
2. *Daily News*, August 4, 1897.
3. *Daily News*, July 9, 1898.
4. Elliott, 1900, pp. 30–31, 89.
5. Cook 1991, pp. 45–70. Cook 1989, pp. 80–93.
6. Cook 1991, pp. 63–66.

Appendix 1

1. *Daily News*, July 26, 1895.
2. Willson, 1897, pp. 171–176.
3. *Daily News*, May 12, 1898.
4. *Daily News*, July 1, 1898.
5. *Daily News*, September 13, 1898.
6. Morris, 1899, pp. 17, 24, 35.
7. Selous, 1907, pp. 59–60, 99.
8. Harvey, 1900, pp. 127–133.
9. *Daily News*, January 4, 1902.
10. Prichard, 1910, pp. 83, 87–88.
11. Koch, 1908, pp. 4–7, 9.
12. Thomas, 1913, pp. 181–183, 221, 265.
13. Ware, 1908, pp. 39–40.
14. Rogers, 1912, pp. 160–163.
15. Cashin, 1976, pp. 101–103.
16. McGrath, 1911, pp. 64–68.
17. Progress, 1911, pp. 73–74.
18. Prowse, 1912, pp. 85–86.
19. Hawkins, 1914, pp. 1–4, 8–9, 24–25, 307–308.
20. Gray, 1922, pp. 45–47.
21. Quoted in Penny & Kennedy, 2003, p. 87.
22. Bartlett, 1925, pp. 179–181.
23. Seitz, 1926, pp. 237–238.
24. Pigot, 1928, pp. 198–199.
25. Rogers, 1911, p. 178.
26. Worcester, 1932, p. 198.
27. Clarke, 1935.
28. Tait, 1939, pp. 146–148.
29. Cecil, 1942, pp. 52–53.
30. Cook, 1991, p. 11.
31. Lewis, 1954, p. 135.
32. Henderson, 1965, pp. 45–46.
33. Cook, 1989, p. 26.

Appendix 3

1. Koch, 1908, pp. 125–126.
2. Ferre, 1993, p. 131.
3. Swansborough, 1885, pp. 3–8.
4. Murphy, 1910, unpaged.
5. Greenleaf, 1968, pp. 277–278.

Appendix 4

1. Harvey 1900, p. v.
2. Ibid., p. vi.
3. Ibid., p. vii.
4. Ibid., p. viii
5. Ibid., p. ix.
6. Ibid., p. x.

Appendix 5

1. *Daily News*, December 19, 1895.
2. *Daily News*, July 1, 1898.
3. *Daily News*, September 7, 1898.
4. Dicks, 1999, p. 181.
5. Newfoundland Railway timetable, June–December 1929.
6. *The Confederate*, May 31, 1948.
7. Lingard, 2000, p. 45.

Bibliography

Books

Adams, Ramon F. *The Language of the Railroader*. Norman, OK: University of Oklahoma Press, 1977.

Baggs, Bill. *All Aboard!* Grand Falls — Windsor, NL: W. N. Baggs, 1994.

_____. *All Aboard! Vol. 2*. Grand Falls — Windsor, NL: W. N. Baggs, 1997.

_____. *All Aboard! Vol. 3*. Grand Falls — Windsor, NL: W. N. Baggs, 2003.

Bartlett, A. Eugene. *Least Known America*. New York: Fleming H. Revell Co., 1925.

Brown, Addison. *Newfoundland Journey*. New York: Carleton Press, 1971.

Bruce, Harry. *Lifeline*. Toronto: 1977.

Burpee, Lawrence J. *Sandford Fleming, Empire Builder*. London: Oxford University Press, 1915.

Carpenter, Frank G. *Canada and Newfoundland*. Garden City, NY: Doubleday, Page and Co., 1925.

Cashin, Peter. *My Life and Times*. Portugal Cove, NL: Breakwater, 1976.

Cecil, Lord Harmsworth. *A Little Fishing Book*. London: Frederick Muller, 1942.

Chadwick, St. John. *Newfoundland: Island into Province*. Cambridge: Cambridge University Press, 1967.

Chafe, W. J. *I've Been Working on the Railroad: Memoirs of a Railwayman, 1911–1962*. St. John's, NL: Harry Cuff Publications, 1992.

Chodos, Robert. *The C.P.R.: A Century of Corporate Welfare*. Toronto: James Lewis and Samuel, 1973.

Clarke, Dennis. *Public School Explorers in Newfoundland*. London: Putnam, 1935.

Cook, Clayton D. *The End of the Line: The Newfoundland Railway in Pictures*. St. John's, NL: Harry Cuff Publications, 1989.

_____. *Tales of the Rails: The Newfoundland Railway*. St. John's, NL: Creative Publishers, 1991.

_____. *Tales of the Rails, Vol. II: The Newfoundland Railway*. St. John's, NL: Jeff Blackwood, 1995.

_____. *Tales of the Rails, Vol. III: The Newfoundland Railway*. St. John's, NL: Robinson-Blackmore, 1996.

_____. *Tales of the Rails, Vol. IV: The Newfoundland Railway*. St. John's, NL: Flanker Press, 2005.

Cramm, Frank. *The Construction of the Newfoundland Railway, 1875–1898*. St. John's, NL: Memorial University Master's Thesis, 1961.

Cross, Walter J. *The Man from Mars Looks at Newfoundland*. Montréal: Atlantic Guardian, 1947.

Davis, Samuel T. *Caribou Shooting in Newfoundland*. Lancaster, PA: New Era Printing House, 1895.

Dicks, Brendan D. *The Railway Ties ... That Bind*. Corner Brook, NL: Robinson-Blackmore, 1999.

Dorin, Patrick C. *The Canadian National Railways Story*. Seattle: Superior Publishing Co., 1975.

Elliott, James Rupert. *To the Old Capitals by the New Way*. Boston: J.R. Elliott, 1900.

Encyclopedia of Newfoundland and Labrador. St. John's, NL: Newfoundland Book Publishers / Harry Cuff Publications, 1981–1994.

Fairford, Ford. *Newfoundland*. London: Adam and Charles Black, 1912.

Fay, C. R. *Life and Labour in Newfoundland*. Toronto: University of Toronto Press, 1956.

Ferre, Sandrine. *Once upon a Train: A Study of the Railway in Newfoundland: Reality of the Past, Legend of the Present*. Thesis (M. De L.). L'Université de l'Ouest (Angers), 1993.

Fleming, Sandford. *The Intercolonial*. Montreal: Dawson Brothers, 1876.

Gray, Prentiss N. (Edited by Theodore J. Holstein, Jr.; Susan C. Reneau). *From Peace to the*

Fraser. Missoula, MT: The Boone and Crockett Club, 1994.
Greenleaf, Elisabeth Bristol. *Ballads and Sea Songs of Newfoundland*. Hatboro, PN: Folklore Associates, 1968.
Guillet, Edwin C. *The Story of Canadian Roads*. Toronto: University of Toronto Press, 1966.
Harvey, M. *Newfoundland in 1897*. London: Sampson Low, Marston and Co., 1897.
_____. *Newfoundland in 1900*. New York: The South Publishing Co., 1900.
Hatton, Joseph, and M. Harvey. *Newfoundland*. Boston: Doyle and Whittle, 1893.
Hawkins, Chauncey J. *Ned Brewster's Caribou Hunt*. Boston: Little, Brown and Co., 1914.
Henderson, Dorothy. *The Heart of Newfoundland*. Montréal: Harvest House, 1965.
Hillier, James K. *The Newfoundland Railway 1881–1949*. St. John's, NL: Newfoundland Historical Society, 1981.
Johnson, Paul, and Henry A. Cuff. *Herbert J. Russell, C.B.E.: The Man, His Work, His Words*. St. John's, NL: Johnson Family Foundation, 2004.
Jones, Kenneth W. *Romantic Railways*. London: Arlington Books, 1971.
Kearley, Wade. *The People's Road: On the Trail of the Newfoundland Railway*. St. John's, NL: Harry Cuff Publications, 1995.
Koch, Felix J. *A Little Journey to Northern Wilds*. Chicago: A. Flanagan & Co., 1908.
Lavallee, Omer. *Narrow Gauge Railways of Canada*. Montréal: Railfare Enterprises, 1972.
Legget, Robert F. *Railroads of Canada*. Vancouver: Douglas, David and Charles, 1973.
Lewis, Oswald. *I'd Like to Go Again: Being Some Further Impressions of Travel in Many Lands*. London: Newman Neame, 1954.
Lingard, Mont. *The Newfie Bullet: The Story of the Passenger Train Service in Newfoundland*. Grand Falls — Windsor, NL: Mont Lingard Publishing, 2000.
_____. *Next Stop, Gaff Topsails: Chats, Stats and Snaps of the Newfoundland Railway*. Grand Falls — Windsor, NL: Mont Lingard Publications, 1996.
_____. *Next Stop St. John's: Chats, Stats and Snaps of the Newfoundland Railway*. Grand Falls — Windsor, NL: Mont Lingard Publications, 1999.
_____. *Next Stop Trinity Loop: More Chats, Stats and Snaps of the Newfoundland Railway*. Grand Falls — Windsor, NL: Mont Lingard Publishing, 1998.
_____. *Next Stop, Wreckhouse: More Chats, Stats and Snaps of the Newfoundland Railway*. Grand Falls — Windsor, NL: Mont Lingard Publications, 1997.
Lodge, T. *Dictatorship in Newfoundland*. London: Casell and Co., 1939.
McGrath, P. T. *Newfoundland in 1911*. London: Whitehead, Morris and Co., 1911.
McGuire, C. R. *The Newfoundland Post Office, Mail Assorting Office*. [s.l.]: C. R. McGuire, 1980.
MacKay, R. A. *Newfoundland*. Toronto: Oxford University Press, 1946.
Marsh, James H., ed. *The Canadian Encyclopedia*. Second Edition. Edmonton: Hurtig, 1988.
Mika, Nick, and Helma Mika. *Railways of Canada*. Toronto: McGraw-Hill Ryerson, 1972.
Millais, J. G. *Newfoundland and Its Untrodden Ways*. New York: Longmans, Green and Co., 1907.
Morine, Alfred B. *The Railway Contract, 1898, and Afterwards*. St. John's, NL: Robinson and Co., 1933.
Morris, Isaac C. *The Dawn of the Twentieth Century As Pertaining to Newfoundland*. St. John's, NL: G. S. Milligan, 1899.
Murphy, James. *Newfoundland Poems*. St. John's, NL:[n.p.], c. 1910.
Murray, Alexander. *Summary of the Newfoundland Railway Survey*. St. John's, NL: House of Assembly, 1876.
Naylor, R. T. *The History of Canadian Business*. Toronto: James Lorimer and Co., 1975.
Neary, Peter, ed. *The Political Economy of Newfoundland, 1929–1973*. Toronto: Copp Clark, 1973.
Nock, O. S. *Railways of Canada*. London: A & C Black, 1973.
Noel, S. J. R. *Politics in Newfoundland*. Toronto: University of Toronto Press, 1971.
Noseworthy, Randy P. *The School Car: Bringing the Three R's to Newfoundland's Remote Railway Settlements 1936–1942*. Whitbourne, NL: R.P.N. Publishing, 1997.
O'Neill, Paul. *The Oldest City*. Don Mills, ON: Musson Book Co., 1975.
_____. *A Seaport Legacy*. Don Mills, ON: Musson Book Co., 1976.
Peacock, Kenneth. Ed. *Songs of the Newfoundland Outports*. Ottawa: National Museum of Canada, 1965.
Penney, A. R. *Centennial Newfoundland Railway, 1881–1981*. St. John's, NL: Canadian National, 1981.
_____, and Fabian Kennedy. *A History of the Newfoundland Railway*. St. John's, NL: Harry Cuff Publications, 2003.
Phillips, R. A. J. *Canada's Railways*. Toronto: McGraw-Hill, 1968.
Pigot, R. *Twenty-Five Years Big Game Hunting*. London: Chatto & Windus, 1928.

Prichard, H. Hesketh. *Hunting Camps in Wood and Wilderness.* London: William Heineman, 1910.

Prowse, D. W. *A History of Newfoundland.* London: Macmillan and Co., 1895.

Rae, W. Fraser. *Newfoundland to Manitoba.* London: Sampson, Low, Marston, Sparle and Rivington, 1881.

Rogers, Sir John. *Newfoundland, Historical and Geographical.* Oxford: Clarendon Press, 1911.

_____. *Sport in Vancouver Island and Newfoundland.* Toronto: Musson Book Co., 1912.

Rowe, Frederick W. *Education and Culture in Newfoundland.* Toronto: McGraw-Hill Ryerson, 1976.

_____. *A History of Newfoundland and Labrador.* Toronto: McGraw-Hill Ryerson, 1980.

Russell, Franklin. *The Secret Islands.* New York: W. W. Norton, 1965.

Seitz, Don C. *The Great Island.* New York: The Century Co., 1926.

Selous, F. C. *Recent Hunting Trips in British North America.* London: Witherby & Co., 1907.

Smallwood, Joseph R., ed. *The Book of Newfoundland, Vol. III.* Edinburgh: Thomas Nelson, 1968.

Smith, Frederick Edwin, First Lord of Birkenhead. *The Story of Newfoundland.* London: Horace Marshall and Son, 1920.

Smith, J. Harry. *Newfoundland Holiday.* Toronto: Ryerson Press, 1952.

Stevens, C. R. *History of the Canadian National Railways.* New York: Macmillan, 1973.

Swansborough, W. *The Newfoundland Railway Guide.* St. John's, NL: [n.p.], c. 1885.

Tait, R. H. *Newfoundland.* [s.l.]: Harrington Press, 1939.

Thomas, William S. *Trails and Tramps in Alaska and Newfoundland.* New York: G. P. Putnam's Sons, 1913.

Thompson, Frederick F. *The French Shore Problem in Newfoundland.* Toronto: University of Toronto Press, 1961.

Ware, Richard D. *In the Woods and on the Shore.* Boston: L. C. Page & Co., 1908.

Whitehouse, P. B., and P. Allen. *Round the World on the Narrow Gauge.* Garden City, NY: Doubleday, 1966.

Williams, Sir Ralph. *How I Became Governor.* London: John Murray, 1913.

Willson, Beckles. *The Tenth Island.* London: Grant Richards, 1897.

Worcester, Elwood. *Life's Adventure: The Story of a Varied Career.* New York: Charles Scribner's Sons, 1932.

Articles

Alderman, Tom. "Now the Newfoundland Line Is a Mighty Fine Line," *Imperial Oil Review,* February 1965, p. 24–28.

Allan, J. M. "Arrival of Dog-Trains with Mail." *Newfoundland Quarterly,* March 1909. In: *75th Anniversary Special Edition Newfoundland Quarterly,* 1976, p. 60.

Brown, Andrew H. "Newfoundland, Canada's New Province," *National Geographic Magazine,* June 1949, p. 777–812.

Chirgwin, W. L. "Story of the Bruce," *Newfoundland Quarterly,* Fall 1962. In: *75th Anniversary Special Edition Newfoundland Quarterly,* 1976, p. 191.

Coish, Calvin. "Newfoundland's Railways," *Atlantic Advocate,* December 1976, p. 9, 413–42.

Cooke, Ernest J. "C. N. R.'s Explosion of Progress," In: *The Book of Newfoundland,* Vol. III. St John's, NL: Newfoundland Book Publishers, 1967.

Cormack, William Epps. "Narrative of a Journey Across the Island of Newfoundland in 1822," *The Beothucks or Red Indians of Newfoundland.* Cambridge: Cambridge University Press, 1915.

Eadie, Thomas, W. "Mr. Eadie Remembers: Part II — The Newfoundland Project," *The Blue Bell,* June 1965, p. 4–8.

Grant, G. M. "Newfoundland and Canada," *The Canadian Magazine,* 11 (October 1898), p. 467–472.

Harding, Les. "The Battle of Foxtrap," *Canada West: The Pioneer Years,* summer 1980, Vol. 10 (2), p. 84–87.

_____. "The Great American and Short Line Railway," *Atlantic Advocate,* April 1980, Vol. 70 (8), p. 60–62, 65.

_____. "The Harbour Grace Railway and the Great Newfoundland Newspaper War," *Newfoundland Quarterly,* summer 1987, Vol. 83 (1), p. 20–21.

_____. "Life on the Line in Newfoundland," *Canadian Rail,* October 1991 (424), p. 159–162.

_____. "The Newfie Bullet," *Newfoundland Quarterly,* Spring-Summer 1982, Vol. 78, p. 1–2, 16–18.

_____. "When the Going Was Bad: St. John's to Port aux Basques by Rail," *The Beaver,* February–March 1992, Vol. 71 (1), p. 34–36.

Harrington, Michael Francis. "The Extraordinary Saga of the Newfie Bullet," *Atlantic Advocate,* June 1969, p. 41.

Hiller, J. K. *The Newfoundland Railway 1881–*

1949. St. John's, NF: Newfoundland Historical Society, Pamphlet No. 6, 1981.

McGrath, P. T. "The Railway Question in Newfoundland," *The Canadian Magazine*, 16 (February 1901), p. 329–334.

Mifflen, Jessie B. "Salute to the Newfie Bullet," *Newfoundland Quarterly*, 69 (December 1972), p. 7–9.

Mitchell, Harvey. "Canada's Negotiations with Newfoundland, 1887–1895," In: Rawlyk, G. A., ed. *Historical Essays of the Atlantic Provinces*. Toronto: McClelland and Stewart, 1967.

Murray, Alexander. "Geography and Resources of Newfoundland," *Journal of the Royal Geographical Society*, 47 (1877), p. 266–278.

Newfoundland Railway Monthly Bulletin, June 1, 1930.

Penney, Alfred R. "The Newfoundland Railway: Newfoundland Epic," In: *The Book of Newfoundland,* Vol. III. St. John's, NL: Newfoundland Book Publishers, 1967.

Perlin, A. B. "Canadian National Railways in Newfoundland," In: Perlin, A. B. (Ed.), *The Story of Newfoundland*. St. John's, NL: [n.p.], 1959 p. 85–88.

Pratt, E. J. "Carlo." *Canadian Forum*, Vol. 1 (November 1920), p. 55.

"Progress: The Ferryland Railway." *Newfoundland Quarterly*, July 1911. In: *75th Anniversary Special Edition Newfoundland Quarterly*, 1976, p. 73–74.

Prowse, D. W. "Opening of the Bonavista Railway." *Newfoundland Quarterly*, Spring 1912. In: *75th Anniversary Special Edition Newfoundland Quarterly*, 1976, p. 85–86.

Skinner, Charles M. "The Railway in Newfoundland," *Bulletin of the American Geographical Society*, 37 (November 1905), p. 658–665.

Wragg, Mike. "The Newfoundland Railway," *Canadian Rail*, 388, September–October 1985, p. 148–183.

Newspapers

St. John's *Evening Telegram*
St. John's *Newfoundlander*
St. John's *Daily News*
St. John's *Evening Herald*
St. John's *Patriot*
St. John's *Public Ledger*
St. John's *Times*
Methodist Monthly Greeting

Other

Colonial Office Dispatches
Debates of the House of Commons, Canada.
Journal of the House of Assembly of Newfoundland. St. John's, NL: The House of Assembly, 1880.

Index

Numbers in ***bold italics*** indicate pages with illustrations.

Accommodation Train 89–95, 167
Alexander Bay 150, 165, 167
All-Red-Route 24, 25, 26, 27, 29
Alphabet Fleet 138–144
American Pacific Railroad 16
American syndicates 9–10, 16, 79
Andrews, Charley 19, 22
Anglo-Newfoundland Development Company 147–148
Argentia 102–103, 130, 137, 154
Argyle, SS 140
Arnold's Cove 56, 104
Astor, Jacob 19
Atlantic Charter ***101***
Austin, W.A. 30, 31, 33, 34
Austin, Texas 59
Australia 26, 56, 60, 158
Avalon Peninsula 28, 30, 33, 183
Avondale 91, ***115***, ***122***, ***124***, ***127***, ***128***, ***129***, 136

Baldwin Locomotive Works 144
bank crash 70, 73, 74, 76
Bareneed 1
Basques 7
Battle of Foxtrap 15–23, 39
Bay de Verde branch line 100
Bay of Islands ***20***, ***21***, 66, 90, 135, 151, 169, 170, 172, 173, 178, 191, 193
Bay Roberts 49
Bear Cove Bridge ***108***
Belgium 77
Bell Island 191
Bellairs, W.G. 27, 28, 29, 30, 34
Beothuks 7, 8, 28, 147
Birchy Cove 136
Bishop's Falls 113, 130, 131, 137, 145, 165, 173
Black River 32, 33
Blackman, A.L. 40, 41, 44, 46
Blondell, Joan 1, 108–109

Bolivia 131
Bonavista Bay 139, 141, 173, 174, 175
Bonavista branch line 56, ***93***, 130, 137, 153, 154, 165, 175–176, 180, 186
Bond, Robert 51, 70, 80, 81, 82, 83
Bonne Bay 141, 174
Boston & Maine Railroad 205
Botwood 2, 144
bridges 11, ***38***, 71, 86, ***87***, 113, 155, 165
Brigus 36, 49, 57, 173, 199
Brigus branch line 49, 94
British Columbia 27, 139
Brittany 7
Broad Cove 173, 174
Bruce, SS 78, 89, 132, ***133***, 134, ***138***, ***139***, 159, 160, 161, 164, 168, 170, 187, 188, 204
Bruce II, SS 139
Buffalo, New York 59
Bull Arm 32
"Bullet" 1, 2, 11, 13, 25, 106, 107, 108, 115, 117, 118, 119, 124, 127, 130
Burke, Johnnie 21

Cabot, John 7, 159, 176, 187
Cabot Strait 24, 134, 140, 164, 168, 183, 187, 188
Calvert, George 199
Canada, HMS 46
Canada Science and Technology Museum 2
Canadian National Railways 2, 13, 65, 71, 110, 111, 112, 114, 117, 118, 119, 124, 130, 140, 145, 146, 147, 185, 210
Canadian Pacific Railway 26, 27, 29, 60, 63, 85, 86, 98, 158, 161, 164, 172, 205
Canadian Transport Commission 119, 124
Cape Ray 66, 117, 151, 152, 164, 174, 187, 189

Carbonear 49, 94, 130, 137, 172, 173, 174, 199
Caribou, SS ***134***, 140, 183
caribou hunting 8, 163, 166–168, 170, 176–177, 177–178, 181, 195, 196
Caribou passenger train 119, ***120***
Carty, Police Inspector 16, 22
Cashin, M.P. 174
Chaleur Bay 25
Chamberlain, Joseph 80
Chile 131
Christof V. Doornum, SS 144
Churchill, Winston ***101***
Clarenville 145, 153, 161–162, 165, 173, 174
Clode Sound 165
Clyde, SS 140, 141, 144
coastal boats *see* Newfoundland Railway Steamship Service
Codroy 66, ***87***, 155, 164, 171, 172, 174, 190, 191
Colonial Building 52
Colonial Office 35, 36, 66, 76, 77, 78, 81
Colorado River 60
Come By Chance 1, 30, 32, 33, 104, 180, 198
Conception Bay 8, 9, 16, 44, 46, 49, 161, 165, 172, 173
Confederation with Canada 1, 9, 15, 16, 22, 25, 26, 27, 35, 37, 38, 39, 73, 109, ***109***, 110, 111, 185, 210
Conservative Party 15, 16, 37, 52, 53, 54, 55, 70, 77, 79, 80, 81, 82, 83
contract of 1898 11, 76–85, 139, 145, 146
Convention of Sunday Schools 46
Cormack, William Epps 8, 28, 29, 30, 34
Corner Brook 66, 74, ***96***, 102, 113, 130, 172, 181
Cross-Country Express 1, 11, 76, 86–95, 96, 108, 112, ***114***, ***134***,

138, 160, 167, 171, 179, 180, 183–184, 188, 193

Daily News 80, 83, 84
Davenport, Colonel 48
Deer Lake *17*, 137, 165, 174, 195, 196
Delaware and Hudson Railroad 9
Delaware River Gap 60
Dempsey, Patrick 53
Depression 99, 144
Dildo 1
dispatching office 137
dog sleds 135–137
dry dock *see* Newfoundland Railway Dry Dock
Dundee, SS 140–141

Empire Commerce, SS 144
English West Country 7, 8
Ethie, SS 140, 141, 202–203
Evening Telegram 37, 38, 39, 41, 43, 44, 45, 79, 85
excursion trips *10*, 44–46, 47, 160–161, 207–208
Exploits River 31, 32, 72, 165, 173

Ferryland branch line 174–175, 199
Fife, SS 140
fishery award 35, 39
Fleming, Sir Sandford 1, 24–26, 27, 28, 29, 40
forest fires 71, 148–149
Fort Erie, Ontario 59
Fortune Bay 51
Foxtrap 1, 15–23
French Shore 35–36, 66

Gaff Topsails 12, 67, 69, 88, 98, 112, *114*, 130, 134, 146, 165, 170, 172, 178, 181, 196, 197
Gambia 66
Gambo 90, 154, 165, 173
Gander 2, 30, 66, 103, 104, 137, 155, 165, 173, 184, 198
Geological Survey of Newfoundland 27
George V, King 46
Glencoe, SS 140, 169
Gleneagles 153
Glenwood 89, 152, 165, 176, 177, 198
Glover, John Hawley 48
Goobies 1
Goose Cove 153–154
Grand Falls 69, 172, 181, 185
Grand Lake 170, 171, 174, 195, 196
Grand Narrows Bridge 60
Grand Trunk Railroad 206
Grate's Cove 173, 174
Great American and Shortline Railway 24–26, 27, 40

Great Fires of 1846 and 1892 8, 9, *68*, 69
Great Northern Peninsula 7, 134
Greene, J.N. 40
Greenland 7

Halifax, Nova Scotia 24, 132, 159, 160
Hall's Bay 36, 37, 39, 40, 41, 48, 66, 67, 69, 158
Hall's Bay Railroad 54, 55, *55*, 58, 61, 62, 63, 200
Harbour Grace 1, 3, 6, 16, 26, 36, 38, 39, 41, *43*, 46–48, 49, 57, 132, 144, 173, 191, 199
Harbour Grace Railway 35–50, *43*, *47*, 51, 54–55, 58, 78
Harry's Brook 153
Heart's Content 1, 4, 9, 22, 173, 174, 180
Heart's Content branch line 100
Heart's Delight 1, 180
Heart's Desire 1, 180
Henry VII, King 7
Hercules, SS 30
Hill, Stephen 29
Holyrood 43, 44, 49, *106*, 150, 165, 173
Home, SS 140
Honduras 79
Howley 163, 166, 168, 169, 181, 196
Humber 54, 135, 136, 138, 145, 164, 165, 170, 171, 172, 173, 178, 184, 194, 195, 196

Iceland 7
Indian Pond 18, 46, 150
Intercolonial Railway 24, 25, 27, 35, 60, 132, 138, 204
Inverness, SS 140
Ireland 24, 25, 26

journalism 15, 37, 79, 80, 84, 141
Joy's Crossing *110*

Kelligrews 1, 160
Knipple and Morris 38, 39
Kyle, SS 87, 140, 143, 177

Labrador 78, 87, 134, 138, 139, 143, 144
Lachine, Québec 60
Lake Superior 58, 60
L'Anse aux Meadows 7
Laredo, Texas 59
last spike ceremonies 46, 47, 48, *91*, 174–175, 175–176
Leopard, SS 31
Lethbridge 153
Lewisporte 137, 138, 155, 173, 180
Liberal Party 15, 16, 37, 41, 51, 52, 55, 70, 71, 83, 84
Light, A.L. 29, 30, 38

Lintrose, SS 140
liveyers 7–8
locomotive shop 144–145
locomotives *42*, 43, 44, *45*, *47*, *49*, *54*, *55*, 56, 71, 88, 90, 91, *92*, 93, 96, *97*, *99*, *102*, 103, 104, 106, *106*, *107*, *108*, 110, *110*, 112, *113*, 114, *119*, *125*, *126*, *128*, 144–145, 148, 160, 161, 162, 170, 198, 207
London 25, 26, 73, 74, 82
Long Range Mountains 74
Lynch, F.J. 30, 32, 33, 34

Macaulay, Thomas Babington, Lord 10
Macdonald, John A., Sir 26
McCallum, Henry 81, 82, 84
McDougall, Emily 4
McDougall, Lauchie 1, *3*, 4, 118
Maine Central Railroad 205
Manuels 199, 207
Marconi, Guglielmo 166
Marine Atlantic 4
Meigle, SS 140, 144
Merlin, SS 44, 35
Methodist Monthly Greeting 80
Mexico 59
Micmacs 30, 31, 32, 56
Middle Brook 169
Middleton, George H. 58, 69
Mikado-type locomotives 145
Millais, J.G. 89–95
Millertown 137
Millo 43
Montréal 59, 73, 85, 132, 147, 168
Moore, P.F. 175
Morgan, R.C. 97, 98
Morine, Alfred B. 69, 77, 80, 81, 82, 83, 84
Morison, D. 174
Morning Post 8
Morris, Edward 81, 82, 175
Mullock, John 9
Munn, R.S. 48
Murray, Alexander 27, 30, 32, 33, 34
Murray, Sir Hubert 77, 79, 80, 81

narrow-gauge railway 9, 11, *17*, *18*, *19*, *20*, *21*, 34, 36, 39, 40, 42, 58, 72, 74, 88, 110, 112, 115, *129*, 130, 176, 180, 183
navvies 11, 51, 53, 54, 55, 61, 62–65, 70, 71, 72, 74, 76, 81
New Founde Land 7
New Orleans 25
New York 8, 24, 25, 26, 132, 177
New York, New Haven & Hartford Railroad 206
Newcastle 143
Newfoundland and Its Untrodden Ways 89
Newfoundland dog 141–143

Index

Newfoundland Express **52**
Newfoundland Forest Protection Association 148
Newfoundland Government Railway 98
Newfoundland Northern and Western Railway 73, 150, 151
Newfoundland Railway 13, 13, 40, 46–48, 53, 64, 65, 67, 71, 73, 78, 99, **101**, 103, 104, 106, 110, 111, **120**, 132, 140, 144, 145, 147, 159, 183, 186, 190, 200–201
Newfoundland Railway Dry Dock 78, 79, 81, 110, 140, 145–146, 163, 172, 173
Newfoundland Railway Steamship Service 78, 79, 81, 83, 84, 85, 99, 110, 113, 132, 137–143, 164, 180
Newfoundlander 41, 44
Niagara River 59
Nicaragua 131
Nigeria 131
Norris Arm 173
North Arm **49**
North Sydney, Nova Scotia 89, 113, 137, 138, 139, 140, 164, 168, 177, 183, 187
Northcliffe, Lord 147
Northern Bight 153, 165
Notre Dame Bay 139, 165, 173, 198
Nova Scotia, SS 39

Ocean Pond 106, 135
Old Glory airplane 143–144
Ottawa 59, 73
outports 8, 9, 13, 51, 80, 92

Panama Canal 64
Petty Harbour 146, 180
Philadelphia 144
Placentia 22, 41, 53, 54, 55, 56, 57, 132, 133, 138, 139, 145, 161, 169, 172, 173, 179, 198, 199
Placentia Railway 51–57, 58, 61, 73, 78, 93, **139**
Plunkett, E.W. 40
poetry and song 200–203
Poldhu, Cornwall 166
Poor, John 24
Port aux Basques 4, 11, 12, 36, 64, 66, 76, 78, 85, 86, 87, 89, 113, 114, **120**, 124, 127, 134, 138, 139, 140, 145, 147, 151, 160, 161, 163, 164, 165, 166, 168, 170, 171, 174, 176, 177, 178, 183, 187, 189, 191
Port Blandford 90, 138, 153, 173
Portugal 7
Portugal Cove 8
Pratt, E.J. 141–143
Prince Edward Island Railway 43, **45**, 71

Privy Council 10, 41, 55
Professor Bennet's Brass and String Band 44
Prowse, Daniel Woodley, Judge 17, 19, 20, 22, 53

Quidi Vidi **126**

rail travel 56, 57, 86–95, 115, 116, 117, 119–131, 157–186, 187–199
Railway (Amendment) Act 83
Railway Coastal Museum **125**
railway fever 9, 10, 51–53, 55, 157–159
Railway Fire Patrol 148–149
Railway Hotel, St. John's **49**
railway mail service 78, 79, 93, 132–136, 160, 194, 195
Railway (Settlement) Act 98
railway stations **67**, **68**, 74, 78, 99, **103**, 132, 133, **136**, 137, 176–177, 190
Ramsay, Thomas 30, 31, 34
Rattling Brook 1
Red Indian Lake 30, 31, 32
Reid, Harry Duff 70, 78, 160, 161
Reid, Robert Gillespie 11, 56, 58–61, **59**, 62, 63, 64, 66–75, 76–85, 96, 133, 138, 140, 144, 151, 152, 157, 158, 159, 162, 194, 196, 207
Reid, Robert Gillespie, Jr. 70, 175, 179
Reid, William Duff 70, 72, 78, 85, 175
Reid Newfoundland Company **54**, 78, 83, 84, 86, 96, 97, 98, 132, 137, 140, 144, 145, 166, 167, 174, 178–179
Renews 175, 180
Rhodes, Cecil 11
Rio Grande 59
Roadcruiser bus service 2, 119, 124, 127, 147
roads 8, 35, 54, 92, 99, 102, 148
Rocky Mountains 11, 114
rolling stock 71, 72, 73, 83, 88, 89, 90, 91, 96, **98**, **100**, 103, **104**, 110, **111**, 112, **112**, 114, **115**, 116, **116**, 117, **117**, **121**, **122**, **123**, **124**, **126**, **127**, **128**, 131, **135**, 145, 147, 164, 185
Roosevelt, Franklin D. **101**
Royal Canadian Air Force 103, 137
Royal Canadian Navy 140

St. Andrew's 18
St. Fintan's 155
St. George's Bay 25, 26, 28, 29, 30, 34, 35, 36, 164, 174, 192
St. John's 2, 8, 9, 10, 11, 12, 15, 16, 21, 22, 24, 25, 26, 29, 30, 31, 32, 33, 34, 35, 36, 39, 41, 42, 43, 46, 48, 49, 52, 53, 55, 56, 57, 65, 69–70, 74, 76, 78, 82, 84, 86, 89, 90, 91, 95, 102, **102**, 108, 113, **122**, 124, **125**, 130, 132, 133, 134, 137, 144, 145, 146–147, 152, 158, 159, 160, 161, 162, 164, 165, 166, 167, 170, 171, 172, 173, 174, 180, 182, 183, 184, 185, 190, 199
St. John's Light and Power company 78, 79, 81, 84
St. John's Street Railway 11, 78, 81, 84, 146–147, 202
St. Shotts 144
Salmon River Bridge 155
Sandy Point 192, 193, 196
Sault Ste. Marie 60
Schools on Wheels 147–148
Scotland 59, 78, 139, 140, 144
screech 107
Senegal 66
Shawnawdithit 147
Shea, Ambrose 23, 46
Ship Harbour **101**
Shippigan, New Brunswick 25, 26
Shoal Harbour 175
Short Ocean Passage 24
Signal Hill 166
snow fighting 1, 12, 34, 67, 69, 71, 86, 88, 90, 93, 103, 104, 112, **117**, **121**, **122**, 135, 146, 178, 180, 181, 189,
Sons of St. Andrew 46
Spaniard's Bay 49
Stabb, Henry 8–9, 24
Standard, SS 41
standard gauge railway 8, 11, 34, 35, 36, 40, 114
standard time 26
Steady Brook **107**
Stephenville 2, **111**
Stockton and Darlington Railway 9
Strait of Belle Isle 140
surveyors 16–22, 27–34, 38, 39, 40, 66, 67, 69, 83
Sydney, Nova Scotia 44, 78, 132, 133, 134, 138, 158, 159
Sydney and Louisbourg Railway 139

Table Mountain 4, 12, 89
telegraph system 11, 73, 78, 79, 81, 83, 84, 93, 137, 146, 152, 163
Terra Nova 91, 163, 165, 166, 167, 173
Terra Transport 2, 130, 146
Thorburn, Richard 52
Tickle Harbour 1, 165, 198
Tiger, SS 31
Tilton 47
Tipple, George 130
Topsail 18, 44, 45–46, 49, 160, 173, 199, 202

Total Abstinence and Benefit Society 45
T'Railway 131
Trans-Canada Highway 67, 69, 185
Treaty of Utrecht 35, 36
Trepassey branch line 49, *91*, 100, 174, 175, 180
Trinity 28, 139, 145, 173, 175, 198
Trinity Loop 86
truck system 51
tunnels 11, 86
Twillingate 145

U-69 140
United States Army Corps of Engineers 102

Upper Gullies 150, 180

Valentia 25, 26
Vancouver 26, 27
Victoria, Queen 24, 80
Vikings 7
Viscount, HMS 140
Voyager, SS 32

Waterford Valley 173
Whitbourne 53, 54, 55, 57, 90–91, *103*, *104*, *105*, *116*, *121*, 145, 161, 165, 173, 180, 199, 207
Whiteway, William, Sir 15, 22, 23, 35, 36, 37, 46, 48, 55, 56, 58, 70, 71, 163
William IV, King 57

Williams, Ralph, Sir 94–95, 175
Wind 4, 12–13, 71, 86, 89, 197, 117, 118, 181, 189
Winter, James 77, 79, 80, 81, 82
Witless Bay 175
World War I 96, 179
World War II 2, 13, 100, 102–109, 137, 140, 144, 146, 153–154
Wreckhouse 4, 12, 117, 118
wrecks, collisions and accidents 2, 15, 16, 46, 49–50, 72, 86, 89, 90, 91, 93, 94–95, 104, 106, 118, 138–139, 140–144, 150–156, 162, 169, 189, 202–203

www.ingramcontent.com/pod-product-compliance
Lightning Source LLC
Chambersburg PA
CBHW081553300426
44116CB00015B/2859